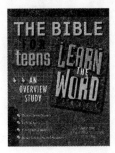  

• **Learn more at www.learntheword.com** •

### The Bible for Teens—Learn the Word™ Series

Who says Bible study has to be boring? Finally, there is a Bible commentary that meets the needs of today's teens by explaining biblical principles and Scripture in a fun, informative, and entertaining format. Adapted from *The Bible—God's Word for the Biblically-Inept*™.

(trade paper)   ISBN 1892016516   $14.99

### Bible Bytes for Teens: A Study-Devotional for Logging In to God's Word

Teens can focus on byte-sized Scripture passages and related teaching to get clear spiritual direction for their day. Also included are reflective study questions and a power-packed design that teens will love.

(trade paper)   ISBN 1892016494   $13.99

### What's in the Bible for . . .™ Teens

*By Mark Littleton and Jeanette Gardner Littleton*

Written to teens, this book explores biblical themes that speak to the challenges and pressures of today's adolescents, such as relationships and peer pressure. Helpful and eye-catching "WWJD?" icons, illustrations, and sidebars are included.

(trade paper)   ISBN 1892016052   $16.95

# LEARN THE WORD™

SERIES

# The Bible for Teens

LEARN THE WORD • LEARN THE WORD • LEARN THE WORD • L ARN

# LARRY RICHARDS

STARBURST PUBLISHERS®

P. O. Box 4123, Lancaster, Pennsylvania 17604

**www.starburstpublishers.com**

*The Bible for Teens: Learn the Word*™ is an adaptation of *The Bible: God's Word for the Biblically-Inept*™.

*If you don't know the Word, you can't live it!*™

CREDITS:
  Written by Larry Richards
  Adapted for teens by Tim Baker
  Cover Design by David Marty Design
  Text design and composition by John Reinhardt Book Design
  Illustrations by Melissa A. Burkhart and Mark Ammerman
  Cartoons by Randy Glasbergen

Unless otherwise indicated all Scripture was taken from the HOLY BIBLE: NEW INTERNATIONAL VERSION®. NIV®. Copyright © 1973, 1978, 1984 by International Bible Society. Used by permission of Zondervan Publishing House.

**LEARN THE WORD**™

First printing, October 2001
ISBN: 1-892016-51-6
Library of Congress Catalog Number 2001088292
Printed in the United States of America

# WHAT'S IN THIS BOOK?

## PART 2: THE NEW TESTAMENT

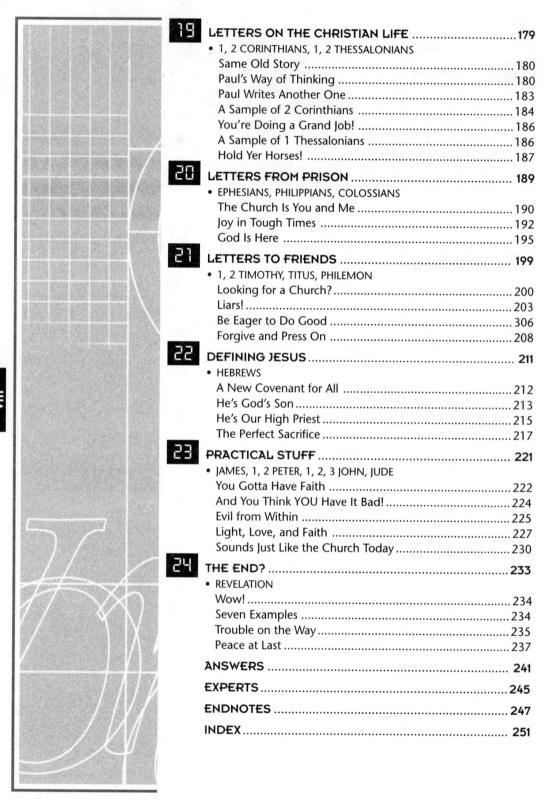

viii

# ILLUSTRATIONS, MAPS, AND TIMELINES

## ILLUSTRATIONS

## MAPS

## TIMELINES

Having trouble understanding the Bible? Tired of books that don't hold your interest? Don't worry! This book will teach you all the ins and outs of Scripture without boring you. Here's how the pages will look with explanations of the features.

## Who's Who

Get the straight scoop on characters in the Bible—who they are and why they're important.

## What?

Have you ever read a word that made you stop and ask, "What?" This feature helps you with those words. Whenever you see a word in boldface, you'll find its definition in the sidebar.

## Bible Summary

This is a summary of big chunks of Scripture.

## Go!

Whenever you see something that's underlined, you'll find the "Go!" feature in the sidebar. This tells you where to go in the Bible to find additional information about the underlined word or phrase.

## Gimme the Basics

Find out right away all the really important stuff about each book in the Bible—Who, What, Where, When, Why?

---

**GIMME THE BASICS**

 **1, 2, 3 JOHN**

. . . how to love and obey

| | |
|---|---|
| WHO | The apostle John |
| WHAT | wrote these letters |
| WHERE | while living in Ephesus |
| WHEN | near the end of the first century |
| WHY | to encourage love for others and obedience to God. |

**WHO'S WHO ???**

JOHN : The apostle John was really close to Jesus during his life on earth. John outlived the other apostles of Jesus and spent most of his life ministering in Asia Minor. These letters, and the Book of Revelation, were written near the end of the first century when John was in his nineties.

**LIGHT, LOVE, AND FAITH**

With the crowning of Emperor Domitian in A.D. 81 the persecution of Christians became state policy. Even though John himself was later **exiled** the apostle's letters ignore the external threat. John is primarily concerned with the inner life of God's people. He focuses on the need to live in intimate fellowship with God and fellow believers.

*exiled: banished from one's home*

> **Bible Summary: 1, 2, 3 John**
> Each of John's three letters encourages fellowship with the Lord and with other Christians. There are three major themes in John. John wants Christians (1) to live in the light, (2) to live lovingly, and (3) to live by faith.

**What's Up with 1 John?**

1 Don't love the world (1 John 2:15–17). Sinful cravings, lust, and bragging about what we have are the results of loving the world more than God. The person who is "worldly" is in the grip of the same desires that motivate the lost—desires which are totally out of harmony with God's nature and of

**GO!**
1 Corinthians 3:3
(worldly)

**Check It Out**

Want to read more about a Bible topic or story? Check out the passage in your Bible.

which he is not the source. Why is it foolish as well as wrong to adopt the values of human society? John says, *"The world and its desires pass away, but the man who does the will of God lives forever"* (1 John 2:17).

2 The call to love one another (1 John 4:11–24). John frequently reminds his readers of the importance of loving one another. God himself is love, so a failure to love fellow Christians is a sign that the believer is out of touch with God. John's got a lot to say about loving our **brothers**.

>>>CHECK IT OUT:

1 John 3:18–27
1 John 4:1–3

**brothers:** fellow believers

OUTSIDE CONNECTION

Rachel Scott: A friend is someone who can look into your eyes and be able to tell if you're alright or not . . . A friend is someone who can say something to you without telling them anything and their words hit the spot."

**Outside Connection**

This feature gives you quotes from other people. Want to know what Josh McDowell thinks? How about Charles Swindoll? You'll find out when you read "Outside Connection."

Why is loving others important for believers?_____

_____

What things make it difficult to love others?_____

_____

What are the benefits to loving others?_____

Your Move

**Your Move**

Here's where you can have a say! Simply answer the questions on the lines provided.

GET REAL

Do you have a friend that you have a hard time loving? Are you bullied by a sibling and come close to hating him or her? What's the secret to loving people that are totally unlovable? Here's a hint: Look at them like God does. See them as broken, hurting people. Then, reach out to them. Even if they make fun of you? Yup. Even if their teasing gets worse? You got it. John's words in these passages don't command us to run from people . . . they urge us to love others no matter what.

**Get Real**

Listen to straight talk about the Bible that brings things down to an everyday level.

REVELATION • ONE

xi

# INTRODUCTION

Welcome to *Learn the Word*! If you want to go deep into God's Word without getting bored, here's the answer! Books in this series are designed to make studying Scripture simple, rewarding, and fun! So sit back, kick up your feet, and let's *Learn the Word*!

## WHAT IS THE BIBLE?

Most people think of the Bible as just one book, but actually the Bible is a collection of *sixty-six* books, written by many different authors. You'll find a list of these ancient books in the front of your Bible.

There are two sections in the Bible: an "Old" Testament with thirty-nine books and a "New" Testament with twenty-seven books. The Old Testament was written between 1400 and 400 **B.C.** The New Testament was written between **A.D.** 40 and 100. The Old Testament deals with events before the birth of Jesus Christ. The New Testament tells about Jesus' birth, life, death, resurrection, and about the movement begun by people who believed that Jesus was the Son of God.

Centuries later, scholars divided the Bible into chapters and verses. So, Genesis 12:3 refers to the twelfth chapter of the Book of Genesis and the third verse in that chapter. This helps readers locate specific Bible stories and teachings.

**B.C.:** *before Christ*

**A.D.:** anno Domini, *Latin for "in the year of our Lord"*

## WHY STUDY THE BIBLE?

**BECAUSE** . . . For over two thousand years, millions of people have viewed the Bible as a message from God. We can't see God. But what a really cool thing it would be if God would speak to us! And that's what the Bible is: God speaking to human beings. Over 2,600 times the writers of the Bible claim to speak or write *God's words*—not their own.

**BECAUSE** . . . Even people who do not believe that the Bible is God's Word need to know what's in the Bible. It's the best-selling book in history! Its stories and images have shaped Western civilization. Its moral code is the original source for most of our laws.

No person can claim to be "educated" without some knowledge of this book that has done so much to shape our world.

**BECAUSE** . . . The Bible offers answers to our questions. Where did our universe come from? Are human beings special? Where can I find meaning for my own life? How can I be a better person? How will the world end? What will happen to me after I die? If God is real, how can I know him? Whether you accept the answers the Bible gives or not, you owe it to yourself to find out what the biblical answers are.

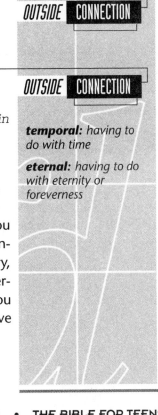

**OUTSIDE CONNECTION**

*Helen Keller:* The Bible gives me a deep, comforting sense that "things seen are **temporal**, and things unseen are **eternal**."[1]

**OUTSIDE CONNECTION**

*Duffy Robbins:* One thing I love about the Bible is that it's so practical. Through writers like the apostle Paul, God has given us examples we can identify with and make sense of in everyday life.[2]

**temporal:** *having to do with time*

**eternal:** *having to do with eternity or foreverness*

## WHY DO PEOPLE NEED A GUIDE TO THE BIBLE?

The only way to understand the Bible is to read it. But if you just open the Bible and start reading, you're likely to get confused. Why? Because even though the Bible tells a single story, this story has many different parts. It's important to understand how each part fits into the story as a whole. Once you know this, you can open the Bible anywhere, and you'll have a solid foundation for understanding its meaning.

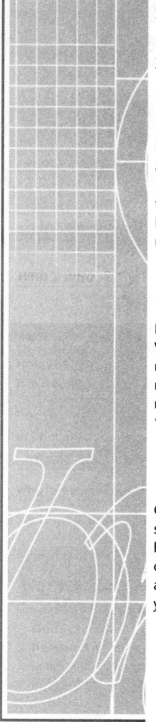

## CHAPTER CHECKUP

At the end of each chapter you'll see a number of questions. These are to help you remember all the great stuff you've learned. You can answer them by yourself or in a group. And you'll find the answers in the back of the book (see page 241).

## WHY USE THE NEW INTERNATIONAL VERSION (NIV)?

I've tried to look at the Bible as the experts would, but I have also tried to write it for those who really want to *Learn the Word*. I want it to be easy to read and understand. That's why this book uses the New International Version (NIV) of the Bible. It's a scholarly translation that accurately expresses the original Bible in clear and contemporary English.

## ABOUT DATES . . .

Many experts have different opinions about dates in the Bible. Variations of one or two years in some cases are not uncommon. But archaeologists keep making new discoveries so that many of the dates are now known and thought to be accurate. In the timelines remember that "c." indicates "circa" or "around" that date.

## ONE FINAL TIP

God, who gave us the Bible, is present whenever we read it, so it helps to read the Bible prayerfully. People who open their hearts to God and ask him to speak to them say that he really does. Open your heart, ask God to speak to you as you read, and you'll be surprised how wonderfully the Bible will enrich your life!

# PART 1

# THE OLD TESTAMENT

GLASBERGEN

"YOUR MOTHER AND I WERE GETTING PRETTY TIRED
OF YOUR BAD ATTITUDE. THAT'S MUCH BETTER!"

 ## WHAT'S THE OLD TESTAMENT?

The Old **Testament** is a collection of thirty-nine books, written between 1450 and 400 **B.C.** The Old Testament is all about the Jewish people. Through this people God revealed himself to everybody. Using this people God drew up a plan that would save anyone who believed in him from the terrible consequences of **sin**.

 ## WHAT'S SO "OLD" ABOUT IT?

It's called the "Old" Testament in contrast to the "New" Testament, which is a collection of twenty-seven books that were written in the first century. The New Testament continues and finishes the story begun in the Old Testament.

**testament:** *another word for covenant—contract, oath, promise, or binding agreement*

**B.C.:** *"before Christ," as opposed to* A.D., *which stands for the Latin phrase* anno Domini, *which means "in the year of our Lord"*

**sin:** *any violation of God's will*

**LEARN ABOUT GOD**

Different people have different ideas about who God is and what he does. One of the best places to learn about God is in the Old Testament. Why? Because God is the major character in the Old Testament. By looking at the Old Testament you'll see how he interacts with human beings—like us!

**OKAY, SO WHAT'S IN THE OLD TESTAMENT?**

*Pentateuch: the first five books of the Old Testament*

The Old Testament can be divided into five different types of writing: **Pentateuch**, History, Poetry, Major Prophets, and Minor Prophets. Within each different type of writing you'll find answers to fascinating questions. Check out the illustration below.

### THE PENTATEUCH

| Genesis, Exodus, Leviticus, Numbers, Deuteronomy | Where did the universe come from?<br>What makes human beings special?<br>Why do people do wrong and evil things?<br>Does God care what happens to us?<br>How can I know what God expects of us? | |

### HISTORY

| Joshua, Judges, Ruth, I, II Samuel, I, II Kings, I, II Chronicles, Ezra, Nehemiah, Esther | What is God's plan for the world?<br>Does God control what happens in history?<br>Does it pay a nation to honor God? | |

### POETRY

| Job, Psalms, Proverbs, Ecclesiastes, Song of Songs (Song of Solomon) | Can I find meaning in life apart from God?<br>How do I communicate with God?<br>How can we survive suffering?<br>What guidelines help me make wise choices? | |

### MAJOR PROPHETS

| Isaiah, Jeremiah, Lamentations, Ezekiel, Daniel | Does God ever reveal the future?<br>What prophecies have already come true?<br>What sins is God sure to judge?<br>How will the world end? | |

### MINOR PROPHETS

| Hosea, Joel, Amos, Obadiah, Jonah, Micah, Nahum, Habakkuk, Zephaniah, Haggai, Zechariah, Malachi | How much does God love us?<br>Do people really "get away with" being wicked?<br>What kind of society will God bless?<br>What kind of society is he sure to punish?<br>Is our country in danger today? | |

# How It All Began

### GENESIS 1–11

**CHAPTER CAPTURE**

- Creation
- Adam and Eve
- Satan and the Fall
- Sin
- Noah and the Flood

 **LET'S DIVE IN**

Wouldn't it have been cool to watch God mold the universe? To watch him make Saturn or create molecules? And since no one was there, it makes you wonder . . . How did Moses know what happened so he could write the first five books of the Old Testament?

Simple. God told him. Basically, it goes like this. The Bible is a book of *revealed truth*, also known as **revelation**. God revealed to Moses what happened, and Moses wrote it down.

*revelation: what God has communicated to us*

 **GENESIS**

*. . . chock full o' beginnings*

| | |
|---|---|
| WHO | Moses |
| WHAT | wrote Genesis |
| WHERE | while traveling in the wilderness |
| WHEN | about 1400 B.C. |
| WHY | to tell us the truth about God and his relationship to people. |

**GIMME THE BASICS**

KEY POINT

Genesis tells us
where we come
from, not when
God did all the
work.

*image and likeness:*
*we have emotions, an*
*intellect and a will . . .*
*just like God.*

*dominion:* *responsibil-*
*ity to care for stuff*

---

Bible Summary: Genesis 1:1–2:3

The famous, ever popular words about creation are penned.
The Bible begins, *"In the beginning God created the heavens and*
*the earth."* The rest of this passage goes on to describe how
God shaped our universe. He created earth to be a place where
humans could live and be happy.

 ### GOD'S HANDIWORK

### What's Up with Genesis 1:1–2:3?

**1** *A different creation story.* There were a lot of other creation
accounts floating around when Moses walked the earth.
But the Genesis account is totally different from these other
accounts. Moses didn't borrow his ideas about creation from
anyone . . . God *told* him what to write.

**2** *A fascinating focus.* The word "God" appears thirty-two
times in Genesis 1:1–2:3, so needless to say God is the
focus. We can learn a lot about God from this passage. We
learn, for example, that God is only one being and that God is
the creator of the world.

**3** *God created humans!* God created us in his **image and**
**likeness.** He gave us **dominion** over his creation. That
means we're in charge! We're unlike any other creature, and
God loves us.

**4** *The world's age is a mystery.* How old do you think the
world is? A million years? A few million years? Maybe even
a *billion* years? This is a question that's plagued scholars for a
long time. Genesis doesn't give us a clue about when the world
was created. It tells us *where* we came from, not *when* God did
all the work.

---

**OUTSIDE CONNECTION** | **Billy Graham:** Intellectually, it is much more difficult not
to believe in God than to believe in him.[1]

**OUTSIDE CONNECTION** | **R. C. Sproul:** The whole realm of nature shouts of the
design of the universe. This design must have a designer.[2]

What impresses you most about God's creation?_____

_____

Have you ever seen something in nature that surprised you? What was it?___

_____

_____

What are some great things about being human?_____

_____

_____

**Your Move**

**GET REAL**

Have you ever gone camping and looked up at all the stars? Have you ever noticed all the different colors in a sunset? Have you ever been surprised by a clap of thunder? God is the one who created all of these natural wonders. When you see or hear or taste or touch or smell something amazing within creation, you are experiencing the work of God's hands.

**Bible Summary: Genesis 2:4–25**

God went to work on Adam. When God was finished, he put Adam in the incredible Garden of Eden. Adam went exploring and gave the animals names. Then God created Eve by using one of Adam's ribs. Adam took one look at her and went, "Shazam!" In other words, he fell instantly in love.

**>>>CHECK IT OUT**

Genesis 2:8–23

### What's Up with Genesis 2:4–25?

**1** *The scoop on God's creation of humans.* Here's how he did it. God took dirt from the ground and used his hands to form humans. That's right, he used his hands to make our hands. He looked into our eyes as he formed them. Then he did the unbelievable. He used his own breath to bring us to life. God gave special and unusual attention to form us. Cool, huh?

*Ray C. Steadman:* No matter how we may feel, or what may be our attitude toward God, we are bound, as creatures dependent on his love and grace, at least to give thanks to him as our Creator.[3]

*OUTSIDE* **CONNECTION**

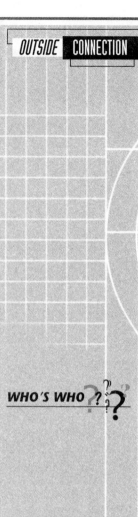
**Ronald F. Youngblood:** *"Create" is a special verb in the Old Testament. It always has God as its subject; it is never used of human activity. You and I may make or form or fashion, but only God creates.*[4]

**2** *A holy babe.* No, this isn't Jesus in the manger; we're talking about Eve here. God saw that Adam would be lonely. He saw that Adam needed help. He saw that Adam would need someone to take to the prom. God wanted man and woman to be life partners . . . working together to further God's kingdom on earth.

> **Bible Summary: Genesis 3**
> Satan came in the form of a serpent. He tempted and tricked Eve into disobeying God. Adam followed Eve and disobeyed God. And their sin rippled through all of history.

 **DA DEBIL MADE ME DO IT**

**SATAN:** Can you hear the suspenseful music starting? Can you feel the lights dimming? Here comes Satan . . . and he ain't happy. Satan (and his angels) hate God. They live to do whatever they can to put God's plans on the skids. So, Satan goes into the garden to wreck God's creation. He uses a deceptively simple plan to get Adam and Eve to sin.

*tree of the knowledge of good and evil:* is the symbol of the ability to know the difference between good and evil

God told Adam and Eve not to eat from the "**tree of the knowledge of good and evil.**" Even though God made himself absolutely clear, Adam and Eve ate from the tree anyway. Ever disobey your parents? That's what's going on here. When Adam and Eve disobeyed God, their natures became twisted and warped. And they passed this twisted and warped nature on to their offspring. Then their offspring passed that nature on. Then, well, you get the picture.

**WHY?**

So, why in the world did God put the tree of the knowledge of good and evil in the Garden of Eden? Here's why. God did not want to force people to love him, because if love is forced, it isn't love. He wanted them to have the free choice. Only then

6

would it be real love. By placing the tree in the garden, God gave Adam and Eve the opportunity to show genuine love for him by being obedient.

### What's Up with Genesis 3?

1 *Extreme vulnerability.* Eve was tempted. Why was she so vulnerable to **temptation**? Well, for starters, she didn't know what God had said (compare Genesis 3:4 with Genesis 2:16–17). She also doubted God (check out Genesis 3:4) and finally Eve relied on her judgment rather than simply obeying. She wanted to decide for herself what was good for her, rather than trust what God told her (check out Genesis 3:6). What was the result? Total disaster!

**temptation:** *an inward pull toward doing wrong*

2 *Double death . . . a really bad thing.* How would you like to hear this: "Take a bite, but if you do you'll die!" That's basically what's going on here. God put the tree in the garden and Eve ate from it, then Adam took a bite too. This is what scholars call the "fall." And a lot of bad stuff happened after the fall.

3 *The fall fallout.* Before Adam and Eve sinned, the Bible says, *"The man and his wife were both naked, and they felt no shame"* (Genesis 2:25). After they sinned, they became aware of their nakedness, and it wasn't a pleasant experience (check out Genesis 3:7).

Also, even though Adam and Eve knew God loved them, they became afraid of him and tried to hide (check out Genesis 3:8, 10). Finally, they felt really guilty, blaming each other and God.

**Kevin Johnson:** *From way back Satan has headed an alternative kingdom. Led every charge in the war against God. Been living proof that lots of times Bad Guys Finish First.*[5]

**OUTSIDE CONNECTION**

4 *More fallout!* What else? Is there really more? Yep. Ever since the fall women have looked to men for approval, and men have tried to rule over women. Men have worked the land, but weeds have always been a step ahead. Also, women experience pain in childbirth.

>>>**CHECK IT OUT**

Genesis 3:12–13

**GO!**

Leviticus 17:11
(sacrifice)

***sacrifice for sins:***
*death of someone in
our place for our sins*

**GO!**

Ephesians 2:1–4 (sin)

***sin nature:*** *the desire
and tendency to choose
to obey God*

**>>> CHECK IT OUT:**

Genesis 4–5

**5** *The first sacrifice.* Here's the amazing thing. God didn't turn his back against Adam and Eve. When they hid, he went looking for them. He used an animal skin to cover them, which means he had to kill an animal for them. That makes this the first __sacrifice__ **for sins**.

> **Bible Summary: Genesis 4–5**
> These chapters show us that Adam and Eve's __sin__ **nature** is passed down to their kids. How do we know? Cain killed Abel. Awhile later Lamech, Cain's kid, took on two wives and justified murdering someone. Then in Noah's day people got even *more* wicked.

### What's Up with Genesis 4–5?

**1** *The spread of sin.* So, we've got sin and a fallen humanity. What might happen next? Unfortunately . . . the spread of sin. The sin nature was transferred to Adam and Eve's off-spring. This answers the age old question . . . Why do people do wrong things? It's simple really. People aren't sinners be-cause they do wrong things. Instead, they do wrong things because they're sinners. You can do all the good deeds you want, but you'll never change this fact of human nature. What do we need? God's inner transformation. Only he can do it. And, boy, do we need it!

**2** *Long lives.* No matter how long you live, you probably won't outlive the guys in Genesis 4–5. We're talking, these guys lived *hundreds* of years. Is this really possible? Yep. Doc-tors have discovered that diseases accumulate over time, so people who lived right after Adam and Eve would have had few if any diseases to deal with.

> **Bible Summary: Genesis 6–9**
> A flood covered the earth and wiped out everybody but Noah and his family. God used Noah to build an ark, which pro-tected animals and his family so that eventually living things would return to earth.

**>>> CHECK IT OUT:**

Genesis 6:9–22;
7:17–24

**A FLOODED EARTH, AND NO TOWELS!**

**NOAH:** You've heard all about this guy. Noah walked with God even though everyone around him was <u>wicked</u>. This is how it happened. God told Noah that he was going to wipe out everyone on the earth (because they were all so wicked) using a massive flood. Even though it sounded ridiculous, Noah built the ark God told him to build, so his faith is praised in the New Testament. (Wanna see what the ark probably looked like? Check out a picture of it below.)

### What's Up with Genesis 6–9?

**1** *The flood's cause.* Human sin is what caused the flood, and the flood is evidence that God is a **moral judge** who punishes the guilty. So, the story of the flood is a warning to us. If we think God is unaware of our sins . . . bzzzzzt, we're wrong!

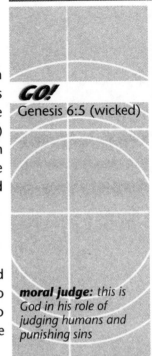

*GO!*
Genesis 6:5 (wicked)

*moral judge:* this is God in his role of judging humans and punishing sins

6

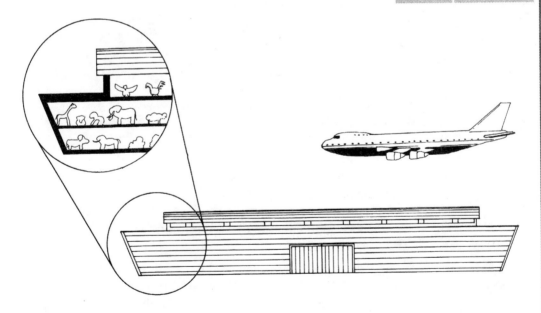

***Noah's Ark***

*Noah's ark was a large wooden boat without an engine. It was 450 feet long, 75 feet wide and 45 feet high. It took Noah and his sons 120 years to build.*

**2** *God makes a promise.* God made it clear he wasn't destroying the earth for fun. He did it to cleanse the world of sin. Then he promised he would never do it again. And to seal this promise, he placed a rainbow in the sky.

### Okay, So Did It Really Happen?

Do you think the flood was just a figment of some writer's imagination? Guess again. People from the Middle East to China and even in the jungles of South America have recorded that a flood wiped out the human race. So, if you think this is just a story, think again. This flood thing really happened!

**Josh McDowell:** There are good reasons to believe that Genesis relates the original story. Only in Genesis is the year of the flood given, as well as dates for the chronology of Noah's life. In fact, Genesis almost reads like a diary or ship's log of the events.[6]

> **Bible Summary: Genesis 10–11**
>
> Genesis 10 contains a *table of nations,* which mentions places where different groups of people lived. Genesis 11 records the building of a big tower; it also tells us when God made these ancient people speak different languages. Why? Because Noah's descendants failed to spread out and populate earth like God asked them to. They also built the tower to *"make a name for themselves"* (Genesis 11:4). In other words, they were being prideful. The last verses of Genesis 11 get us ready to meet Abram. Abram is one important dude in the Bible.

### Something to Bungee Off

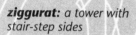
*ziggurat: a tower with stair-step sides*

Pop quiz. What's a **ziggurat**? For those of you who missed this one, don't feel too bad. You don't see many ziggurats today, but that's what the Jews built. They called it the "tower of Babel." Basically, a ziggurat is a pyramid-like building that was common in the Middle East and South America (see illustration, page 11). Ancient peoples used these towers as places of worship. They invented their own religions and tried to reach God by their own efforts.

*A Ziggurat*

Towers like the Ziggurat were constructed by the people of Mesopotamia over five thousand years ago and by the people of Central America two thousand years ago.

### God Goes First

We all want to be appreciated, but sometimes our desire for appreciation can take us in a bad direction. Take the Jews. One of the reasons they built the tower was so that people would admire them. But God didn't like this. He knew the Jews were putting themselves before him, so he confused them all by giving them different languages. The moral of the story? Put God first, not yourself.

## CHAPTER CHECKUP

1. What difference does it make whether God created the world?
2. What makes human beings special?
3. How does the Bible explain evil?
4. What was the fall and what were the consequences of it?
5. What does the flood tell us about God?

### CRASH COURSE

▶ Genesis gives us a unique account of the origin of the universe. No other perspective is like it in the ancient world. (Genesis 1)
▶ God created human beings in his own image, making human beings special. (Genesis 1:27; 2)

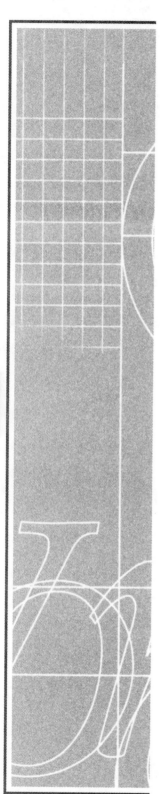

- When Adam and Eve disobeyed God, they died spiritually and transmitted their sin nature to all their offspring. (Genesis 3)
- The truth of the Bible's account of the fall is seen in the big and little evils that mar society and each person's experience.
- The Genesis flood revealed God as a *moral judge* who must and will punish sin. (Genesis 6)

# Setting the Course:

## GENESIS 12–50

 LET'S DIVE IN!

So, you've got the first eleven chapters of Genesis that give a basic understanding of where humans came from. What happens next? Genesis 12 is about Abraham. Abraham was God's choice to be the father of the Jewish people. And (get this one) the rest of the Old Testament—all 905 chapters of it—follows the history of the Jews.

God revealed himself through Abraham's family, he dealt with sin, and then he reopened the way for us to have a personal relationship with God. That's a lot of responsibility for one family! Check out the timeline below to see who was important in early Israelite history, and when they lived.

*Timeline of Genesis 12–50*

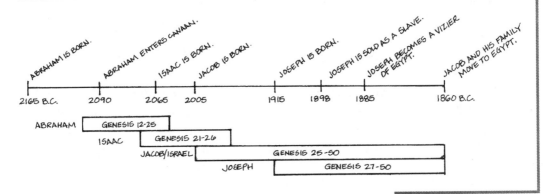

## The Fertile Crescent

*The area outlined like a half-moon is known as the Fertile Crescent. The area was perfect for growing things and was a great trade route.*

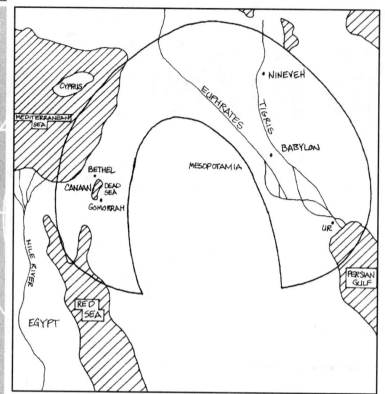

### GO!

Genesis 12:1–3, 7 (Abrahamic Covenant)

**Abrahamic Covenant:** *these are specific promises God made to Abraham*

### >>>CHECK IT OUT:

Genesis 2:8–23

Bible Summary: Genesis 12

God appeared to Abraham and made a bunch of promises. All of the promises God made are known as the **Abrahamic Covenant**. How did Abraham respond to God? He left his home like God commanded and went to the land that God showed him.

## The World Famous Covenant

You've heard all about it, right? Read it in your school newspaper too, huh? Well, okay . . . maybe not. But the covenant God made with Abraham is really important. God made these promises in a special ceremony, like all legal arrangements were made in Abe's day. Some of God's promises were fulfilled in Abe's time. The rest will be fulfilled when history is over.

## Abe's Faith

Abraham was a weak man . . . like everyone. Hey, he was human! The Bible is open and honest; it says he made mistakes. But even through his mistakes Abraham had strong faith in God. When he was a hundred (and his wife was ninety), God promised them a son. Imagine how odd that must have sounded. Even though it was a very strange thing for God to promise, Abe believed God, so God chose to view him as **righteous**.

**righteous:** *sinless in God's eyes*

*Max Lucado: You do not impress the officials of NASA with a paper airplane. You don't claim equality with Einstein because you can write $H_2O$. And you don't boast about your goodness in the presence of the perfect [God].*[1]

*Kay Arthur: What does the Word of God mean when it speaks of faith? Faith is simply taking God at his Word.*[2]

## God's Big Promises

| Reference | God's Promise . . . | The Promise Kept . . . |
| --- | --- | --- |
| Genesis 12:2 | I will make you into a great nation. | From Abraham sprang both the Jewish and Arab peoples. |
| Genesis 12:2 | I will bless you. | God protected and enriched Abraham during his lifetime. |
| Genesis 12:2 | I will make your name great and you will be a blessing. | Jews, Muslims, and Christians honor Abraham as founder of their faith. |
| Genesis 12:3 | I will bless those who bless you, and whoever curses you I will curse. | Throughout history peoples who have persecuted the Jews have experienced national disaster. |
| Genesis 12:3 | All peoples on earth will be blessed through you. | Abraham's descendants gave the world the Bible and Jesus. |
| Genesis 12:7 | To your offspring I will give this land. | Israel remains the promised land of the Jewish people, to be occupied at history's end. |

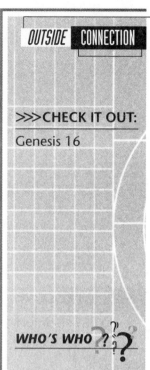

>>>CHECK IT OUT:

Genesis 16

*Duffy Robbins:* Any honest study of history and archaeology will turn up ample evidence that demonstrates that the Bible is a book that can be trusted. That doesn't mean that Christian scholars have an answer for every question, or that there aren't areas of confusion. But judging the Bible solely on the basis of human intellect is like trying to find the sun with a flashlight.[3]

## WHAT HAPPENED AFTER ABE?

**Bible Summary: Genesis 21–27**
Want to know about Isaac? Check out the story in these chapters. Isaac is an important guy, because he inherited the covenant that God made with Abraham.

WHO'S WHO

**ISAAC:** Abe and Sarah had a son. He inherited the covenant promises that God made with Abraham. Isaac married Rebekah and their son, Jacob, inherited God's promises to Abraham.

How would you have felt if you were Abraham when God promised him a son?_____

_____

In what areas of your life do you need faith right now?_____

_____

Why is it sometimes difficult to exercise faith like Abraham did?_____

_____

God makes promises to us. Stop and think about that for a minute. The creator of the universe binds himself to us by promising us stuff. And God doesn't just go around making empty promises. He fulfills what he promises. That means God's promises in his Word are true. When he promised Abraham a son, he wasn't messing around. He meant (and did) what he promised. It's the same with us. God makes us promises. We might look a little weird believing in what he promises, like Abraham did, but it's totally worth it!

## Bible Babes

Don't be offended, but in Bible times women had a slightly different role than in today's world. In Bible times men were responsible to provide for their wives and daughters. The inheritance was passed through the male line. So, what you've got in the Bible is a bunch of stories about men. But don't get confused. This doesn't mean women aren't important to God, or to history. In fact, Genesis 24 talks about Abraham's concern to find the right wife for Isaac. It was a big deal.

### Bible Summary: Genesis 25–50

Interested in learning about Jacob? Read these chapters. He was next (after Isaac) to inherit the covenant promises. Esau, Jacob's older twin brother, would have been his father's heir, but Esau didn't like God and traded his **birthright** to Jacob for a bowl of soup. Later Jacob tricked his father into giving him a **blessing** that was originally intended for Esau. Jacob fled to a place called Haran when Esau threatened to kill him. While he was there, Jacob married and had many children. Then, a little later in his life, Jacob and his family moved to Egypt to escape a famine. Jacob and his family, who made up all of the **Israelites** at that time, stayed there for four hundred years.

**JACOB:** You know that he's the grandson of Abraham and Sarah, and the son of Isaac, but is there anything else? God spoke to Jacob several times during his lifetime. One time Jacob actually wrestled with God! After the match God changed his name from Jacob, which means "deceiver," to Israel, which means "God preserves." Jacob's descendants were called Israel or the Israelites.

## JEALOUS OF JOSEPH

### Bible Summary: Genesis 36–50

Joseph is a real hero. He was the favorite son of his father, Jacob, so his brothers got jealous and sold him into slavery. After a lot of tough stuff, Joseph became a chief official, and God helped him help Egypt through a famine. Joseph saved the lives of his father and brothers during the famine by moving them to Egypt.

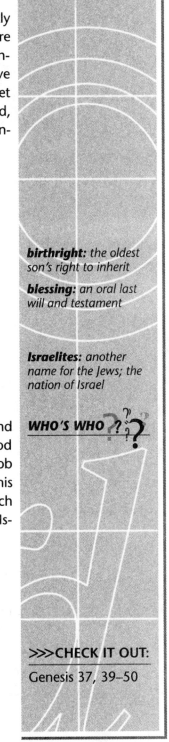

**birthright:** *the oldest son's right to inherit*

**blessing:** *an oral last will and testament*

**Israelites:** *another name for the Jews; the nation of Israel*

17

**WHO'S WHO** ??

>>>**CHECK IT OUT:**
Genesis 37, 39–50

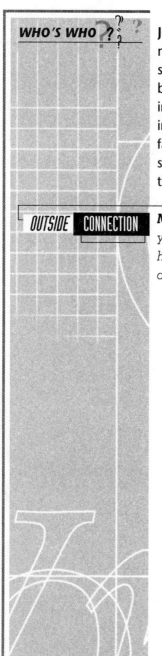

**JOSEPH:** If you're feeling down and need a little encouragement . . . try reading this story. Joseph followed God despite some real turkeys in his life. His brothers betrayed him. His boss's wife falsely accused him of rape. His cellmates left him in the dust. After all of that, God raised him to be head honcho in prosperous Egypt. Joseph's story is filled with heartache, family love, loss, and triumph. If you're looking for a great story about following God when things are tough, you need to read this!

**OUTSIDE CONNECTION**

**Mother Teresa:** *Make sure that you let God's grace work in your souls by accepting whatever he gives you, and giving him whatever he takes from you. True holiness consists of doing God's will with a smile.*[4]

## CHAPTER CHECKUP

1. What was special about Abraham?
2. What is a covenant?
3. Why is it important to understand the Abrahamic Covenant?
4. Who inherited the covenant promises after Abraham died?
5. Why is faith important for a person seeking a personal relationship with God?

### CRASH COURSE

▶ God gave Abraham covenant promises for himself and his descendants. The covenant promises outlined what God intended to do in the future. (Genesis 12:1–3)
▶ Abraham believed God's promise, and God credited it to him as righteousness. (Genesis 15:6)
▶ The covenant promises given to Abraham were passed on to Isaac, Jacob, and to their descendants, the Jewish people.
▶ The rest of the Old Testament is the story of the Jewish people and how God worked out his covenant promises through history.

# The Long Trip Home

3

## CHAPTER CAPTURE

- Moses
- Miracles
- The Ten Commandments
- A Portable Tabernacle

### EXODUS

 **LET'S DIVE IN!**

Slaves. That's what the **Israelites** are at the beginning of Exodus. God calls a man named Moses to free his people. Exodus is the story of how God broke the power of Egypt and freed the Israelites. God led the freed slaves to Mount Sinai (look at the map on page 20), where he gave them the Ten Commandments.

**Israelites:** *God's covenant people; the descendants of Abraham, Isaac, and Jacob*

19

### Timeline of Exodus

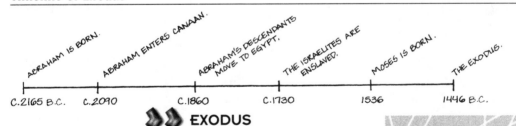

ABRAHAM IS BORN. | ABRAHAM ENTERS CANAAN. | ABRAHAM'S DESCENDANTS MOVE TO EGYPT. | THE ISRAELITES ARE ENSLAVED. | MOSES IS BORN. | THE EXODUS.

C.2165 B.C. — C.2090 — C.1860 — C.1730 — 1536 — 1446 B.C.

### EXODUS

. . . exit to freedom

| | |
|---|---|
| WHO | Moses wrote |
| WHAT | the story of the Israelites' deliverance from slavery |
| WHERE | in Egypt |
| WHEN | around 1440 B.C. |
| WHY | to record God's power and his commitment to Abraham's descendants. |

GIMME THE BASICS

## Places in Exodus

This map will help you locate some of the major places mentioned in the Book of Exodus.

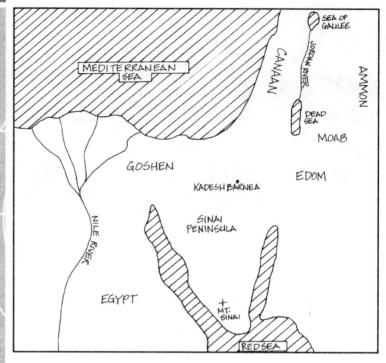

 NO WAY, GOD!

### NO WAY, GOD!

**MOSES:** Who was Moses? He was an Israelite adopted into Egypt's royal family as an infant. When Moses was eighty years old, God called him to confront **Pharaoh** and free his people. God struck Egypt with ten plagues to win Israel's freedom, and Moses led all two million of the freed slaves to Mount Sinai. There God gave the Israelites the Ten Commandments and a code of law to follow. Moses led the Israelites for forty years and died at age 120.

### What's Up with Moses?

God chose Moses to do four specific things.

1. *Moses was God's choice to deliver the Israelites from slavery.*
2. *Moses was God's choice to give us the Ten Commandments.*
3. *Moses was God's choice to give Israel his law and is honored in* **Judaism** *as the lawgiver.*
4. *Moses was God's choice to write the first five books of the Old Testament. Moses was also the first* **prophet**.

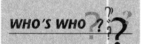

### WHO'S WHO

**Pharaoh:** *a title for the ruler of ancient Egypt*

**Judaism:** *the Jewish religion*

**prophet:** *someone who speaks for God*

## A High Priest

**AARON:** Aaron was Moses' brother and his companion during the Exodus period. He became the Israelites' first high **priest**.

> ### Bible Summary: Exodus 1–6
> Moses was a member of the royal family (he was adopted into Egypt's royal family after his river ride in the basket. You can check that story out in Exodus 2:1–10). After killing an Egyptian slave driver, Moses fled to the Sinai desert. Forty years later God told Moses to return to Egypt and free his people. Moses told God he didn't feel up for the job, but God promised to be with Moses. God promised Moses he would be successful.

## What's Up with Exodus 1–6?

**1** *The Israelites lived a brutal life.* We often think the plagues were too rough on the Egyptians. But after over four hundred years of enslaving the Israelites, the plagues were the right punishment.

**2** *God's words to Moses help us understand what kind of person God is.* We get to see that God keeps his promises, hears the prayers of his people, and responds to their suffering. He is a God who will act to deliver his people, and who has planned a wonderful future for them.

**3** *Moses made major excuses.* God replied by telling Moses God's personal name. In Hebrew the name God uses (YHWH in Hebrew, or Jehovah) means "the one who is always present." God made it crystal clear. Moses wouldn't succeed because he was buff. He would succeed because God was present with him. The name God revealed to Moses is simple to translate—"I AM."

*Kay Arthur:* Of all the names of God, Jehovah is the name most frequently used in the Old Testament (6,823 times).[1]

**WHO'S WHO**

*priest:* a middleman between God and the Israelites

**>>>CHECK IT OUT:**

Exodus 1; 3:1–4:17; 6:2–8

**KEY POINT**

**God keeps his promises.**

**OUTSIDE CONNECTION**

21

 **MIRACLES!**

**Bible Summary: Exodus 7–19**

It reads like a modern-day action movie. Pharaoh refused to free his Israelite slaves. Moses announced a series of plagues. Ten terrible **judgments** devastated Egypt, and Pharaoh was forced to let the Israelites go. When Pharaoh changed his mind and pursued God's people, the Lord gave the Israelites an escape route by parting the sea. The waves came down just in time to drown the entire Egyptian army, and God's people were free to travel to Mount Sinai!

*judgments: acts of God intended to punish*

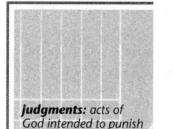

**OUTSIDE CONNECTION**

**Norman L. Geisler:** *If God exists, then miracles are possible.*[2]

### What's Up with Exodus 7–15?

**1** *God told Moses he would harden Pharaoh's heart and that Pharaoh would refuse to let the Israelites go.* You might be wondering if it was fair for God to harden Pharaoh's heart. Okay, here's the explanation. God didn't really "harden" Pharaoh's heart. God progressively revealed more and more of his power. The more Pharaoh saw of God's power, the more stubborn he got. There wasn't any way he was going to give in to God—he was going to stand his ground, even though he'd eventually lose.

**2** *On the first **Passover**, a lamb was killed and its blood was sprinkled on the doorways of Israelite homes.* When the angel who struck the firstborn sons of Egypt saw the blood, it "passed over" those homes. The New Testament recalls this event in Jesus' title, the "Lamb of God." It teaches that Jesus shed his blood in payment for our sins, that we might be saved from punishment for our sins.

**3** *God told the Israelites to remember what he had done to free them by eating a Passover meal every year.* They were to serve the same food the people ate in Egypt on the night that God struck the firstborn sons of the Egyptians but spared his own people. Jewish families still celebrate Passover each spring. (You can check out what they ate in Exodus 12:8.)

>>> **CHECK IT OUT:**

Exodus 7:3–5; 7:13; 8:15

*Passover: the meal that Hebrews shared on the night that God "passed over" their homes but struck dead the firstborn sons of Egypt*

>>> **CHECK IT OUT:**

Exodus 12:1–14; 21–28; John 1:29–34

22

**4** *God's actions and miracles help us understand him better.* God is known throughout the Bible as the Creator who made the world, and as the Redeemer whose mighty acts in history won the freedom of his people. Through these acts we get a better understanding of who God is and how much he loves us.

 **WRITTEN IN STONE**

> **Bible Summary: Exodus 20–24**
> Moses led the Israelites through the wilderness to Mount Sinai. Clouds and lightning covered the mountain as God spoke to his people. God called Moses to the top of the mountain and gave him the Ten Commandments along with additional laws for the Israelites to follow. Imagine meeting God face-to-face and getting the laws that everyone would follow for generations. Cool!

### What Are the Ten Commandments?

The Ten Commandments teach basic morality. The first four reveal what it takes to have a good relationship with God. The rest show how to have good relationships with others.

>>>**CHECK IT OUT:**
Exodus 20:1–17

*Bob Briner: Consecration precedes conquest. Before we can win, we must have committed our course of action to God. We must put our own desires, goals, motives and plans aside in favor of God's direction.*[3]

**OUTSIDE CONNECTION**

### What's Up with Exodus 20–24?

**1** *God gave these commandments to his own people.* God did not give the commandments to strangers and say, "Keep them and you will become my people." In other words, you don't obey God to get his acceptance. You're already accepted by God, but people who have been saved by God will *want* to live the kind of life his commandments describe.

>>>**CHECK IT OUT:**
Exodus 20:1

23

## A Good Relationship with God . . .

| Scripture | Command | How to Do It |
| --- | --- | --- |
| 1. Exodus 20:3 | Do not put any other gods before God. | Put God first always! |
| 2. Exodus 20:4–6 | Don't worship idols. | Reject false ideas about God. |
| 3. Exodus 20:7 | Don't take God's name in vain. | Never act like God isn't watching. |
| 4. Exodus 20:8–11 | Keep the Sabbath holy. | Set aside a day of rest and remember God. |

## A Good Relationship with Others . . .

| Scripture | Command | How to Do It |
| --- | --- | --- |
| 5. Exodus 20:12 | Honor your father and mother. | Show respect for your parents. |
| 6. Exodus 20:13 | Do not murder. | Don't harm others. |
| 7. Exodus 20:14 | Don't commit adultery. | Be faithful to your spouse. |
| 8. Exodus 20:15 | Don't steal. | Show respect for others and their stuff. |
| 9. Exodus 20:16 | Do not testify falsely. | Respect others . . . their lives and their property. |
| 10. Exodus 20:17 | Do not covet. | Care about others, not about their possessions. |

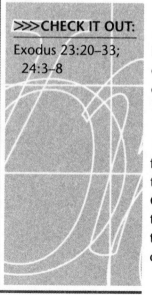

>>>**CHECK IT OUT:**

Exodus 23:20–33;
24:3–8

**2** *God did not force the Israelites to accept his laws.* He first explained what he expected of them. He warned of punishment for disobedience and promised blessings if they obeyed. The people promised to obey God. Did they *actually* do that? Hmmmm . . . keep reading!

**3** *The Law Covenant.* In ancient times a *covenant* might be an oath, a contract, or a treaty. The Law Covenant is different from the covenant God made with Abraham. What are the differences? Basically, the Abrahamic Covenant involved God only (meaning God was the only person committed in the covenant) and the Law Covenant involved both God and the Israelites (meaning both parties were committed in the covenant).

**WORSHIP ON THE GO!**

**Bible Summary: Exodus 25–40**

Moses received more than the Ten Commandments. With the law God gave him the blueprint for a **worship** center. God gave specific details about what he wanted the temple to look like and what furniture he wanted in the temple. Moses and the Israelites followed God's instruction and completed the worship center, which was called the **tabernacle**. When it was finished, Moses and the people got together to **dedicate** the tabernacle to the Lord.

### >>>CHECK IT OUT:
Galatians 3:17–22

**worship:** *honoring God with our praise*

**tabernacle:** *a tent, also called the "tent of meeting"*

**dedicate:** *to set apart for the service of God*

## What's Up with Exodus 25–40?

**1** *A place to worship.* Why were God's directions so specific? Because each detail of the tabernacle taught a spiritual truth. For instance, God said there should be only one door leading into the worship center to show there is only one way to approach God—his way!

### >>>CHECK IT OUT:
Exodus 32:1–35;
40:34–38

Have you ever set up a "golden calf" or an idol in your life? How did it affect your relationship with God?_____

 Your Move

_____

_____

When have you felt like Moses wandering in a "desert"? What can you learn from that experience?_____

_____

_____

What are some things you can do to keep your focus on God during worship?

_____

_____

 **GET REAL**

God loves you. He hates it when you wander away from him. But when you do, he lovingly reaches out for you . . . gives you a few simple rules to follow to keep your life straight, then sends you on your way. Your job? Simple. DO what God asks. It's not too much, and, hey, NOT doing what God asks can REALLY hurt your life.

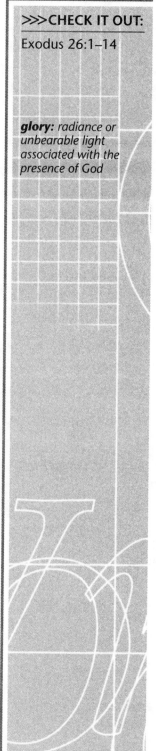

**glory:** *radiance or unbearable light associated with the presence of God*

**2** *The golden calf.* While Moses was on Mount Sinai, the Israelites begged Aaron to make an idol in the form of a calf. Many worshiped the idol, giving it credit for freeing God's people from Egypt. God punished the Israelites who worshiped the calf. Even though God's people broke his law, God remained faithful to his promise to Abraham. When the tabernacle was completed, God filled it with his **glory** to show he truly was present with his people.

## CHAPTER CHECKUP

1. Why is Moses such an important person in the Old Testament?
2. What is a miracle? Name one miracle you've read about in the Old Testament.
3. What miracles did God perform to free the Israelite slaves?
4. The Ten Commandments help you have good relationships with whom?

### CRASH COURSE

▶ Exodus tells the story of the Israelites' deliverance from slavery in Egypt.
▶ Moses was God's choice to confront Egypt's Pharaoh and to announce the miraculous judgments that forced the Egyptians to free their slaves.
▶ After God freed the slaves, he gave them the Ten Commandments to teach them how to maintain a healthy relationship with him and with each other.
▶ God promised to bless his people, if they kept his commandments.
▶ God also gave Moses plans for a portable worship center, the tabernacle, where they could worship and offer sacrifices.

26

# Extreme Adventure!

## LEVITICUS • NUMBERS • DEUTERONOMY

**CHAPTER CAPTURE**

- Laws You Can Live By
- How to Make a Sacrifice
- Lost in the Wilderness
- The Law a Second Time

 **LET'S DIVE IN!**

When we begin Leviticus, the Israelites have just been delivered from slavery in Egypt and have traveled to Mount Sinai. Moses gives them God's laws (a.k.a. the Ten Commandments) and even a blueprint for a new worship center. While they're at Mount Sinai, God reveals other rules for **holy living**.

Next the Israelites head for the promised land that God promised to Abraham's descendants years before. Unfortunately, the Israelites rebel (yeah, like you couldn't have guessed that one!) and spend thirty-eight years wandering in the desert. (Check out the map of their wanderings on page 28.)

Only when a new generation of Israelites grow up and replace the older, more disobedient Israelites are they able to cross the borders of Canaan. And there, just beyond the Jordan River, Moses reviews the covenant for the new generation.

*holy living: living like Jesus, living set apart from the world*

27

*Timeline of Leviticus, Numbers, and Deuteronomy*

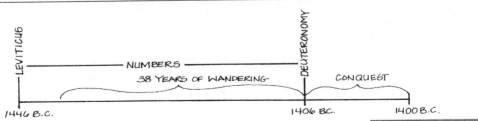

## The Israelites' Wilderness Wanderings

When the Israelites left Mount Sinai, they traveled northeast to Kadesh Barnea and rebelled against God. After wandering for thirty-eight years they traveled north to the plains of Moab. While there, Moses publicly reviewed God's law for them.

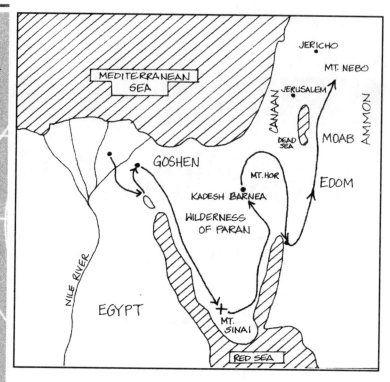

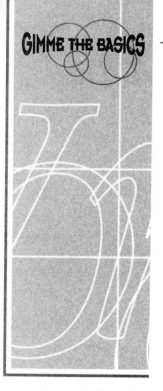

GIMME THE BASICS

 **LEVITICUS**

*. . . laws for living holy*

| | |
|---|---|
| WHO | Moses wrote this |
| WHAT | book of laws |
| WHERE | at Mount Sinai, |
| WHEN | around 1446 B.C., |
| WHY | to remind the Israelites they were God's special people. |

 **LAWS, LAWS, LAWS**

### Bible Summary: Leviticus

You want laws? You got 'em. Leviticus means "about the Levites," and this book contains rules for the Levites—the priests and worship leaders. But this book is about more than the Levites. It's chock full of rules that apply to *all* the Israelites. They are intended to remind God's people that they belong to him.

## What's Up with Leviticus?

**1** *Offerings and sacrifices (Leviticus 1–7).* Let's say you're an Israelite. How would you approach God? What would you do? Well, for starters, you'd make an **offering**, also known as a **sacrifice**. If you want to approach God to express thanks, you'd offer one type of sacrifice. If you've sinned, you'd offer a different type of sacrifice. These chapters in Leviticus help us understand the *type* of sacrifice you'd offer depending on what you wanted to say to God.

**offering:** *a gift*

**sacrifice:** *death of something to pay for our sins*

>>>**CHECK IT OUT:**
Leviticus 5:1–10

**2** *Priesthood (Leviticus 8–10).* Aaron and his sons, who were Levites, were called to be priests in a solemn ceremony, and the newly finished tabernacle was dedicated. Only Aaron's relatives were allowed to present Israelite offerings or sacrifices to the Lord.

>>>**CHECK IT OUT:**
Leviticus 9

**3** *Loads of laws (Leviticus 11–15).* Okay, there's two basic kinds of law in the Old Testament. The first kind is called *moral* law. Moral law is all about what is right and wrong and about the way we treat God and other people. The other kind of law is **ritual** law (sometimes called ceremonial law). Ritual laws were rules the Israelites were to live by simply because they were God's people.

>>>**CHECK IT OUT:**
Leviticus 11–15

**ritual:** *having to do with worship practices*

**Joni Eareckson Tada:** *God is telling his people what he expects of them in their worship. God wants his people to understand that all of life is spiritual; all of life's activities come under his domain. How we plow our fields or how we shop at the market. How we mate our animals or even how we talk to a gas station attendant. Everything we do can be a way of worshiping him.*[1]

**OUTSIDE CONNECTION**

**4** *Ritual laws (Leviticus 11–15).* These laws were really important. They gave Israelites instructions about what they could and could not eat, what they were supposed to do when a person was born, when a person contracted an infectious skin disease, died, etc. These ritual laws reminded the Israelites of one important life issue: God is interested in every aspect of their lives—no matter what!

>>>**CHECK IT OUT:**
Leviticus 13:45–46; 16:14–16; 16:29–34

29

**GO!**

Leviticus 16:31
(blood sacrifice)

**>>>CHECK IT OUT:**

Leviticus 18:6–18;
19:12–18; 20:22–
26

**worship:** *praising God for who he is and what he has done*

**5** *The Day of Atonement (Leviticus 16).* The long list of sacrifices in Leviticus 1–7 were sacrifices that could atone only for unintentional sins. So, what about the sins an Israelite committed knowingly, fully aware that he or she was doing wrong?

Solution? Once a year on the Day of Atonement the high priest took a <u>blood sacrifice</u> into the inner room of the tabernacle, the Holy of Holies, to make an atonement *for all the sins of the Israelites.*

**6** *Laws of practical holiness (Leviticus 17–22).* Want to be a good friend? Interested in being the perfect kid for your parents? These chapters will help you hit that target! These chapters contain a variety of laws that the Israelites were to follow. Many of the laws were moral laws about relationships between people.

**7** *Worshiping God (Leviticus 23–25).* These chapters describe special festivals when the Israelites gathered to **worship** God. Some of these same festivals are still celebrated today!

Read Leviticus 19:12–18. Why do you think God made these laws?

_____

_____

Which ones do you think are the most difficult to follow?_____

_____

Who do you know that has lived a "holy life"? Why does this person come to mind?_____

_____

It's not easy to follow all of the laws that are in the Bible. God doesn't make us robots. He doesn't want to implant a microchip in our brains to make us do everything he wants. He wants us to *choose* to obey him.

**8** *Conditions for blessing (Leviticus 26–27).* The last chapters of Leviticus are super important. They remind the Israelites about the covenant God made with them on Mount Sinai. The covenant promised blessings to those who obeyed God, and punishment to those who disobeyed him.

 **NUMBERS**

*. . . a real long trip*

| WHO | Moses wrote this |
|-----|------------------|
| WHAT | narrative history |
| WHERE | after reaching the borders of Canaan |
| WHEN | around 1406 B.C. |
| WHY | to remind the Israelites what happens when you rebel against God. |

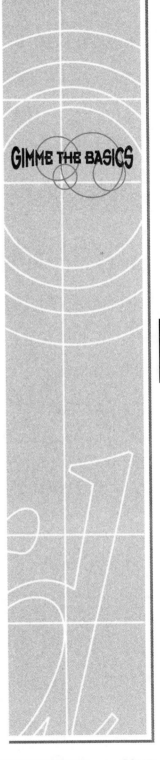

GIMME THE BASICS

 **WE WON'T BE THERE TOMORROW**

**Bible Summary: Numbers**

Why in the WORLD is this book called Numbers? Well, numbers is filled with numbers—various accounts of how many Israelites were wandering through the desert. After camping for a year at Mount Sinai, the Israelites headed for Canaan. When they got there the Israelites refused to trust God and rebelled. For the next thirty-eight years the Israelites wandered in the desert. (Scope out the time line on page 27 to see exactly when this was.) While they were in the desert God provided for all their needs. When all the adults who had been freed from Egypt had died, Moses led the new (and more trusting) generation back to Canaan. Numbers has three main sections:

- Preparation for the Journey (Numbers 1–10)
- Journeying toward Canaan (Numbers 11–21)
- Waiting on the plains of Moab (Numbers 22–36)

**promised land:** *the land that God promised to Abraham's descendants. Known today as Palestine.*

>>> CHECK IT OUT:

Numbers 13:26–
14:25

### KEY POINT

**God is with us on the journey of life.**

>>> CHECK IT OUT:

Numbers 15:1–21

## What's Up with Numbers?

**1** *Trip prep (Numbers 1–10).* There were tons of things to do while they were camped at the mountain. First the Israelites took a census that said there were 603,550 men. With women and children, the people numbered over two million! Then they constructed and dedicated the tabernacle and its furnishings. God set the descendants of Levi apart to care for the tabernacle, and jobs were assigned to various Levite families. When all these tasks were completed, the Israelites were ready to leave for the **promised land**. Finally!

**2** *The Canaan vacation (Numbers 11–21).* What an experience! Imagine having God with you as you journey to the land he's promised you. He leads you with a pillar of fire. He feeds you with manna from heaven. Surely the Israelites stuck with God, right? Nope! Instead of being grateful, the Israelites grumbled and complained.

When they reached the borders of Canaan, Moses sent a search force to explore the land. The men reported that Canaan was fertile, but that its inhabitants were powerful and their fortified cities looked mighty scary. Terrified by the report, the Israelites refused to obey God's command to attack and seize the promised land.

Under the Law Covenant, direct disobedience called for punishment. But Moses prayed for the people, and the Lord pardoned their sin. Yet the Israelites could not avoid the consequences of their unwillingness to obey the Lord. Until the entire generation of those who were unwilling to obey God died out, the Israelites were forced to wander in the wilderness—waiting.

**3** *God reaffirms his faithfulness (Numbers 15–21).* Want a reminder of God's faithfulness? Check out the first words of Numbers 15. The Israelites had rebelled, but God immediately told Moses, *"Speak to the Israelites and say to them, 'After you enter the land I am giving you . . .'"* (Numbers 15). Despite repeated failures to trust and obey God, God intended to keep his promises and give the Israelites the promised land.

**4** *Waiting on the plains of Moab (Numbers 22–36).* As the years of wandering came to a close, the Israelites followed a major trade route east of Mount Sinai. They avoided some of their enemies but fought others. Balak, ruler of Moab, was frightened, and sent for a man named <u>Balaam</u>, who was supposed to have supernatural powers. The ruler of Moab hoped Balaam would be able to curse the Israelites. Balaam tried to curse the Israelites, but God intervened and Balaam was forced to bless them instead.

**5** *Balaam's advice.* Balaam wanted to earn the money the Moabites offered him, but Israel could not be cursed. So he suggested the Moabites try to turn God against his own people! Following Balaam's advice, the Moabite ruler sent young women to seduce Israelite men and invite them to sacrifice to idols. Balaam reasoned God would punish the Israelites himself, and they would be defeated by his Moabite clients. God administered punishment alright, but only to the guilty. He remained faithful to his promises to the people as a whole.

**6** *The second census.* When they set out to take the second census, adults who left or had died were replaced by a new crop of Israelites. A second census showed that despite these deaths, the Israelites were as numerous as before, with over 600,000 men. The new generation learned from their parents' failures. This generation obeyed the Lord their God.

**7** *The Moabites are thrashed.* Various laws are reviewed in chapters 27–30. Chapters 31–33 talk about how the Moabites were defeated and how several of Israel's tribes requested land that the Moabites had lived on.

**8** *Moses defines the boundaries of Canaan and makes plans.* Moses explained to the Israelites how territory will be distributed to each tribe.

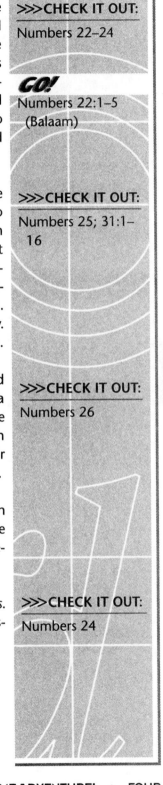

>>>**CHECK IT OUT:**

Numbers 22–24

*GO!*

Numbers 22:1–5
 (Balaam)

>>>**CHECK IT OUT:**

Numbers 25; 31:1–16

>>>**CHECK IT OUT:**

Numbers 26

>>>**CHECK IT OUT:**

Numbers 24

33

**GIMME THE BASICS**

 **DEUTERONOMY**

*. . . a pop quiz on the law*

| WHO | Moses preached |
|---|---|
| WHAT | sermons reviewing God's law |
| WHERE | on the plains of Moab |
| WHEN | about 1406 B.C. |
| WHY | to remind the new generation of Israelites what God expects. |

## PAY ATTENTION THIS TIME!

**Bible Summary: Deuteronomy**

Deuteronomy means "second law." The new generation of Israelites was about to enter the promised land, so Moses takes some time to remind them about all that God had done for them. He summarized the way God's people were to live in order to enjoy his blessing. The book ends with an account of Moses' farewell blessing and his death. Here are some of the major sections of Deuteronomy:

- Remembering the journey (Deuteronomy 1:1–4:43)
- Reviewing God's law (Deuteronomy 4:44–11)
- Rules to remember (Deuteronomy 12–26)
- Consequences to consider (Deuteronomy 27–28)
- Covenant commitment (Deuteronomy 29–30)
- Moses' farewell and death (Deuteronomy 31–34)

### What's Up with Deuteronomy?

**1** *Remembering the journey (Deuteronomy 1:1–4:43).* Moses talks about the thirty-eight-year journey from Mount Sinai to the border of the promised land. He urged the new generation to learn from history, and especially to develop a sense of wonder at the special relationship they had with the God of the universe.

>>> **CHECK IT OUT:**

Deuteronomy 4:32–40

**OUTSIDE CONNECTION**

*Josh McDowell: When you belong to God he already sees you as his eternally loveable, infinitely valuable, and thoroughly competent daughter or son. Nothing you do on your own attracts God's attention or wins his care for you. Your status as God's child and all the blessings that come with it stem from what he has made you and what he has done for you because of Christ.[2]*

34

**2** *Reviewing God's law (Deuteronomy 4:44–11:32).* Moses restated a number of laws given at Mount Sinai, including the Ten Commandments. When you read these, you might have some of the following questions:

**Q:** What does it mean to "fear the Lord"?
**A:** It doesn't mean "be afraid of God." The phrase means "show respect for God" by seeking to please him.

**Q:** What does "love" have to do with law?
**A:** Love moved God to give Israel the law, and love moves people to keep it. The law showed how to express love for God.

**Q:** Why did God tell the Israelites to destroy the Canaanites?
**A:** God was punishing the immorality and idolatry of the Canaanites. If allowed to remain, their practices would have corrupted God's people.

**3** *Rules to remember (Deuteronomy 12–26).* There's some review here. A lot of what's here is also in Leviticus. A few new themes are also introduced. Deuteronomy 17:14–20 limits the rights of any future king, while Deuteronomy 20 sets out humane rules for warfare. Deuteronomy 18 warns against seeking guidance through any **occult practice** and promises that God will provide prophets to guide them in his way.

**4** *Consequences! (Deuteronomy 27–28).* The Law Covenant is a contract covenant: When the Israelites kept the law, God blessed them. When they disobeyed, God disciplined them. These chapters spell out both blessings for obedience and punishments for disobedience.

**5** *Commitment . . . puuuuulease! (Deuteronomy 29–30).* Moses called on the Israelites to make a choice and to keep the covenant they had made with the Lord their God.

**6** *Moses' ultimate good-bye speech (Deuteronomy 31–34).* God chose a successor who would lead the Israelites after Moses. Moses blessed the people whom he had led for years.

*occult practice: any practice of devotion with satanic powers*

**>>>CHECK IT OUT:**

Deuteronomy 18:9–22

**>>>CHECK IT OUT:**

Deuteronomy 29:15–20

35

Then Moses went to the top of Mount Nebo and looked over the Jordan River, where he was able to see the promised land. Moses died there, and God himself buried his faithful servant (see Deuteronomy 34:5–6).

# CHAPTER CHECKUP

1. What's the theme of Leviticus?
2. What Bible terms are linked with Leviticus's teaching on sacrifice? Why is it so important for us to understand these terms?
3. What is the difference between ritual law and moral law?
4. Why did the Israelites have to wander in the wilderness for thirty-eight years?
5. What roles does love play in the law God gave to Israel?

## CRASH COURSE

▶ God gave the Israelites laws for holy living, which are found in Leviticus. The sacrifices mentioned in Leviticus show us that everyone sins and the penalty for sin is death.
▶ The offerings and sacrifices specified in Leviticus teach us that blood atonement is required if we are to be forgiven. Two different types of laws are pointed out: moral laws and ritual laws.
▶ Numbers tells us about the rebellion of the Israelites. As a result, God required them to wander in the desert for thirty-eight years.
▶ Deuteronomy records Moses' last words to the Israelites as they were about to enter the promised land.

CHAPTER CAPTURE

- Canaan (a.k.a. the Promised Land)
- Obedience and Victory
- The Judges
- Blessing by Trusting

# Conquest and Collapse

## JOSHUA • JUDGES • RUTH

 **LET'S DIVE IN!**

After all of that history . . . wandering in the desert, disobeying God, receiving the law . . . a new generation of Israelites was ready to take possession of the promised land. Why? Because this was finally a generation that was willing to trust and obey God. They learned from their ancestors' mistakes and decided not to make the choices they did. So everything should be hunky-dory, right? It should be smooth sailing now, shouldn't it? Well, not exactly. You see, this generation's obedience was fleeting. Eventually, they went astray too and soon found themselves under the attack of other nations.

 **JOSHUA**

### . . . the conquest of Canaan

| | |
|---|---|
| WHO | An unnamed author wrote |
| WHAT | a history lesson in |
| WHERE | the promised land (Canaan) |
| WHEN | around 1400 B.C. |
| WHY | to emphasize the importance of obedience to the Lord. |

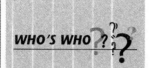

**JOSHUA:** Joshua became the leader of the Israelites after Moses died. He loved God and was faithful to him. And he learned a lot about leadership from Moses, as he stood by his side throughout Moses' life. During Joshua's reign, the Israelites stayed close to God.

> **Bible Summary: Joshua**
>
> Led by Joshua, the Israelites crossed the Jordan River and defeated a number of other nations (check out the illustration below). They became a mean, lean spiritual machine. The Israelites flourished during Joshua's reign, and Joshua was the one who divided the Israelites into twelve tribes, too. Check out the stuff this book covers:
> - Getting ready to invade (Joshua 1–5)
> - Invading the land (Joshua 6–12)
> - Free Land Day! (Joshua 13–21)
> - Joshua's good-bye speech (Joshua 22–24)

*Israelite Conquests*

*This is a map of the conquests of Israel. Canaan was not a united nation, making it easier for the Israelites to invade their land. Joshua's first battle in the country split the country in two sections, and then the Israelites defeated both sections.*

SIDON

MEROM

MT. HERMON

MISREPHOTH MAIM

HAZOR

SEA OF GALILEE

MEDITERRANEAN SEA

ACHSHAPH

SHIMRON

MEGIDDO

CANAAN

BETH HORON  AI  GILGAL

GIBEON  JERICHO  SHITTIM

LIBNAH  MAKKEDAH

JERUSALEM

EGLON  HEBRON  DEAD SEA

DEBIR

38

## What's Up with Joshua?

**1** *Getting ready to win! (Joshua 1–6).* The Israelites sharpened their weapons and planned their strategy for the fight ahead.

**2** *Invading the land (Joshua 6–12).* Most of Joshua 6–8 is devoted to the fall of Jericho. Here's what happened. Jericho was surrounded by walls. The Israelites couldn't penetrate the walls, so Joshua instructed his army to walk around the city six times. On the seventh day God told them to walk around the city seven times and blow their trumpets. When they blew their trumpets, guess what happened? The walls fell down and the Israelites conquered!

**3** *Free land day! (Joshua 13–21).* Joshua gave the newly conquered land (Canaan) to the Israelite **clans** and families. It went like this. Everybody drew **lots** to find out how much land they received. And because they believed God was in charge of the lots, everyone felt as though God had personally distributed the land.

**4** *Joshua's good-bye speech (Joshua 22–24).* Many years after the victory over the Canaanites, Joshua called the Israelites and reminded them of all God had done. He challenged them to serve the Lord. Then he died. Joshua's final challenge is still relevant today: *"Choose for yourselves this day whom you will serve"* (Joshua 24:15).

 **JUDGES**

*. . . the long decline*

| | |
|---|---|
| WHO | Someone |
| WHAT | wrote this short history of |
| WHERE | events in Canaan |
| WHEN | from about 1375 to 1050 B.C. |
| WHY | to show us how important it is to be committed to God. |

>>> CHECK IT OUT:

Joshua 1:6–9; 2:8–11; 4:1–14; 5:1–10

>>> CHECK IT OUT:

Joshua 6:1–25; 7–9

>>> CHECK IT OUT:

Joshua 16; Numbers 35:6–25; Joshua 20:1–9; 21:1–3; Leviticus 24:8

**clans:** *groups of closely related families*

**lots:** *an object used as a counter in determining a question by chance; like drawing straws*

>>> CHECK IT OUT:

Joshua 24:1–27

39

Joshua learned a lot from Moses. How might God use a strong leader in your life?_____

_____

What walls has God called you to tear down for him?_____

_____

What things has God given you? How have you shown him that you appreciate those gifts?_____

_____

Getting new stuff is always cool. Every year we look forward to Christmas with expectations of getting a new video game or skateboard or whatever. God loves to give us stuff. But we can't take his gifts for granted. God's gifts require our obedience. We need to do what God asks us to do. And when he gives us stuff, we need to remember to thank him for his awesome gifts.

 **I'LL KEEP YOU IN LINE!**

### Bible Summary: Judges

Okay, so you'd think that after everything they'd seen God do, the people would continue serving God, right? Bzzzzzzzt. After Joshua died, the Israelites turned to worshiping the **pagan** idols of their neighbors. What happened next? The Israelite nation became oppressed by enemies. This lasted until the people of Israel once again returned to him and prayed for deliverance. Then God provided leaders called **judges** who threw out the oppressors. During the judges' rule, the Israelites did not remain faithful to God. The Book of Judges has three main sections:

- Major problems (Judges 1:1–3:5)
- Stories of the judges (Judges 3:6–16:31)
- What happens when you stray (Judges 17–21)

*pagan: refers to the worship of false gods*

*judges: Israelite leaders; spiritual, political, and military leaders*

>>>CHECK IT OUT:

Deuteronomy 7:1–6; Judges 1:27–2:4

### What's Up with Judges?

1 *Major problems (Judges 1:1–3:5).* As the Israelites took over the land, they were told to get rid of the Canaanites, so

the Israelites wouldn't be corrupted by the Canaanites. Well, not all of the Israelites did this. As a result, they were affected by Canaanites' false spiritual beliefs. The result was that the Israelites' spiritual lives totally fell apart.

**Josh McDowell:** *If you want to experience fulfillment, you need to enter through the door of trusting obedience, accepting his care as a gift, counting on God enough to eagerly discover and do his plan. God has a way for you to go. He has marked a path. A good plan. His set of life-giving instructions. But what he wants for you and from you is even more special and specific than that. God's plans are so solid and sure that the Bible calls them his will.*[1]

**2** *Stories of the judges (Judges 3:6–13).* Here's a question for you. . . . What was a judge? A judge was an individual God raised up to lead one or more Israelite tribes. These people were gifted and exercised power to make important decisions. They made legal and governmental decisions. Many of them were also military leaders. And you didn't get this job because your dad had been a judge; you got it because God gave it to you. Here are some examples of judges; we'll start with Deborah.

**DEBORAH:** All ancient societies were **patriarchal** (PAY-tree-ar-cuhl), and Israel was no exception. Priests, town elders, political and military leaders, like the heads of households, were men. But here's Deborah! She blew the doors off the concept of a patriarchal society. She was a prophetess and emerged as the acknowledged leader, the judge, of several of the northern Israelite tribes. God gave her the gifts she needed to be a good ruler. What matters today is not how society limits us, but how God enables us!

**GIDEON:** You remember the famous story about Gideon, right? The one where he and his small army of three hundred took on a huge army and won? What's more incredible is that Gideon knew about his weaknesses and still obeyed God. The lesson? Even a weak person is strong when they're called by God.

**OUTSIDE CONNECTION**

41

**WHO'S WHO**

*patriarchal:* run by men

**>>>CHECK IT OUT:**
Judges 4:1–16

**WHO'S WHO**

**>>>CHECK IT OUT:**
Judges 6–7

**OUTSIDE CONNECTION**

**WHO'S WHO** ??

**Philistines:** *people from Crete, who liked war and who controlled coastal Canaan*

**>>>CHECK IT OUT:**

Judges 16

42

**GIMME THE BASICS**

---

**Martin Luther:** *When God contemplates some great work, he begins it by the hand of some poor, weak human creature, to whom he afterward gives aid, so that the enemies who seek to obstruct it are overcome.*[2]

**SAMSON:** Samson is the dude everyone remembers for his long hair and his amazing strength. He was a judge, but he never had the chance to lead the Israelites out of oppression from the **Philistines**. Samson was a passionate man, and his passion led him to fall in love with a prostitute. He gave her the secret of his strength, and with this secret the prostitute had him killed. Samson was super strong, but it takes complete commitment to God to do great things for him.

**3** *The results of wandering (Judges 17–21).* This book closes with a description of three incidents that reveal what happens when a society loses its direction by turning away from God's Word and his ways.

 **RUTH**

*. . . simple faith*

| | |
|---|---|
| WHO | An unnamed author |
| WHAT | wrote this beautiful story of a young woman who honored God |
| WHERE | in Bethlehem |
| WHEN | during the days of the judges |
| WHY | to show that when a society abandons God, individual commitment is honored. |

 **A PILLAR OF FAITH**

**Bible Summary: Ruth**

This book of the Bible takes its name from the daughter-in-law of Naomi. Naomi left Israel during a famine and returned years later after her husband and sons died. Ruth committed herself to Naomi and to Israel's God. Although in poverty, Ruth's virtue and character won the admiration of Naomi's husband's relative, named Boaz. Boaz married Ruth, and the union led to the birth of Obed, the grandfather of Israel's greatest king, David.

**RUTH:** Ruth's famous words to Naomi express her commitment. *"Where you go I will go, and where you stay I will stay. Your people will be my people and your God my God"* (Ruth 1:16). Ruth's modesty and obvious commitment to her mother-in-law won the admiration of the community and the love of Boaz.

### What's Up with Ruth?

**1** *Stories for the heart.* This awesome story reminds us that even when the things we rely on break down, we can still live faithful and fulfilling lives.

**2** *An example of commitment.* People through the years have looked at Ruth's and Naomi's relationship as a guide for how to love their friends and even their spouses. Lots of people include some words from this story (specifically Ruth 1:16) in marriage ceremonies.

**3** *Boaz . . . the redeemer.* When a man died childless, a relative could marry the widow. Any son of the resulting union would gain the first husband's inheritance. But to rescue the lost estate, the redeemer had to be closely related to the widow, and he had to be willing to accept the responsibility.

## CHAPTER cHECkUp

1. What is the main message of the Book of Joshua?
2. What is the main message of Judges?
3. What was a judge, and what did the judges do for the Israelites?
4. What is the main message of the Book of Ruth?

**CRASH COURSE**

▶ Joshua tells the story of the Israelites' conquest of Canaan. The miracle at Jericho taught the Israelites that obedience to God's commands assures victory, and their failure at Ai taught Israel that disobeying God leads to defeat.

▶ Judges relates incidents that happened during a long period of time. The judges were political, military, and reli-

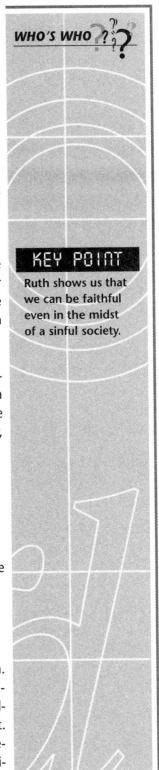

**WHO'S WHO ?? ?**

**KEY POINT**

Ruth shows us that we can be faithful even in the midst of a sinful society.

43

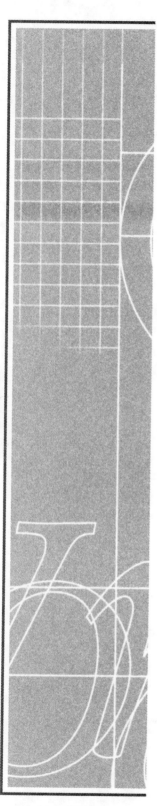

gious leaders whom God provided when the Israelites looked to him for help. The Israelites didn't stay faithful to God, so they suffered greatly.

▶ Ruth reminds us that people can find blessing by trusting God even when their friends have turned away from him.

44

**CHAPTER CAPTURE**

- The Last Judge
- A King with a Flaw
- God's Anointed
- One Buff Nation
- The Davidic Covenant

# A New Beginning

## 1, 2 SAMUEL • 1 CHRONICLES

 **LET'S DIVE IN!**

Israel was a really disjointed, unorganized group of people. During the age of the judges Israel was barely surviving in the promised land. Samuel **anointed** Saul in 1050 B.C. and made Saul Israel's first king. After a few years, David took over as king. David united the country, defeated every enemy they encountered, and established Jerusalem as Israel's political and religious capital. When David died in 970 B.C. the Israelites occupied ten times as much territory as when he became king.

**anointed:** *set apart for a task by a ceremony that included pouring oil on a person's head*

45

### Recycling Stories

The stories that we get from these times in the Bible are really important. They've been told and retold throughout history. Want to know more about the time that we're talking about? Check out the chart on the next page.

 **1 SAMUEL**

*. . . the beginning of the monarchy*

| | |
|---|---|
| WHO | We're not sure who wrote this |
| WHAT | history of |
| WHERE | events in Canaan |
| WHEN | from 1050 to 1010 B.C. |
| WHY | to record how Israel became a united nation ruled by kings. |

 GIMME THE BASICS

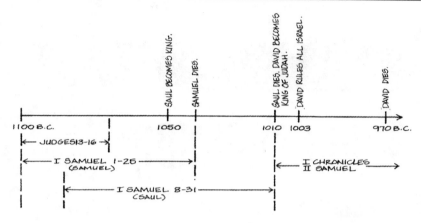

 **DEDICATED TO THE LORD**

> **Bible Summary: 1 Samuel**
> This book begins with the birth of Samuel and his dedication to the Lord. It goes on to talk about Samuel's ministry and how he lived out his old age. The Israelites pressured Samuel, their last judge, to give up his position and anoint a king. Then the focus of the book shifts to Saul, whose flaws lead God to reject him. David comes on the scene, and the book traces the relationship between David and Saul. Eventually David becomes king. Here's an outline:
> - Samuel (1 Samuel 1–7)
> - Saul (1 Samuel 8–15)
> - Saul and David (1 Samuel 16–20)

**WHO'S WHO ?**

**SAMUEL:** When Samuel was just three years old (really young, huh!?), his mom dedicated him to serve in the tabernacle as God's servant. Samuel was Israel's last judge, and he had the opportunity to chase the Philistines into Israel's land. As he got older, the people demanded a king, and God eventually gave them what they wanted. He instructed Samuel to anoint Saul as king.

### What's Up with 1 Samuel 1–7?

**>>> CHECK IT OUT:**

1 Samuel 1–2

1 *Hannah's prayer (1 Samuel 1–2).* Hannah prayed a ton for a son; God answered her prayer with Samuel. When the

child was three, she took Samuel to the tabernacle and there he served God as priest, prophet, and as Israel's last judge.

**2** *Israel's defeat (1 Samuel 4–6).* The **ark of the covenant** was popular in ancient Israel. People thought it had magic powers. A Philistine army invaded the land and two Israelite priests brought the ark of the covenant to the battlefield at Aphek, counting on its magic powers to help them. The Philistines defeated Israel and captured the ark. But the trophy, which symbolized God's presence, caused such terrible plagues the Philistines quickly returned it to Israel.

**3** *Victory at Mizpah (1 Samuel 7).* Twenty years after the defeat at Aphek, Samuel removed idolatry from Israel and led the people back to God. When they were attacked again by the Philistines, Samuel prayed, and Israel won a great victory at Mizpah. It was such complete victory that it ended any immediate threat from the Philistines throughout Samuel's judgeship.

***ark of the covenant:*** *Israel's holiest object; the gold-covered box contained the Ten Commandments and symbolized God's presence on earth*

**>>>CHECK IT OUT:**

Exodus 25:10–22;
1 Samuel 6

**>>> CHECK IT OUT:**

1 Samuel 7:3–14

## >>> ARE YOU A CHICKEN?

**SAUL:** Saul, Israel's first king, was a tall young man who won people over. The people were very devoted to Saul, but he was morally corrupt. When Saul faced problems, he failed to trust God and was unwilling to obey him. The result was that God eventually rejected his kingship.

*WHO'S WHO*

### What's Up with 1 Samuel 8–15?

**1** *What's the hurry? (1 Samuel 8).* Israelites demanded a king not because they thought having a king was the best idea, but because other nations had a king, and they wanted to be like other nations. Without a king, Israel was different. They were directly subject to God's laws. But they rejected God to be like everybody else—a SERIOUS mistake!

**2** *Saul's errors (1 Samuel 13; 15:1–26).* Israel's kings were different from, say, the United States president. Their kings were political *and* spiritual leaders. The king's commitment to

**>>>CHECK IT OUT:**

Deuteronomy 17:14–20; 1 Samuel 8:1–7; 12:6–25

**>>>CHECK IT OUT:**

1 Samuel 13:3–13; 15:9–31

God set the tone for the nation. Saul did two things that reveal he wasn't interested in following God and therefore did not deserve to be king.

**Saul's First Mistake.** A massive Philistine army got together to attack Israel. Samuel told Saul to wait, and that within seven days he would come and intercede with God. Saul waited, but his army started to leave. Finally Saul got impatient and offered a sacrifice to God—a huge no-no. Only a descendant of Aaron was qualified to offer a sacrifice. Samuel found out and said, "*You acted foolishly.... You have not kept the commandment the L*ORD *your God gave you....*" (1 Samuel 13:13).

**Saul's Second Mess Up.** God told Saul to destroy the Amalekites. Saul failed to do this and began making excuses for why he didn't destroy them. He said things like, "*I was afraid of the people* [his own army] *and so I gave into them*" (1 Samuel 15:24). This rejection of God's eternal authority resulted in God's rejection of Saul's earthly authority.

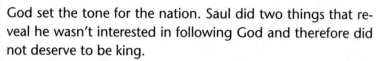 **OUTSIDE CONNECTION**

**Duffy Robbins:** *Real life is no fairy tale. Every decision really does count. We face real choices and real consequences.... Each decision we make today affects the chapters in tomorrow's story. We don't have the option of coming back in nine months or ten years and saying, "Let's do that one again."*[1]

## ▶▶ LETTING JEALOUSY RUN YOUR LIFE

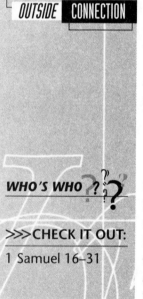 **WHO'S WHO ??**

**>>>CHECK IT OUT:**
1 Samuel 16–31

**DAVID:** David is one important guy in the Old Testament. He's the youngest kid in his family, and the family's guard for their sheep. As he lived and worked outdoors he developed a love and respect for God and his creation. And while he protected his family's sheep, David learned to trust God's presence and power. David gained Saul's attention when he went head-to-head with Goliath—a mean monster of a dude—and David killed him. David enlisted in Saul's army and married one of Saul's daughters. His military victories won the affection of the people, but Saul began to get jealous—so jealous that he tried to kill David several times!

## What's Up with 1 Samuel 16–31?

**1** *David is God's choice (1 Samuel 16).* God sent Samuel to anoint Saul's successor. Samuel was thrown off by David's size, but David, who was physically unimpressive, was chosen because he had a heart for God.

**2** *David vs. Goliath (1 Samuel 17).* This incredible event illustrates David's confidence in God. The defeat of Goliath (check out the illustrations on page below) led to a great Israelite victory.

**3** *David as a boy (1 Samuel 18–31).* Unfortunately, David and Saul had a difficult relationship; read some scriptural stories about them to find out more about these guys.

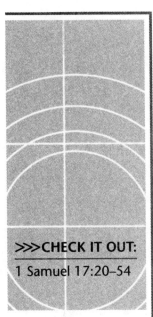

>>>**CHECK IT OUT:**

1 Samuel 17:20–54

### Goliath

*The Bible says he was "six cubits and a span." That's over nine feet tall!*

### Sling

*It looked like a doubled rope with a leather pocket in the center.*

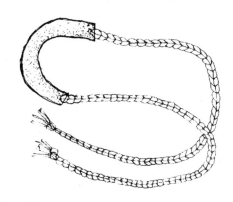

### Stones

*Sling stones found on Israelite battlefields were the size of baseballs. Ouch!*

 ## 2 SAMUEL

### . . . the forty-year reign of King David

| | |
|---|---|
| WHO | An unnamed author |
| WHAT | wrote about the origin |
| WHERE | of Israel's royal line |
| WHEN | from 1010 to 970 B.C. |
| WHY | to establish the right of David's descendants to the throne. |

**Bible Summary: 2 Samuel**

If you're looking for a public record of David's reign as king of Israel, take a close look at this book. You'll find out about David's great strengths and personal failures. The book reviews:

- David's rule in Judah (2 Samuel 1–4)
- David's uniting of Israel (2 Samuel 5–24)

 ## 1 CHRONICLES

**GIMME THE BASICS**

### . . . David's forty-year reign

| | |
|---|---|
| WHO | An unnamed author |
| WHAT | describes David's reign |
| WHERE | over a united Israel |
| WHEN | from 1003 to 970 B.C. |
| WHY | to encourage exiled Jews in the 500s B.C. |

**Bible Summary: 1 Chronicles**

This book tells all about David's accomplishments. All of this is mentioned to remind the Jews in exile in Babylon that God has not forgotten them. He will restore the monarchy ruled by a descendant of David, Israel's second king. The book contains:

- A record of David's acts (1 Chronicles 11–29)
- Genealogies (1 Chronicles 1–10)

 ## A KING AFTER GOD'S OWN HEART

2 Samuel and 1 Chronicles present a grown-up David who rules as king of Israel. David doesn't rule like an ordinary king who forgets that he represents God or boasts of his own ac-

complishments. David's unbelievable accomplishments aren't because he's strong, smart, or persuasive. They're because he puts his trust in God.

**Michelle Akers:** *I make it a point to spend time doing things that keep me close to Him and in His will. Plus, now I spend time with God out of love, whereas I used to do it out of fear. I really miss it if I don't spend time with Him. God has answered my prayer for a desire to pray by rewarding my effort and obedience with answered prayer, a closer, more intimate relationship, and fruitful works.*[2]

## What's Up with These Books?

**1** *The family tree (1 Chronicles 1–10).* There's an endless list here of really strange names. Each name was a reminder to the Israelites that God's hand was at work throughout history; he was directing the future. People (especially guys like Abraham, Isaac, and Jacob) were special reminders of God's living presence and power.

**2** *David's run in Judah (2 Samuel 1–4).* After Saul's death the tribe of Judah chose David to be king. However, the northern Hebrew tribes (Israel) supported a son of Saul named Ish-bosheth. Only after seven years, in 1003 B.C., was David named king of all the Israelites.

**3** *David's a great general.* Aided and guided by God, David's armies imposed crushing defeats on the nations that surrounded Israel. The victories expanded the territory controlled by Israel by ten times (check out the map on page 52). By winning all of these wars David, his army, and the Israelite nation had control of the trade routes, which brought great wealth to Israel.

>>>CHECK IT OUT:
2 Samuel 5:17–25;
1 Chronicles 20:4–
8; 2 Samuel 8:2

**4** *The Davidic Covenant (2 Samuel 7; 1 Chronicles 17).* God made a major promise to Abraham when he said, *"All peoples on earth will be blessed through you"* (Genesis 12:3), but God did not explain to Abraham how he would keep that promise. The Davidic Covenant revealed that God intended to keep his promise through a descendant of David.

**Israel's Territory before and after David's Reign**

*This map shows the Israelites' territory before and after David's reign. David expanded Israel's borders and gave his people ten times as much land as they occupied when Saul was king. The striped area of land indicates the extent of Israel's kingdom before David's reign. The dashed line indicates the extent of Israel's kingdom at the end of David's reign.*

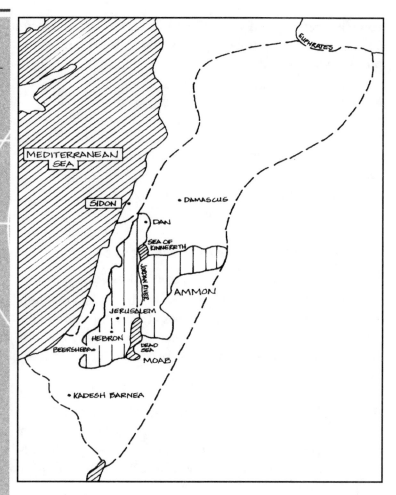

**house:** *used in this way it's both a temple and a dynasty*

>>>**CHECK IT OUT:**

Psalm 89:2–8;
Jeremiah 33:14–26;
2 Samuel 7:1–17;
Matthew 1:1–16;
1 Corinthians
15:20–28

One of King David's great dreams was to build a temple in honor of God. However, God wouldn't let him. God shot back with a promise to build *David* a **house**. And he said there would always be a descendant of David qualified to inherit Israel's throne. This is what people are referring to when they speak about the "Davidic Covenant."

The Davidic Covenant is a really important Old Testament prophecy. It describes a time of peace when the entire world will be ruled by one of David's descendants. When you read the Gospels it's clear that the person who's being talked about here is Jesus.

**5** *David's human too! (2 Samuel 11–18; 24).* Sometimes history glorifies the victories of kings, while ignoring their failures, but the Bible describes in graphic detail the failures of

King David. David is no mythical hero; he is a flesh-and-blood human being whose great strengths are matched by great weaknesses. Each story sketched below describes a sin or failure of Israel's greatest king. Take a moment to read some of these.

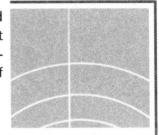

## The Sins of King David

| 2 Samuel 11 | 2 Samuel 13 | 2 Samuel 14 | 2 Samuel 24 |
|---|---|---|---|
| David seduces Bathsheba and when she becomes pregnant, David arranges for her husband's death in battle. | When one of David's sons rapes a half sister, David fails to act. The girl's full brother, Absalom, murders the rapist. | David neither punishes nor forgives his son Absalom. The alienated Absalom plans a rebellion in which many lose their lives. | David conducts a military census, which displays a lack of trust in God. |

**St. Augustine:** *The confession of evil works is the first beginning to good works.*[3]

**Think back to a time you sinned; what effect did the sin have on your life and the lives of those around you?**_____

_____

**Now think back to a time you confessed your sin to God and asked for forgiveness; how did you feel after doing this?**_____

_____

## GET REAL

Sin is not fun. Uh, let's change that a bit. Sinning might *feel* fun, but the effects of sin are no fun at all! David knew this all too well. We know it too. God wants us to stay away from sin, and live for him. But when you do sin, confess it to God right away. He wants to forgive you.

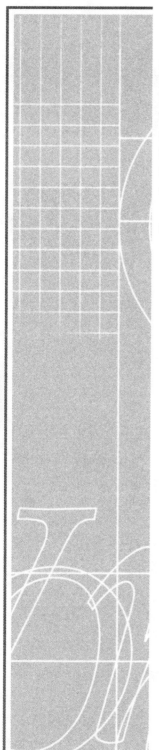

**6** David makes religious changes (1 Chronicles 22–26; 28–29). Early in his reign David brought the ark of the covenant to Jerusalem. When David finished expanding Israel's territory, he focused his attention on worship. He made detailed plans for the temple his son Solomon would build. He gave a lot of money to the project and used only the best building materials. He also wrote job descriptions for the Levites who served the temple. And what's really important is that David wrote tons of songs that we use today at church! Many of these are written down in the Book of Psalms in the Old Testament.

When David died in 970 B.C., he left a powerful, wealthy, and united Hebrew nation, eager to honor and celebrate God.

## CHAPTER CHECKUP

1. What three key figures marked the transition to monarchy?
2. What were conditions like in Israel when Samuel was born?
3. How had conditions changed by the time David died?
4. How did God's promise to David in 2 Samuel 7 relate to the covenant promises God made to Abraham?
5. What are some of the things that we might learn from a study of David's life?

### CRASH COURSE

▶ 1 Samuel records the beginning of the Israelites' transition from a loose association of tribes to a nation ruled by kings.
▶ Samuel, Israel's last judge, anointed Saul king about 1050 B.C.
▶ Saul failed to trust or obey God and was not allowed to found a dynasty.
▶ David succeeded in building Israel into a dominant nation of the Middle East.
▶ God gave a promise covenant to David, guaranteeing that a descendant of his would rule forever.

# Israel at Its Best

## 1 KINGS 1–11 • 2 CHRONICLES 1–9
## JOB • PSALMS • PROVERBS
## ECCLESIASTES • SONG OF SONGS

## 🔹🔹 LET'S DIVE IN!

Everyone likes a good time, right? Well, Jews in Old Testament times weren't any different. During the eighty years that David and his son Solomon ruled, things in the nation were going really great. This is often referred to as Israel's Golden Age. The Jews were loving life, and their kings were doing a great job. The nation was rich and powerful. Great books were written. A temple was built in Jerusalem. Things were really, really good.

## 🔹🔹 EVEN SMART PEOPLE STUMBLE

**SOLOMON:** Solomon followed David as king of Israel. He was one smart guy. He wrote thousands of proverbs and over a thousand songs. He also became a botanist, recording plant life, and a zoologist, researching the habits of animals. Solomon found time to carry out many building projects, including construction of the magnificent Jerusalem temple, which was one of the wonders of the ancient world. Solomon's wealth was legendary. He made twenty-five tons of gold each year!

*WHO'S WHO* ??

>>>**CHECK IT OUT:**
1 Kings 1–11;
 2 Chronicles 1–9

# What's Up with Solomon's Reign?

>>> **CHECK IT OUT:**

1 Kings 3:1–15; 9:1–9

**1** *God appeared to Solomon (1 Kings 3; 9; 2 Chronicles 1; 7).* God spoke to Solomon twice. At the beginning of Solomon's reign the young king asked for *"a discerning heart"* (1 Kings 3:9). This unselfish request pleased God, who promised Solomon wisdom, wealth, and a long life.

Later in Solomon's reign God spoke to Solomon again. The Lord encouraged Solomon to *"walk before me in integrity of heart and uprightness"* (1 Kings 9:4) and warned Solomon about the danger of disobedience.

>>> **CHECK IT OUT:**

2 Chronicles 3–6

**2** *Solomon constructed the Jerusalem temple (1 Kings 5–8; 2 Chronicles 2–7).* Ten of the twenty chapters that feature Solomon are devoted to the construction and dedication of the Jerusalem temple (check out the illustration below). Why was the temple important? First, the temple was the place where God met with his people. It was the only place where sacrifices could be offered, and prayers to God were to be made facing toward the temple. Second, throughout Solomon's reign the spiritual state of God's people was reflected in either their neglect or their devotion to temple worship.

## Solomon's Temple

*This is a picture of what Solomon's temple probably looked like. He decked it out with tons of gold just to honor God. At today's prices, Solomon's temple would be worth five billion dollars!*

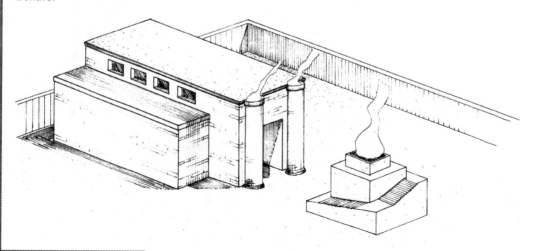

**3** *Solomon ignored God (1 Kings 11).* Solomon's early promise was never fulfilled. Despite his youthful dedication to God, Solomon turned away from the Lord in his later years. In disobedience to God's law, he cemented treaties with other nations by marrying women of foreign royal families. That choice led directly to tragedy.

>>>CHECK IT OUT:

Deuteronomy 20:7

*Charles Swindoll: In Chapter 11, the hinge of 1 Kings, Solomon slips from fame to failure, from success to sensuality, from temple-builder to idol worshiper. His spiritual troubles, as with his father David, started at home. Solomon indulged his desire for foreign women—he had seven hundred wives, princesses, and three hundred concubines. And they turned his heart away from the Lord to worship their false gods.*[1]

OUTSIDE CONNECTION

 **POETRY: WRITING THAT INSPIRES**

Let's stop here in our study of the Bible and explore the Old Testament's five books of poetry. Israel's golden age was a time of great literary achievement. David started work on a collection of praise poems, the Book of Psalms, and his son Solomon recorded many of the brief sayings found in the Book of Proverbs.

The following biblical book, Job, is poetry too. But Hebrew poetry is unusual. Rather than depending on **rhyme and meter**, Hebrew poetry depends on setting ideas side by side in a pattern called "parallelism."

*rhyme and meter: placing emphasis on syllables*

 JOB

. . . *the mystery of suffering*

| | |
|---|---|
| WHO | An unknown author |
| WHAT | related the story of Job |
| WHERE | in Mesopotamia |
| WHEN | some two thousand years before Christ, |
| WHY | to explore faith's response to human suffering. |

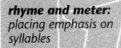

GIMME THE BASICS

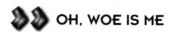

## OH, WOE IS ME

### Job's Story

>>>CHECK IT OUT:

Job 1–2

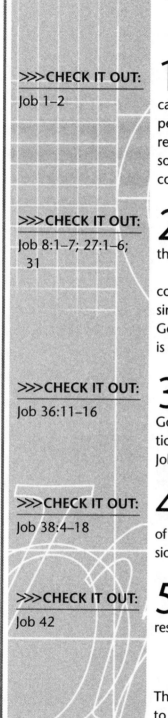

1 *Job 1–2.* Job is a man singled out by God himself as *"blameless and upright."* When Satan argues that this is only because God has blessed Job and protected him from harm, God permits Satan to attack Job. Job is stripped of everything, but remains true to God. Even when Satan gives Job really gross sores all over his body, Job remains faithful. But his suffering continues.

>>>CHECK IT OUT:

Job 8:1–7; 27:1–6; 31

2 *Job 3–31.* Three friends come to console Job and are freaked out at his condition. Job is really ticked off and tells the three that he wishes he'd died at birth.

Job's three friends begin to talk to him. Each of them is convinced that God is just and righteous, and Job must have sinned. Job's friends urge him to confess the hidden sin that God is punishing and to appeal for mercy. But Job's conscience is clear; there is no hidden sin.

>>>CHECK IT OUT:

Job 36:11–16

3 *Job 32–37.* A younger man named Elihu speaks up. He points out that suffering need not always be punishment. God may use suffering to teach, and to get a person's attention. So Job's friends are wrong to attack him as a sinner, and Job is wrong to say God isn't being fair.

>>>CHECK IT OUT:

Job 38:4–18

4 *Job 38–41.* Then God himself speaks to Job. He does not tell Job why he permitted the suffering. He simply reminds Job of two basic truths: God is great beyond human comprehension and human beings are weak and limited.

>>>CHECK IT OUT:

Job 42

5 *Job 42.* Job realizes it is not a creature's place to explain the Creator's doings. God rebukes the three friends and then restores all Job has lost and more.

### Thinking about Job

The Book of Job does not tell us why God allows good people to suffer. It does remind us that believers respond to suffering differently than those without faith. Some, like Job's friends,

feel driven to ask, "Why?" Others, like Job, learn to trust God no matter what comes.

*Max Lucado: God has given us peace in our pain. He covers us all the time. For when we are out of control, he is still there.*[2]

 **PSALMS**

### . . . the book of praises

| | |
|---|---|
| WHO | David and others |
| WHAT | penned these poems |
| WHERE | in ancient Israel |
| WHEN | over a span of centuries |
| WHY | as an aid to private and congregational worship. |

 **LET US PRAISE THE LORD**

### What's Up with Psalms?

**1** *The five "books" within the Book of Psalms.* Each "book" represents a collection of poems. The first book (Psalm 1–41) was collected in the time of David. The last book (Psalm 107–150) was collected around the time of <u>Ezra</u>, about six hundred years later. Many of the psalms were used in worship before being included in one of the official collections.

**2** *The Psalms are like a diary.* One really cool aspect of the psalms is the depth of emotion they express. The psalms remind us that whatever we may feel—anger or pain, thankfulness or joy—we can tell God. As we share our innermost emotions with the Lord, we can be confident that he hears and cares, and that God will work within our hearts as well as in our circumstances.

**3** *The Psalms are life-changing.* More than any other book of the Bible, the Book of Psalms explores the personal nature of our relationship with God. Anyone who wants to know God better will find the psalms an unmatched help and guide.

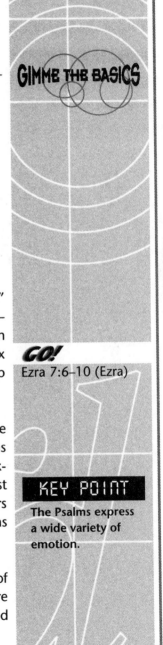

*OUTSIDE* **CONNECTION**

**GIMME THE BASICS**

**59**

*GO!*
Ezra 7:6–10 (Ezra)

**KEY POINT**

The Psalms express a wide variety of emotion.

When have you expressed raw emotion to God? What happened after you did?_____

_____

Why do you think people should praise God?_____

_____

Try writing your own psalm!_____

_____

_____

_____

Expressing yourself is a good thing. God has given you a gift. Maybe you can write. Maybe you can paint. Maybe you're a great public speaker. Whatever you've been gifted to do, God wants to use that. He wants you to use that for him. That's what these guys in the Old Testament did. That's what God wants you to do.

**OUTSIDE CONNECTION**

**Paul Little:** *God enjoys the worship, praise and fellowship of a group of believers gathered in the name of Christ. He is pleased to meet us in chapel, church and prayer groups. But he also likes to meet us alone.*[3]

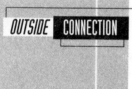

 **PROVERBS**

*. . . guidelines for daily life*

| | |
|---|---|
| WHO | Solomon and others |
| WHAT | contributed wise sayings |
| WHERE | in Israel |
| WHEN | about 900 B.C. |
| WHY | to help readers make good decisions. |

 **WISDOM FOR TODAY**

The Book of Proverbs begins with a statement of purpose. The proverbs are *"for attaining wisdom and discipline, for understand-*

*ing words of insight; for acquiring a disciplined and prudent life, for doing what is right and just and fair"* (Proverbs 1:2–3).

### What's Up with Proverbs?

**1** *They're general and apply to everyone.* These principles apply to everyone, not just to believers. The proverbs are not promises given by God. They describe what will usually happen when a person makes a right choice, not what God guarantees will happen.

**2** *They're all about choices.* The writers are not trying to convey information, but to guide decisions. They're concerned that we do the right thing and avoid the harmful consequences of bad decisions.

**Charles Swindoll:** *Common sense is good, but it's not enough. We need the love of and respect for the Lord to form the basis of our choices. So, take and read the Proverbs—and grow in the knowledge of God (Proverbs 2:5).*[4]

 ## ECCLESIASTES

### . . . *searching for life's meaning*

| | |
|---|---|
| WHO | Solomon |
| WHAT | wrote this book |
| WHERE | as king in Jerusalem |
| WHEN | near the end of his life |
| WHY | to ask if human life has meaning apart from a relationship with God. |

GIMME THE BASICS

 ## SEARCHING FOR MEANING WITHOUT GOD

### The Story behind Ecclesiastes

Near the end of his life Solomon lost his spiritual direction and began to worship the gods of his foreign wives (he had a TON of wives). During this time Solomon decided to search for life's meaning. He used his massive intelligence to test and explore human experience. But he would limit himself to *"all that is*

done under heaven." Solomon would not consider truth revealed by God! He would search for meaning in the brief years human beings have to live here on earth.

Guess what . . . Solomon failed! Despite the fact that he had access to every pleasure, wealth beyond counting, and achievements that won the acclaim of all, Solomon felt it was all meaningless.

### What's Up with Ecclesiastes?

1 *Ecclesiastes is a book of inspiration.* Ecclesiastes is an accurate report of Solomon's reasoning. But not everything Solomon writes is true. This book is in the Bible to remind us of an important truth. We can't find meaning apart from God. Apart from God and his loving purpose for us, human life is meaningless.

**Larry Richards:** *This book is not communication of truth from God, but an inspired report of Solomon's reasoning. What then is the value of this unique Old Testament book? It is not meant for us to use as a source of information. Instead it is meant to communicate in compelling and deeply moving tones a message needed by all mankind. Apart from the perspective on life God's Word provides, life truly is meaningless and empty.*[5]

2 *Where did Solomon look for meaning? (Ecclesiastes 1:12–6:12).* The first half of Ecclesiastes, chapters 1–6, contains a report of where Solomon searched for the elusive answer. Check out this list to see if you've ever tried these:

### KEY POINT

Life is meaningless apart from God.

| Solomon's search for meaning | Scripture |
| --- | --- |
| Can knowledge provide meaning? | Ecclesiastes 1:12–18 |
| Can pleasure provide meaning? | Ecclesiastes 2:1–11 |
| Can accomplishments provide meaning? | Ecclesiastes 2:17–26 |
| Can humans make effective changes to the society? | Ecclesiastes 3:16–22 |
| Is life meaningless? | Ecclesiastes 4:1–16 |
| Do possessions give meaning to life? | Ecclesiastes 5:8–6:2 |
| Can man control his future? | Ecclesiastes 6:3–12 |

**3** *How can our lives have meaning? (Ecclesiastes 7:1–12:8).* Solomon found that human life—if this life is all there is—can have no meaning. But he couldn't resist pointing out that even under the circumstances, some ways to live are better than others.

**Billy Graham:** *Youth is the time to decide for Christ and for Righteousness.*[6]

*OUTSIDE* **CONNECTION**

 SONG OF SONGS

*. . . the celebration of love*

| | |
|---|---|
| WHO | A young Solomon |
| WHAT | wrote this love poem |
| WHERE | in Jerusalem |
| WHEN | during his early reign |
| WHY | as a celebration of married love. |

**GIMME THE BASICS**

 THE LOVE OF A LIFETIME

### The Story behind Song of Songs

Does this poem grow out of an early experience that Solomon had with true love? Or is it simply an **allegory**, intended to depict the love of God for Israel, or of Christ for the believer? This is something a lot of people talk about. Charles Swindoll and many others think this poem is about true love—a love that was lost as Solomon abandoned **monogamous** marriage for politically motivated, multiple marriages.

*allegory: a story used to make a point*

*monogamous: a lifelong commitment to a single spouse*

### What's Up with the Song of Songs?

**1** *The poem is written in three voices.* The voice of the *Lover* is Solomon's. The voice of the *Beloved* is the **Shulamite** woman. The other voice is a *chorus* of the Shulamite's friends.

*Shulamite: a woman from Shunem, near Mount Gilboa in Israel*

**2** *The poem is divided into three sections.*
  1. The Courtship (Song of Songs 1:2–3:5)
  2. The Wedding (Song of Songs 3:6–5:1)
  3. The Deepening Relationship (Song of Songs 5:2–8:14)

**>>> CHECK IT OUT:**

Song of Songs 8:1–14

63

**Josh McDowell:** *As a beloved child of God, you have an importance that will never be matched by anything you ever do. If you were the only person ever created, Jesus would have died for you just to form a relationship with you.*[7]

## CHAPTER cHECKUp

1. Name the two kings who ruled during Israel's golden age?
2. What accomplishments mark Israel's golden age?
3. What four books of Bible poetry were written or begun during the golden age?
4. What is the theme of each of the following books of Bible poetry?

Job _____

Psalms _____

Proverbs _____

Ecclesiastes _____

Song of Songs _____

### CRASH COURSE

▶ The years 1010–930 B.C. were Israel's golden years, marked by power, prosperity, and literary production. David and Solomon were the two kings who ruled during the golden years.

▶ The construction of the Jerusalem temple was Solomon's best known achievement.

▶ Lots of great poetic literary material was written.

▶ Job explores how a person of faith can respond to suffering.

▶ Psalms is a guide to worship and a personal relationship with God.

▶ Proverbs gives practical advice on making wise and right choices.

▶ Ecclesiastes is a search for meaning in life apart from God.

▶ The Song of Songs is a poem exploring the joys of married lovers.

# The Kingdom Up Yonder: Israel

## 1 KINGS 12—22 • 2 KINGS • JONAH
## AMOS • HOSEA

65

### ⟫⟫ LET'S DIVE IN!

Solomon died in 930 B.C. (check out the time line on page 66 to see how Solomon fits into history), and the unified Hebrew kingdom was torn apart. Two tribal groups to the south remained committed to rulers from David's family line. The southern kingdom was known as Judah. But the ten northern Hebrew tribes set up a rival kingdom, which kept the old name of Israel. From the beginning the kings of Israel abandoned God's law in favor of a counterfeit religion (one that totally excluded God). Despite the ministry of prophets sent to call Israel back to God, the northern kingdom continued on its fatal course. In 722 B.C. Israel fell to the Assyrians. Its citizens were taken captive and scattered across the Assyrian Empire.

>>>CHECK IT OUT:

1 Kings 1–11;
   2 Chronicles 1–9

## Timeline of a Divided Kingdom

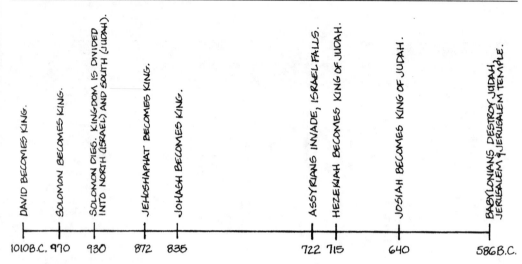

DAVID BECOMES KING.

SOLOMON BECOMES KING.

SOLOMON DIES. KINGDOM IS DIVIDED INTO NORTH (ISRAEL) AND SOUTH (JUDAH).

JEHOSHAPHAT BECOMES KING.

JOHASH BECOMES KING.

ASSYRIANS INVADE, ISRAEL FALLS.

HEZEKIAH BECOMES KING OF JUDAH.

JOSIAH BECOMES KING OF JUDAH.

BABYLONIANS DESTROY JUDAH, JERUSALEM & JERUSALEM TEMPLE.

1010 B.C. 970    930    872    835        722 715        640        586 B.C.

GIMME THE BASICS

 1, 2 KINGS

*. . . a history lesson*

| | |
|---|---|
| WHO | An unnamed author |
| WHAT | evaluated the reigns of kings |
| WHERE | from Israel and Judah |
| WHEN | between 970 and 586 B.C. |
| WHY | to demonstrate the value of obeying and the danger of disobeying God. |

## WE'LL CREATE OUR OWN RELIGION

When Solomon died, the people appealed to his son, Rehoboam, for tax relief. The foolish young king refused. That's when the soap opera–like problems began. The ten northern tribes rebelled and crowned Jeroboam as their king. Jerusalem, the site of Solomon's temple, was in the south. That worried Jeroboam. If the people of the north went to Jerusalem to worship, as God's law required, how long would they remain loyal to him? So Jeroboam created his own religion, one that mimicked the faith God had revealed to Moses. Jeroboam appointed his own priests, set up calf idols at worship centers

66

in Bethel and Dan, and established his own religious holidays. While claiming that this religion was a vehicle for worship of the Lord, every act of worship was in direct violation of God's law. Every ruler of Israel supported this counterfeit religion and *"did evil in God's sight."*

 ## PROPHETIC VOICES

You'd think God would abandon Israel during these times, but he didn't. During the two hundred years (930–722 B.C.) that the northern Hebrew kingdom existed, God sent prophets who warned the Israelites and urged them to return to him.

Basically there are two categories of prophets in the Bible. Some were *speaking prophets*, whose stories are written in a historical narrative. Others were *writing prophets*, whose messages are recorded as books of the Bible. Elijah and Elisha were speaking prophets whom God sent to Israel. Jonah, Amos, and Hosea were writing prophets who preached there.

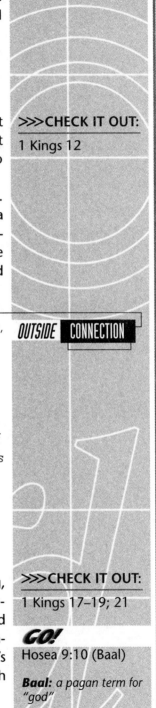

>>> CHECK IT OUT:
1 Kings 12

*Charles Swindoll:* The prophets did a lot more than proclaim, The end is near. They spoke to their times, rebuking kings, priests, and people for such issues as injustice, corruption, idolatry, empty ritualism, violence, divorce, pride, materialism, greed, and the oppression of the poor and helpless. If they would not heed the rebukes, the prophets warned of God's coming judgment against their faithlessness and sin. If they did repent, however, the prophets assured them of God's mercy, comfort, and blessings. . . . Though we don't have prophets today in the biblical sense, the voices of these Old Testament prophets resound with relevant truth.[1]

*OUTSIDE* **CONNECTION**

### Elijah

Elijah was sent to Israel at an important time. Israel's king, Ahab, had married Jezebel, the daughter of a pagan king. Together Jezebel and Ahab set out to replace worship of the Lord with the worship of **Baal**. The royal couple killed God's prophets and brought in hundreds of false prophets from Jezebel's homeland. The effort seemed successful until God sent Elijah to confront the king and show his power.

>>> CHECK IT OUT:
1 Kings 17–19; 21

*GO!*
Hosea 9:10 (Baal)

***Baal:*** *a pagan term for "god"*

67

Elijah called on God to stop the rains. No rain fell for three long years; the land of Israel dried up. There wasn't any food available for Ahab's horses, so his powerful military was easily defeated. Then Elijah reappeared and challenged Ahab to a duel between himself and four hundred prophets of Baal. Thousands of Israelites watch the contest on Mount Carmel.

Baal's prophets cried out all day for their god to send fire and burn up a sacrifice they had laid out. But nothing happened. Then when Elijah called on the Lord to act, fire from heaven burned up the sacrifice and even the stone altar on which it lay. The people were convinced that *"the LORD, he is God."* At Elijah's command the people killed the prophets of Baal.

### Elisha

Elisha was Elijah's apprentice and then took over after <u>Elijah went to heaven</u>. He ministered after the death of Ahab, through the reigns of Ahab's descendants, Ahaz and Jehoram. Elijah and Elisha were different. Elijah was more confrontational; Elisha had a softer approach. Despite the miracles Elisha performed on Israel's behalf, there was no great national return to God. Later Elisha anointed a military commander, Jehu, as the next king of Israel. Jehu wiped out Ahab's remaining family and purged Israel of the worship of Baal.

*GO!*

2 Kings 2:11–12
(Elijah went to heaven)

##  JONAH

*. . . God's reluctant messenger*

| WHO | Jonah |
|---|---|
| WHAT | announced judgment |
| WHERE | in Nineveh |
| WHEN | when Jeroboam II ruled Israel, |
| WHY | and he gave the city an opportunity to repent. |

## ▶▶ SWALLOWED UP

Jeroboam II was an evil and successful ruler. During his forty-one-year reign the northern kingdom became super powerful in the Middle East. This guy expanded the borders almost as much as David and Solomon did. Jeroboam II's victories had been *"in accordance with the Word of the LORD,"* given by a patriotic prophet, *"Jonah the son of Amittai, the prophet from Gath Heper"* (2 Kings 14:25).

But when God called Jonah to go and preach against Nineveh, the capital of the Assyrian Empire, Jonah chickened out and jumped on a ship heading in the opposite direction.

Assyria was the great enemy of Jonah's people. Jonah wanted God to destroy Nineveh, but he was afraid that if he warned the Assyrians, they might repent, and God would not destroy them after all.

> **Bible Summary: Jonah**
> This book contains four short chapters.
>   Chapter 1—Jonah runs away and is swallowed by a great fish.
>   Chapter 2—Jonah thanks God for saving his life.
>   Chapter 3—Jonah goes to Nineveh, and the city repents!
>   Chapter 4—Jonah pouts, and God scolds him for his lack of compassion.

### What's Up with Jonah?

**1** *This story is the real deal (1:17).* Early English versions translated a Hebrew word that means a "great fish" as "whale." The text makes it clear that God had to prepare the great fish that swallowed Jonah so that Jonah would not drown.

**2** *Jonah's second chance (Jonah 3:1–3).* The Lord gave the disobedient Jonah a second chance to obey. This time Jonah delivered God's message to Nineveh, which was this: *"Forty more days and Nineveh will be destroyed."*

**3** *The Ninevites "believed God" (Jonah 3:4–9).* The people of Nineveh **repented** by fasting and wearing **sackcloth**. The king himself demanded that everyone *"give up their evil ways and their violence."*

**repented:** *not just sorry for sin, but a commitment to change*

**sackcloth:** *a very coarse material similar to burlap*

When have you been like Jonah and ran from God?_____
_____

What gifts has God given you to tell others about him?_____
_____

Who do you know who needs to hear about God? What can you do to tell them?
_____
_____

Got love? Jonah did, kinda. He was probably quick to tell others how much he loved God, but the minute God called him to do something tough, he ran. What's the lesson? God's call isn't always easy, but it's necessary. It's necessary to do what God asks. Why? Because he knows the bigger picture. He knows a bunch of stuff that you don't know. When we choose *not* to follow God's plan, we're failing to do what we were created to do.

**OUTSIDE CONNECTION**

**Warren Wiersbe:** *Jesus used Nineveh to illustrate an important point (Matthew 12:38–41). He had preached to that generation for three years and had reinforced his message with his miracles, yet they would not repent and believe. The Ninevites heard one sermon from one preacher, and that sermon emphasized wrath, not love—yet they repented and were forgiven.[2]*

 **AMOS**

*. . . judgment coming*

| | |
|---|---|
| WHO | God sent a rancher from Judah |
| WHAT | to announce judgment |
| WHERE | on Israel |
| WHEN | during the reign of Jeroboam II, |
| WHY | because of the injustice and oppression in Israel. |

>>>CHECK IT OUT:

Amos 7:10–16

70

## The Day of the Lord

Amos was a rancher who lived in Judah when God called him to deliver his message across the border in Israel during the reign of Jeroboam II. Israel was unusually prosperous at the time, but the very wealthy oppressed the very poor. Amos boldly took his message of coming judgment to the retreat of the rich at Bethel, one of the worship centers established long before by Jeroboam I. There the priest Amaziah threatened Amos's life and ordered him not to prophesy. But Amos boldly announced God's judgment on the priest, and finished his message of Israel's impending doom before returning to his ranch in Judah.

About forty years after Amos preached God's Word to Israel (who still refused to repent), the Assyrians under Sargon II crushed that nation and scattered its population throughout the Assyrian Empire.

> **Bible Summary: Amos**
> The Book of Amos contains a series of Amos's sermons to Israel. The topics of the sermons serve as an outline for the book.
> - God will judge Israel's neighbors (Amos 1:1–2:5)
> - God will judge Israel (Amos 2:6–16)
> - Israel's sins are identified (Amos 3:1–6:14)
> - Amos describes five visions of doom (Amos 7:1–9:10)
> - Amos assures Israel of her ultimate restoration (Amos 9:11–15)

### What's Up with Amos?

**1** *God's complaints against Israel.* Amos describes Israel's sins, and the judgment they deserve. Israel follows the false religion set up by Jeroboam I and violates God's laws again and again. The wealthy in Israel oppress the poor. False religion, immorality, and injustice—all of these reveal how far the hearts of God's people are from him.

>>>**CHECK IT OUT:**

Amos 2:6–8; 4:1–6; 5:4–24; 6:4–7

*OUTSIDE* **CONNECTION**

> **Billy Graham:** *From the beginning of time until the present moment, man's ungodly quest for power, his determination to use his gift of free choice for his own selfish ends, has brought him to the brink of doom. The rubble and ruins of many civilizations lie scattered over the earth's surface—mute testimony to man's inability to build a lasting world without God.*[3]

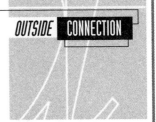

**day of the LORD:** *a time of terrible judgment*

>>>CHECK IT OUT:

Amos 5:18–27

>>>CHECK IT OUT:

Amos 8

**2** *The "**day of the LORD**" (Amos 5:18–27).* The Old Testament prophets talk a lot about the *"day of the LORD."* The day of the Lord is a future moment in time when God will personally intervene in human history.

**3** *Five visions of doom (Amos 7:1–9:10).* Amos describes five visions that God showed him. The visions reveal that while God has withheld punishment in the past, he won't hold back anymore. Amos says, *"The time is ripe for my people Israel: I will spare them no longer"* (Amos 8:2).

**4** *A promise (Amos 9:11–15).* The defeat of the northern kingdom by the Assyrians and the exile of the ten northern Hebrew tribes did not mean that God had voided the covenant promises given to Abraham over a thousand years before. While that generation of Israelites would be torn from the land, eventually God would bring their descendants back to the promised land.

 **HOSEA**

*. . . real love*

| WHO | The prophet Hosea |
|---|---|
| WHAT | contrasted Israel's ungratefulness with God's covenant love |
| WHERE | in Israel |
| WHEN | during the last thirty years of Israel's existence |
| WHY | to explain the reason for Israel's destruction by Assyria. |

 **LOVE TO THE MAX**

This is a book that really shows us what love is. Hosea the prophet was married to an unfaithful wife. Yet he continued to love her deeply. Even though she abandoned him and her children for lovers, Hosea provided for her and ultimately brought her back home. Hosea's personal experience mirrored the experience of God with Israel. Although God loved Israel as a husband loves his wife, Israel had taken his many gifts and turned to idolatry.

Hosea shares his personal story first. Then he explains God's complaint against unrepentant Israel and expresses God's deep, continuing love for his unfaithful people.

> **Bible Summary: Hosea**
> The book has two stories to tell: the story of Hosea and his wife, Gomer, and the story of the Lord and his people Israel.
> I. The unfaithful wife ..................... Hosea 1–3
> II. The unfaithful nation ................. Hosea 4–14
>    A. Israel's sins denounced .......... Hosea 4–8
>    B. Israel's doom announced ...... Hosea 9–10
>    C. God's love affirmed .............. Hosea 11
>    D. Discipline first ....................... Hosea 12–13
>    E. Then blessing ...................... Hosea 14

## What's Up with Hosea?

**1** *Hosea . . . one committed dude! (Hosea 3:1–4).* The commitment that Hosea displayed to his marriage is remarkable. Hosea's willingness to keep on loving despite his deep hurt reminds us that marriage is a commitment that is not to be quickly set aside.

**2** *God's gonna judge Israel (Hosea 4:1–19).* Hosea's message was like that of other prophets. He spoke plainly about the sins that would meet with God's judgment. This wasn't a guy who was scared or timid about what he said. He told sinners what was ahead of them if they kept breaking God's laws.

**3** *God's love is unshakable (Hosea 11).* In one of Scripture's most powerful passages God expresses his love for Israel. God has cared for his people, like a parent teaching them to walk, protecting and caring for them. God's love is so deep that whatever happens, God simply will not let his people go.

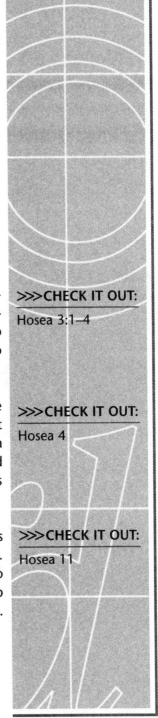

>>>CHECK IT OUT:
Hosea 3:1–4

73

>>>CHECK IT OUT:
Hosea 4

>>>CHECK IT OUT:
Hosea 11

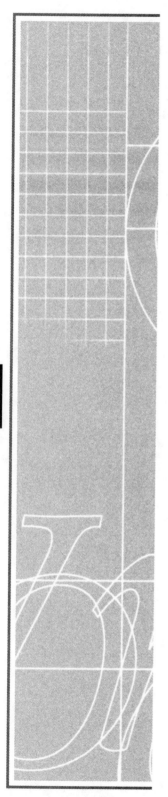

# CHAPTER CHECKUP

1. How were the kings of Israel alike?
2. What two prophets ministered to Israel during the reign of Jeroboam II?
3. What was their message to Israel?
4. What is the *"day of the LORD"*?
5. What sins in Israel called for God's judgment?

## CRASH COURSE

▶ After the death of Solomon the united Hebrew kingdom was divided into a southern kingdom, called Judah, and a northern kingdom, Israel. The northern kingdom, Israel, was ruled by a succession of evil kings.

▶ Even though God sent prophets to warn Israel and turn the nation back to him, the people did not listen, and Israel was conquered by the Assyrians in 722 B.C.

▶ Among the prophets that God sent to Israel were the speaking prophets Elijah and Elisha. The ministry of Elijah and Elisha is important because it occurred during one of three periods in which miracles were common.

▶ Jonah was an Israelite prophet whose mission to Nineveh provided proof that God would withhold judgment if the people repented of their sins.

▶ Amos was a writing prophet whose book contains sermons warning Israel that God would judge them for their idolatry and social injustice.

▶ Hosea was a writing prophet whose commitment to his unfaithful wife mirrored God's love for and commitment to unfaithful Israel.

# The Kingdom on the South Side: Judah

## 1, 2 KINGS • 2 CHRONICLES • OBADIAH
## JOEL • MICAH • ISAIAH

 **LET'S DIVE IN!**

Solomon died in 930 B.C. (check out the timeline on page 66.) When he died the ten northern Hebrew tribes broke away and established Israel (an independent kingdom) whose capital would be Samaria. In the southern kingdom, Judah, descendants of David continued to rule from Jerusalem. Many in the north were unhappy with Jeroboam's decision to establish a counterfeit religion, so they moved south to continue to worship God at the temple Solomon built.

The two rival Hebrew kingdoms existed side by side for over two hundred years, sometimes at war, sometimes co-operating against common enemies. When the northern kingdom fell to Assyria in 722 B.C., Judah survived. Judah continued to be ruled by David's descendants until 586 B.C., when the nation fell to the Babylonians and its citizens were sent into exile.

>>> **CHECK IT OUT:**

1 Kings 1–11;
2 Chronicles 1–9

 **2 KINGS**

GIMME THE BASICS

*. . . a historical account*

| | |
|---|---|
| WHO | Unknown authors |
| WHAT | evaluated the kings |
| WHERE | of Israel and Judah |
| WHEN | from 970 to 586 B.C. |
| WHY | to show why obeying God is so important. |

 **2 CHRONICLES**

GIMME THE BASICS

*. . . a commentary on history*

| | |
|---|---|
| WHO | Unknown authors |
| WHAT | highlighted godly kings |
| WHERE | of Judah |
| WHEN | from 970 to 586 B.C. |
| WHY | to show that when God was honored and worshiped, Judah was blessed. |

 **THE SOUTHERN KINGDOM**

### Moral Leadership

>>>CHECK IT OUT:

1 Chronicles 14–15; 17

The kings of Judah were more than political leaders. They provided moral and spiritual leadership, too. The spiritual and political well-being of the nation were closely linked. In general, the nation prospered under godly kings and suffered under ungodly kings.

OUTSIDE CONNECTION

**King Solomon:** *Righteousness exalts a nation, but sin is a disgrace to any people.*[1]

 **GOD'S PROPHETS**

If you wanted a significant job in Old Testament times, you might want the job of a prophet. There are a lot of *speaking* prophets mentioned in the Old Testament. No less than seventeen of the thirty-nine Old Testament books are composed completely of the messages given by *writing* prophets.

## Dude, Don't Do the Occult!

The **occult** is all over the Old Testament. The Greeks went to Delphi to consult the **oracle** there. The Romans looked for signs in the **entrails** of a slaughtered pig, or in the direction taken by a flight of birds. The people in Old Testament times consulted **mediums** or spiritists who claimed to contact the dead or some spirit. All the religions in ancient times involved some aspect of the occult. Everyone was searching for supernatural guidance.

When the Israelites were about to enter Canaan, God warned them against all occult practices. The Bible forbids every kind of occult practice, labeling all of them *"detestable to the LORD"* (Deuteronomy 18:12).

**occult:** *anything dealing with the mystic arts like Satanism, black magic, witchcraft, etc.*

**oracle:** *a message from God delivered by a prophet*

**entrails:** *internal organs*

**mediums:** *one possessed by or consulting a ghost or spirit of the dead, especially for information about the future*

## True vs. False Prophets

How could God's Old Testament people distinguish a true messenger of God from a pretender? Deuteronomy gives us four tests, and a true prophet could pass them all. Here are the tests:
1. A true prophet urges people to follow the Lord (Deuteronomy 13:1–4).
2. A true prophet is an Israelite, not a foreigner (Deuteronomy 18:15).
3. A true prophet speaks God's word in God's name (Deuteronomy 18:19).
4. A true prophet makes predictions that come true (Deuteronomy 18:21–22).

Today we can be sure that the prophets of the Bible truly were God's messengers. We have hundreds of their predictions in Scripture, which have been fulfilled and proven. But when a prophet delivered a message in his own generation, all four of these tests were needed to prove him or her as God's messenger.

What person has influenced you the most in your life?_____

_____

How do you decide whether you'll allow someone to influence you?_____

_____

How can you spot a false prophet?_____

_____

 Here's a good rule of thumb: whatever has an impact on you ends up influencing those around you. It's just the way things are. If you hang out with people who do wrong things, you'll eventually be influenced by those people. And those around you (like your siblings or your friends at youth group) will eventually be influenced by you. The best way to have a positive influence on others is to hang out with people who have a positive influence on you.

78

**Edomites:** *a group of people from Edom who were the neighbors of the people of Judah*

>>>CHECK IT OUT:
Genesis 36:8–9

 **OBADIAH**

*. . . Edom's doom*

| WHO | The prophet Obadiah |
|---|---|
| WHAT | announced that |
| WHERE | because Jerusalem |
| WHEN | was plundered by the **Edomites**, |
| WHY | God would destroy Edom for attacking his people. |

 **OK, THAT'S ENOUGH!**

Judah was on the Edomites' list. It had everything they wanted, so they went after it. At least four times the Edomites attacked Judah and plundered Jerusalem. After one of these invasions, the prophet Obadiah announced that God would destroy Edom. In his covenant with Abraham God had promised, *"I will bless those who bless you, and whoever curses you I will curse"* (Genesis 12:3).

Obadiah's book is short. It tells how the Edomites marched

through the gates of God's people, seized their wealth, and waited at the crossroads to cut down their fugitives (Obadiah 1:13–14). Therefore God would see to it that the *"house of Esau"* (a synonym for Edom, which was founded by Esau) was consumed (Obadiah 1:18).

 JOEL

### . . . *the judgment cometh*

| | |
|---|---|
| WHO | The prophet Joel |
| WHAT | shared his vision of near and final judgment |
| WHERE | in Judah |
| WHEN | possibly around 825 B.C. |
| WHY | as a warning and a call to repentance. |

 YUK . . . BUGS!

Joel wrote this book just after a great swarm of <u>locusts</u> had stripped Judah of all vegetation. He announced that God sent the locusts to call Judah to repentance.

How are the people of Judah to respond to this message from God? They need to return to the Lord with all their hearts, for *"Who knows? He may turn and have pity and leave behind a blessing"* (Joel 2:14) for Joel's generation.

> **Bible Summary: Joel**
>
> This three-chapter book is divided into two sections. The first section (Joel 1:1–2:27) talks about the locusts that swarmed Judah from the north, which was unusual because most locust swarms came from the south. The second section (Joel 2:28–3:21) is a vision of the coming day of the Lord, a description of events that are a long way off.

### What's Up with Joel?

**1** *Repent! (Joel 1:13–15).* Joel interprets the locust invasion as punishment for Judah's sins. He calls on God's people to turn to the Lord quickly, so nothing else happens.

GIMME THE BASICS

79

*GO!*
Revelation 9:3–11 (locusts)

>>>CHECK IT OUT:

Joel 1:1–12

>>>CHECK IT OUT:

Joel 1:12–14

**2** *True repentance (Joel 2:12–14).* In Bible times people openly displayed grief and sorrow. To show repentance they tore their clothing, smeared dirt on their faces, and wept loudly as they sat in ashes. Joel reminds Judah that God demands true repentance (Joel 2:13).

>>>**CHECK IT OUT:**
Joel 2:25–27

**3** *God's response to true repentance (Joel 2:18–27).* Through Joel God promises to bless and protect his people when they repent and turn to him. He says, *"I will repay you for the years the locusts have eaten"* (Joel 2:26).

**Ron Luce:** *The first step in getting through to the presence of God is to ask him to show you the sin in your life that he wants you to get rid of. When you ask this question, it is amazing how the floodgates of heaven will be opened as he speaks. He always wants to speak to us—we are just asking the wrong questions.*[2]

**4** *The End! (Joel 2:28–3:21).* Joel catches a glimpse of an over-powering human army that will someday invade the **Holy Land.** God would use this to bless his people.

**Holy Land:** *modern-day Israel and Palestine*

**OUTSIDE CONNECTION**

**John Alexander:** *To deny sin is bad news, indeed. The only good news is sin itself. Sin is the best news there is, the best news there could be in our predicament. Because with sin, there's a way out. There's the possibility of repentance. You can't repent of confusion or psychological flaws inflicted by your parents—you're stuck with them. But you can repent of sin. Sin and repentance are the only grounds for hope and joy. The grounds for reconciled, joyful relationships. You can be born again.*[3]

## MICAH

*. . . judgment coming*

| | |
|---|---|
| WHO | The prophet Micah |
| WHAT | warned of the destruction of both Samaria and Jerusalem |
| WHERE | in Israel and Judah |
| WHEN | just before Assyria invaded, |
| WHY | because of the sins of both Hebrew kingdoms. |

GIMME THE BASICS

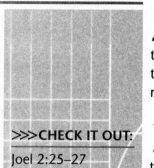

**REPENT OR YOU'LL REGRET IT**

Micah was a prophet who ministered in Judah during the reigns of Jotham, Ahaz, and Hezekiah. These were critical years for both Hebrew kingdoms because Assyria could invade them any day. Micah had a similar message for both Israel and Judah, which he delivered to their capital cities, Samaria and Jerusalem. Basically he said, "Look dudes, destruction is on the way to each city that has turned its back on God." In clear and unmistakable words Micah presented God's **indictment**, spelling out the sins that called for judgment.

**indictment:** *an official charge of wrongdoing*

Israel ignored Micah's warnings. Micah lived long enough to see Israel get kicked around, defeated by Assyria, and exiled. But Micah also saw a godly king, Hezekiah, replace evil Ahaz in the south. Through the influence of Hezekiah and the prophets Micah and Isaiah, Judah turned back to the Lord. While the Assyrians did invade Judah, the southern kingdom, including Jerusalem, survived.

### Bible Summary: Micah

God was about to step into history to judge his idolatrous people. Micah portrays the anguish his actions would cause. While God's sinful people lay awake thinking up how to sin in new ways, God had set his own plan in motion. The present civilization would be destroyed, but a few faithful people would be spared.

### What's Up with Micah?

**1** *Gotta deal with sin (Micah 3:1–7; 6:7–16).* God is a moral judge, who is responsible for punishing sin. Micah draws a picture of political leaders who exploit citizens and of religious leaders who pretend that nothing is wrong. He goes on to describe a **materialistic** society in which the average person is dishonest and deceitful, practicing "religion" but unconcerned with justice.

>>>CHECK IT OUT:

Micah 3:1–7; 6:9–16

**materialistic:** *consumed with gaining more and more possessions*

**2** *Gotta have a Savior (Micah 5:2–5; 7:19–20).* Like other prophets who warned of coming judgment, Micah looked beyond the coming disaster to a day when God would save

>>>CHECK IT OUT:

Micah 7:7–20

his people. In this book (written over seven hundred years before Christ) Micah identified the town where the promised Savior would be born!

 ISAIAH

*. . . the Old Testament gospel*

| WHO | The prophet Isaiah |
|---|---|
| WHAT | warned of judgment |
| WHERE | to the people of Judah |
| WHEN | between 740 and 690 B.C. |
| WHY | and conveyed hope in the coming Messiah. |

 A COMING MESSIAH

Isaiah also lived under the threat of Assyria and witnessed the fall of Israel. Like Micah, Isaiah boldly warned Judah to turn back to God.

---

**Bible Summary: Isaiah**

The prophet's name means *Yahweh is salvation*. No other Old Testament prophet communicates so clearly God's intention to save his people.

---

### What's Up with Isaiah?

>>> CHECK IT OUT:

Isaiah 1; 5:1–7

**1** *God's sick of our sin (Isaiah 1).* The Lord put up with the sinful behavior of Israel and Judah far too long. Even the revivals led by godly kings in the south had not touched the hearts of God's people.

>>> CHECK IT OUT:

Isaiah 10:1–12

**2** *God uses humans (Isaiah 10:1–12).* Isaiah identifies Assyria as the *"rod of [God's] wrath."* The Assyrian invasion was not a random event. God allowed it to punish the sins of Israel and Judah. God is in control of history, and the rise and fall of nations accomplishes his purposes.

82

**3** *Hope was Isaiah's theme.* You wouldn't know Isaiah had hope from reading chapters 1–35. All you'll read in those chapters is destruction, destruction, destruction! But Isaiah frequently assures his hearers that God is committed to them, that he will keep his covenant promises that he made to Abraham and David. Isaiah reveals that God's promises will be fulfilled through the gift of God's Son, who will be born as a human child.

**4** *God's sovereign power (Isaiah 40–48).* The comfort and hope that Isaiah offers to Judah is based on his understanding of the nature of God. The God of Israel and Judah is the Creator, who made and governs the universe. God is the one who has made covenant promises and who will surely keep them. He is the one who knows the future and who reveals it, for he controls the future.

>>>**CHECK IT OUT:**

Isaiah 40:18–31;
  42:5–9; 44:6–20

**5** *God's people have a great future (Isaiah 58–66).* The history of Israel and Judah had been marked by periods of either blessing or devastating tragedy. Isaiah looked beyond history and described a future of endless blessing after the Savior punished sin and established God's rule in the hearts of human beings.

>>>**CHECK IT OUT:**

Isaiah 60:15–22;
  65:17–25

83

### The Message of Isaiah

Isaiah's message to the people of Judah was totally important. He warned his friends about judgment and reminded them that in the end God would clean the universe of sin and bring in a time of endless blessing for all who trust in him.

The Savior, Jesus Christ, described so powerfully by Isaiah, has appeared with the offer of salvation for all. Ultimately Jesus will return to earth, and he'll put everything back where it belongs.

**Charles Swindoll:** *Isaiah may have been 'Prince among Prophets.' But even greater than the man was his message—news of new life, new hope, and a new world under the King of kings and Lord of lords.*[4]

**OUTSIDE** CONNECTION

# CHAPTER CHECKUP

1. What Bible books record the history of Judah after Solomon's kingdom was divided?
2. Why was it important that Judah be ruled by godly rather than evil kings?
3. Why did all pagan peoples adopt occult practices? What was God's alternative to the occult for his people?
4. What were the four tests of a true prophet?
5. Match each of these four prophets to the corresponding message:

| Obadiah | The Savior to be born in Bethlehem |
| Joel | God's sovereign rule |
| Micah | Judgment on Edom |
| Isaiah | A plague of locusts |

## CRASH COURSE

▶ When Solomon died in 930 B.C. his kingdom was divided. The southern kingdom was renamed Judah. Judah was ruled by descendants of David until its fall to the Babylonians in 586 B.C. Many of the kings of Judah were godly and helped begin religious revivals. God also sent both speaking and writing prophets to the kings and people of the south as his spokesmen.

▶ The prophet Obadiah predicted the doom of Edomites who had beat up on God's people.

▶ The prophet Joel was given a vision of terrible judgment to come at history's end before God fully restored his people to himself.

▶ The prophet Micah ministered during the years Israel fell. He not only warned Judah of coming judgment but he also predicted the appearance of the promised messianic king.

▶ The book of the prophet Isaiah contains both warnings and promises. Many passages predict the coming of a king who would also be the Savior.

# The Kingdom Lives!

## 2 KINGS 15–25 • 2 CHRONICLES 29–36
## NAHUM • ZEPHANIAH • HABAKKUK
## JEREMIAH • EZEKIEL

85

 **LET'S DIVE IN!**

The southern kingdom, Judah, survived the Assyrian invasion that destroyed Israel in 722 B.C. God answered the prayers of Judah's godly king, Hezekiah, and threw back the invaders. But the sins that led to Israel's defeat were a big part of Judah as well. Despite revivals under King Hezekiah and later under King Josiah, Judah continued to sin. God kept watching, and he was about to judge them.

## ONE LONELY KINGDOM

When the Assyrian armies crushed Israel, Hezekiah was the ruler of Judah. He made plans to revive Judah's faith in the Lord. The Assyrian armies weren't satisfied with crushing only Israel; they wanted Judah, too. They destroyed the cities that guarded Judah's borders and threatened Jerusalem.

The army was mean, the battle tough. When the Assyrians

**>>>CHECK IT OUT:**
2 Chronicles 29–31;
2 Kings 18–19

appeared outside the capital and ridiculed the idea of depending on God, King Hezekiah and the prophet Isaiah called out to the Lord. God answered their prayers with a sudden plague that killed thousands of Assyrian soldiers, forcing King Senecherib to return home. This event is recounted three times in the Old Testament, in 2 Kings 18–19, in 2 Chronicles 32, and in Isaiah 36–39. We can learn a lot from this. If we're fully dedicated to God, he'll protect and bless us. If God's people were fully dedicated to him, the Lord would protect and bless them.

So the people of Judah remained devoted to God, right? After all, they had once again seen God's mighty acts and his protecting hand. Unfortunately, they didn't take the lesson to heart. Seven kings followed Hezekiah. Only one of the seven, Josiah, was dedicated to the Lord. The nation drifted further into idolatry, and its society became even more immoral and unjust. In 605 B.C. a series of Babylonian invasions began. In 586 B.C. Jerusalem was totally destroyed and its population was transported to Babylon.

 **HAVE IT YOUR WAY**

>>>CHECK IT OUT:

Ezekiel 8–11

This stuff can get confusing. When we read the accounts of godly kings like Hezekiah and Josiah, it's difficult to understand why Judah fell. But the revivals they led were superficial and brought about no permanent change of heart.

The prophet Ezekiel was taken to Babylon as a captive in 597 B.C., and he prophesied to the Jewish community there. He was given a vision of Judah's sins. In his vision Ezekiel saw God's people worshiping pagan deities. As Ezekiel watched, God's glory (his visible presence) rose from the inner room (the Holy of Holies) of the temple and withdrew from Jerusalem. God's people had abandoned him. He would no longer protect them from their enemies.

**Warren Wiersbe:** *Everything that God had given the Jews was taken from them. They had no king on David's throne, nor do they have one today. They had no temple, for it had been burned and its sacred vessels confiscated. Their Holy City was destroyed, and ever since that time has been the*

Has God given you something to tell people? If so, what is it?_____
_____

What is God warning you about?_____
_____

What risks do you take in talking to people about God? What are the benefits?
_____
_____

Telling the truth ain't easy. Imagine being a prophet when these dudes walked the earth. God tells them to say something, and they wrestle with whether they should say it or not. Ever have difficulty telling the truth? Hey, being honest isn't easy, but it is necessary. The Old Testament prophets may have had difficulty saying what God told them to say, but they did it anyway. That's a model we can live by.

focal point for war and unrest in the Mideast. Their land was taken from them, and they were scattered among the nations. Be sure your sins will find you out *(Numbers 32:23)*.[1]

 NAHUM

_ _ _ _ _ . . . *warning from a comforting prophet* _ _ _ _

| | |
|---|---|
| WHO | The prophet Nahum |
| WHAT | described the fall of Nineveh |
| WHERE | while in the Middle East |
| WHEN | while Assyria was still dominant |
| WHY | to tell them God was going to judge them. |

GIMME THE BASICS

 GOD AIN'T GOT NO FAVORITES

Nineveh, the capital of Assyria, repented. (Remember Jonah's story about the whale? He's the prophet that helped them understand their sins.) But before long the success of the

Assyrian armies replaced humility with an arrogant pride. So, when the Assyrians went out to attack Israel, they were brutal. They showed no pity. The prophet Nahum began shouting that Nineveh was about to be judged by God. Here's what he said: *"The LORD is a jealous and avenging God; the LORD takes vengeance and is filled with wrath. The LORD takes vengeance against his foes and maintains his wrath against his enemies"* (Nahum 1:2).

> **Bible Summary: Nahum**
>
> The prophet teaches that divine judgment of the wicked *will* happen. His short book is divided into three parts:
> - God's anger against Nineveh is expressed (Nahum 1:1–15)
> - Nineveh's fall is described (Nahum 2:1–13)
> - The destruction is graphically portrayed (Nahum 3:1–19)

## What's Up with Nahum?

1 *Simple logic (Nahum 1:1–15).* Nahum states the truth clearly: *"the LORD will not leave the guilty unpunished"* (Nahum 1:3). Nahum urges the people of Judah to *"celebrate your [religious] festivals, O Judah, and fulfill your vows"* (Nahum 1:13). In other words they needed to make things right with God.

2 *Nineveh's fall is predicted (Nahum 2:6; 3:8–15).* The prophet describes a flood that would collapse palaces and open river gates to the enemy. Nahum gives specific details about the fall of the city decades before the actual event.

3 *Consolation.* The name Nahum means *consolation.* Cool, huh? God wanted his people to know that he remained in charge of his universe, and that he would punish their oppressors. But the Book of Nahum can also be read as a warning. God plays no favorites. He will punish his own people if they turn out to be wicked.

 **ZEPHANIAH**

### . . . judgment on Judah

| | |
|---|---|
| WHO | Zephaniah |
| WHAT | prophesied judgment |
| WHERE | in Judah and Jerusalem |
| WHEN | during the reign of Josiah |
| WHY | to get the people to repent. |

## LISTEN UP!

Josiah was Judah's last godly ruler. He became king when he was only eight, following his grandfather Manasseh and his father Amon. These two kings, whose combined rule extended over fifty-seven years, had completely corrupted biblical religion, and Judah was filled with idolatry and injustice. In Josiah's eighteenth year a lost book of the law, probably Deuteronomy, was recovered. When Josiah read it, he realized that his nation was in serious trouble. They had strayed far away from the law that God had laid down for the Israelite nation. Josiah got brave. He restored worship in the temple, tore down and burned the idols that infested the land, and got rid of practitioners of the occult. He called all the people together and had God's Word <u>read to them</u> and urged them to follow it. Josiah took huge, brave steps to stand up for God when it wasn't cool to do it.

Despite all his efforts, it was too late to reverse the national spiritual decline. While the nation would be preserved as long as Josiah lived, its sins called out for divine judgment, and judgment would surely come. In other words, a world of hurt was on the way, and Josiah couldn't stop it.

*R. C. Sproul: If there's no God, of course you don't need Jesus. If there is a God, and he is holy and you are holy, you don't need Jesus. But if God is and God is holy, and you are not holy, there is nothing in the universe you need more desperately than Jesus. A Holy God will never negotiate justice. His justice must be satisfied or he is no longer good. He is no longer just. He is no longer holy. He is no longer God.*[2]

**GIMME THE BASICS**

**>>>CHECK IT OUT:**

2 Kings 22–23

**89**

**GO!**

1 Chronicles 34:29–31 (read to them)

**OUTSIDE CONNECTION**

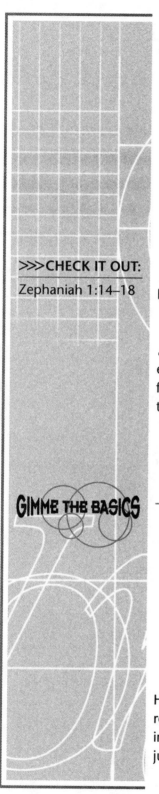

**Bible Summary: Zephaniah**

His mission was to warn Judah of God's judgment that would wipe out Judah and her neighbors. Zephaniah ended his message with a word of hope. After judgment God would bring his people home. The book has three parts:

- Announcement of judgment on Judah (Zephaniah 1:1–2:3)
- Announcement of judgment on the nations (Zephaniah 2:4–15)
- The promise of a future for Jerusalem (Zephaniah 3:1–20)

>>>CHECK IT OUT:

Zephaniah 1:14–18

## What's Up with Zephaniah?

1 *Judgment on Judah (1:1–2:3).* Zephaniah described the *"day of the Lord"* that was coming soon. God was going to judge his people in Judah as well as the nations that oppressed them.

2 *Hope for the future (Zephaniah 3:11–20).* The Old Testament prophets were blunt. They warned their listeners to expect judgment. But they also reaffirmed God's lasting love for his people. Sins would be punished, but God was committed to save his people in the end.

 **HABAKKUK**

*. . . living by faith*

| | |
|---|---|
| WHO | Habakkuk talks with God |
| WHAT | about how God's justice can be understood |
| WHERE | in Jerusalem |
| WHEN | during the reign of Josiah |
| WHY | because the Babylonians were going to invade. |

 **WHASSUP, GOD?**

Habakkuk was upset. Even though Josiah did his best to get a revival going, the city he lived in was still full of violence and injustice. So, Habakkuk asks God how he can allow these injustices to go on. The Lord says he is about to send the

Babylonians to punish his sinning people. This confuses Habakkuk, and he objects—the Babylonians are more wicked than the people living in Judah! Then God shares some secrets with Habakkuk about his plans. Even when wicked people *seem* to be succeeding and being used by God, they're being punished too. Habakkuk is satisfied, and asks God to make it all happen quickly. Ever felt picked on, and forgotten by God? This is good news! He knows what's going on, and he's just waiting for the perfect moment to help you out!

---

**Bible Summary: Habakkuk**

The prophet raises important questions about God's justice. How can God permit sin to rip up human society? Is God really silent and withdrawn? The Book of Habakkuk explores this issue through the prophet's questions and God's surprising answers. The book can be outlined as follows:

- Habakkuk complains (Habakkuk 1:1–11)
- Habakkuk complains again (Habakkuk 1:12–17)
- Principles of present judgment (Habakkuk 2:1–20)
- Habakkuk's prayer (Habakkuk 3:1–19)

### What's Up with Habakkuk?

**1** *Judah's sinful to the max (Habakkuk 1:1–11).* Even though it looked like a revival was going on, Judah's society was really bad. Tons of sinning, lots of injustice. Habakkuk cannot believe a holy God can permit this to go on unpunished. When he prays, God tells him of the coming Babylonian invasion. God will punish sin.

>>> **CHECK IT OUT:**

Habakkuk 1:2–4

**2** *Habakkuk's questions (Habakkuk 1:12–17).* God's answer confuses Habakkuk. He asks, *"Why are you silent while the wicked swallow up those more righteous than themselves?"* The people of Judah are bad, but the godless Babylonians are worse! The success of the wicked makes it seem like God just doesn't care at all.

**3** *God is not silent (Habakkuk 2:1–20).* God says, *"while the wicked swallow up those more righteous . . ."* In other words, God is judging even while the wicked seem to enjoy their greatest success!

>>> **CHECK IT OUT:**

Habakkuk 2:4–20

So, what's the message? Don't envy the wicked. They may appear successful. But even while they appear successful outwardly, inwardly they are unsatisfied and insecure. It just doesn't pay to be wicked!

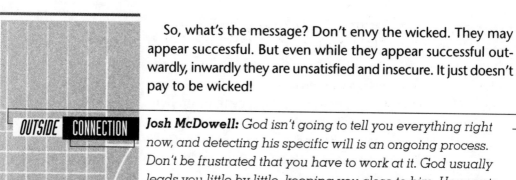

**OUTSIDE CONNECTION**

**Josh McDowell:** *God isn't going to tell you everything right now, and detecting his specific will is an ongoing process. Don't be frustrated that you have to work at it. God usually leads you little by little, keeping you close to him. He counts on you to walk step by step in relationship with Him and learn from him—because, after all, finding your heart's desire is all about delighting in him.*[3]

**OUTSIDE CONNECTION**

**Norman L. Geisler:** *Although often neglected, Habakkuk's prophecy is one of the most influential in the Bible. Habakkuk 2:4 is quoted three times in the New Testament (Romans 1:17; Galatians 3:11; Hebrews 10:38), more than almost any other verse. It served as the basis for the Protestant Reformation and, through Luther's Commentary on Galatians, the conversion of John Wesley. Habakkuk is a book of faith.*[4]

 **JEREMIAH**

### . . . the weeping prophet

| | |
|---|---|
| WHO | Jeremiah |
| WHAT | wrote this book |
| WHERE | urging Judah |
| WHEN | during the last forty years of its free life |
| WHY | to submit to Babylon. |

 **STANDING ALONE**

Jeremiah was a guy who was called by God to urge the people of Judah to submit to the Babylonians. For forty years Jeremiah warned the nation that God was going to punish his people's sins. What was his solution? Surrender. The Israelites not only ignored him; they persecuted him as a traitor. Jeremiah lived long enough to see his prophecies fulfilled, to witness the destruction of Jerusalem and Solomon's temple, and to see the people of Judah taken captive to Babylon.

**GIMME THE BASICS**

## What's Up with Jeremiah?

**1** *Jeremiah's pain (Jeremiah 15:12–18; 20:7–18).* Being a prophet wasn't an easy job. Imagine how isolated and alone Jeremiah felt! He was a sensitive person, who was hurt deeply by the ridicule and hostility he constantly faced. Jeremiah's only recourse was to share his feelings with the Lord, which he records in several passages (like in Jeremiah 15:15; 17–18).

Jeremiah's a perfect example of what to do when we're hurting. Sometimes, when we're feeling emotions that we don't know how to deal with, we want to yell at someone or just run away. Jeremiah teaches us that when our emotions feel like they're too much to handle, we can tell God our hurts. God's never too busy to listen!

**2** *Judah keeps sinning (Jeremiah 5:7–25; 10:1–16).* Jeremiah wasn't a chicken. He boldly confronted the people of his day about the sins for which they'd be judged. But like a lot of people, the people of Judah considered immorality a private matter and refused to repent. If you read Jeremiah's book, it'll feel like you're reading a modern-day newspaper. A lot of similarities exist between the sin of Jeremiah's day and the sin of our own day.

**3** *The punishment is on the way (Jeremiah 25:1–14).* You've heard this one before. Moses had warned God's people of

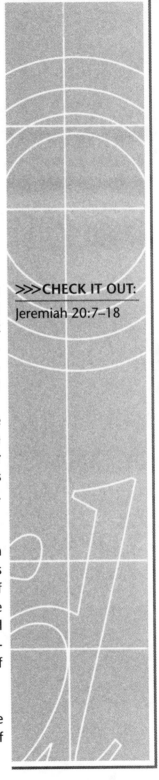

>>>CHECK IT OUT:
Jeremiah 20:7–18

93

>>>CHECK IT OUT:

Deuteronomy
28:49–68

what would happen if they refused to honor and obey God. Now Jeremiah reminds them again and again. He said things like, "*Turn now, each of you from his evil ways and your evil practices.*" But Judah would not listen or pay attention.

**4** *The promise of a New Covenant (Jeremiah 30–31).* Jeremiah's mission was to announce the coming fall of his nation. He was given the privilege of communicating the promise that one day God would make a New Covenant with his people. Check out the New Covenant in Jeremiah 31:31–34.

When we get to the New Testament we'll learn a lot about the New Covenant (by the way, the term New Testament literally means New Covenant). But the important thing to note here is that in the darkest of times, through Jeremiah, God gave his people what is surely the brightest, most wonderful promise in God's Word.

**5** *The flight to Egypt (Jeremiah 40–44).* After Jerusalem was destroyed, most of the Jewish population was deported to Babylon. A few Jews remained under a governor appointed by Nebuchadnezzar. When that governor was assassinated, the remaining Jews were terrified and planned to flee to Egypt, but first they asked Jeremiah to ask the Lord what they should do. Jeremiah prayed and reported what God said. The remaining Jews were to stay in their homeland. God would keep them safe. But if they refused to listen, and went to Egypt, Nebuchadnezzar would attack Egypt, and they would be wiped out.

Instead of listening to Jeremiah the people angrily rejected God's guidance.

**OUTSIDE CONNECTION**

**Warren Wiersbe:** *A nation or an individual life can get to the 'point of no return.' If the clay becomes hard, it can no longer be molded. How important it is to yield to Christ early in life.*[5]

 EZEKIEL

*. . . prophet to the exiles*

| | |
|---|---|
| WHO | Ezekiel |
| WHAT | warned the captives |
| WHERE | in Babylon |
| WHEN | six years before the fall of Jerusalem |
| WHY | to prepare God's people for a lengthy captivity. |

 DRY BONES

The Babylonians invaded Judah three times. Each time they invaded, they took prisoners. In 597 B.C. Ezekiel was taken to Babylon after the second invasion. In 592 B.C. Ezekiel was called to be a prophet when he was thirty years old. His messages to the exiles in Babylon were exactly like the warnings Jeremiah was shouting at the same time in Judah. Through a series of visions Ezekiel described events for the captives that were taking place in Judah long before word from the homeland could reach them.

> **Bible Summary: Ezekiel**
> The book contains a series of messages acted out and preached by the prophet. Ezekiel was a very animated man. Most of the book dates from before the fall of Jerusalem and is about its coming destruction. After Jerusalem was destroyed, Ezekiel spoke of a restored Jerusalem and of a new temple to be built on the same site as the one that had been destroyed.
> - Prophecies against Judah (Ezekiel 1–24)
> - Prophecy against foreign nations (Ezekiel 25–32)
> - Prophecies of restoration (Ezekiel 33–39)
> - Prophecy of the rebuilt temple (Ezekiel 40–48)

### What's Up with Ezekiel?

1 *The emptied temple (Ezekiel 8–11).* The Israelites' thinking went like this. The city has the temple. God lives in the temple. Therefore, the city can't fall, because it has God's pres-

**KEY POINT**

It is important to give your life to Christ as soon as you are presented with the choice.

95

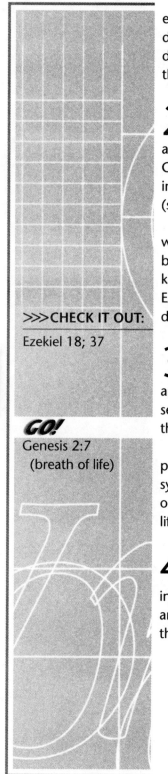

ence. Surely God would not permit his dwelling place to be destroyed by pagans. But in a vision, Ezekiel saw God withdraw his presence from the temple and Jerusalem. Afterwards, the temple was an empty shell. God had left!

**2** *Personal responsibility (Ezekiel 18).* Like most people who heard the prophets, many in Jerusalem blew off Ezekiel's and Jeremiah's warnings. If their forefathers had displeased God, and he was intent on punishing them, there was nothing they could do about it. Ezekiel confronted this attitude (see Ezekiel 18:4).

Ezekiel felt personally responsible for the problems Israel was facing. In the coming invasion God would distinguish between the righteous and the wicked. The wicked would be killed while the righteous would survive to go into captivity. In Ezekiel 18 the prophet gives four examples to show that God deals with human beings individually.

>>>CHECK IT OUT:

Ezekiel 18; 37

**3** *One wacky dream (Ezekiel 37).* Ezekiel has a dream that is out of this world. He's shown a valley filled with scattered and dried bones. He is told to prophesy, and the bones reassemble and are covered with flesh. But they do not live until they are given the breath of life (Ezekiel 37:1–10).

God explains the vision. The bones represented the Jewish people scattered throughout the nations. Their reassembling symbolized the Jews regathering to the promised land. But only when the people are filled with God's Spirit will they have life (Ezekiel 37:11–14).

*GO!*

Genesis 2:7
(breath of life)

**4** *The rebuilt temple (Ezekiel 40–48).* Ezekiel's message ended with hope. The prophet looks forward to a time of blessing at history's end, when God's people will live in their land and worship the Lord at a temple that will be constructed at that time.

## CHAPTER CHECKUP

1. Revival saved Judah when the Assyrians destroyed Israel under what godly king?

2. What sins of Judah did the prophets point to as the cause of the Babylonian victory?
3. Name three of the four prophets who preached in Judah.
4. Name the prophet who preached to the exiles in Babylon before the destruction of Jerusalem.

### CRASH COURSE

▶ King Hezekiah's dependence on God saved Judah from the Assyrians who destroyed Israel.

▶ The prophet Nahum described the fall of Nineveh as divine judgment on the Assyrians.

▶ The prophet Zephaniah warned the people of Judah that God would judge them too.

▶ Habakkuk predicted the Babylonian invasion as a punishment for Judah's sins.

▶ The prophet Jeremiah struggled for forty years to reach the people of Judah. His message was rejected. His predictions came true.

▶ The prophet Ezekiel had visions in which he witnessed the sins of the people in his homeland and the withdrawal of God's presence from the Jerusalem temple.

▶ Despite the sins of Judah that called for judgment, God would deliver the righteous and would keep his promises to Abraham. He would save his people at the end of history.

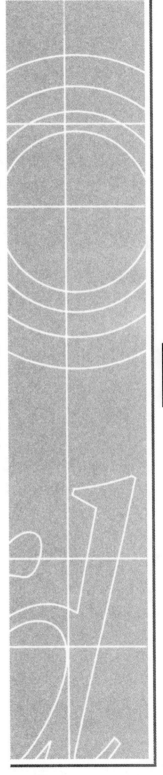

97

# Exile
# and Return

LAMENTATIONS • DANIEL • ESTHER
EZRA • NEHEMIAH • HAGGAI
ZECHERIAH • MALACHI

## LET'S DIVE IN!

The Israelites were bummed out! They were invaded three times by the Babylonians, led by King Nebuchadnezzar. This army stripped Judah of her wealth and population. In 586 B.C. the remaining Jews of Judah were resettled in Babylon, many in the capital city itself. Seventy years later the Babylonian Empire was conquered by the Medes and Persians. The new ruler, Cyrus, reversed the Babylonian policy of resettlement, and permitted captive peoples to return to their homeland. The captivity forced God's people to review their sins and ask a question that floored them: "Has God totally rejected us?"

They get their answer in three different ways, in three different books. But the answer was a resounding, "No, God has not rejected you!"

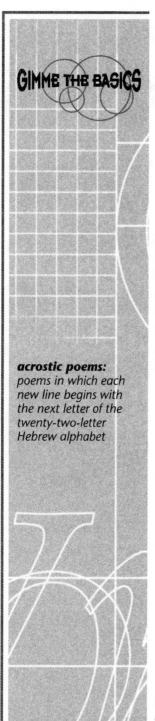

## LAMENTATIONS

### *. . . the agony of defeat*

| | |
|---|---|
| WHO | Tradition says Jeremiah |
| WHAT | wrote these poems |
| WHERE | in Babylon |
| WHEN | after Jerusalem fell |
| WHY | to express the pain felt by the Jewish captives. |

## DUDE . . . I'M SO NOT READY FOR THIS

Ever experience a really drastic consequence? Maybe your parents kept telling you not to do something. Then you did it once again. Then you paid the price. That's what's happening to the Israelites in this book. The people of Judah who ignored the warnings of Jeremiah finally experienced the consequences of abandoning God. Their despair and anguish are captured in five **acrostic poems** that make up Lamentations.

*acrostic poems:*
*poems in which each*
*new line begins with*
*the next letter of the*
*twenty-two-letter*
*Hebrew alphabet*

### Bible Summary: Lamentations

Poems that express sorrow were a common literary form in the ancient Near East. The poems of Lamentations express the loss experienced by the captives in Babylon, who at last realize how foolish they were to have turned away from God. The five "laments" are:

- Jerusalem in mourning (Lamentations 1:1–22)
- Jerusalem in ruins (Lamentations 2:1–22)
- A call for renewal (Lamentations 3:1–66)
- Restitution to come (Lamentations 3:1–22)
- A cry for relief (Lamentations 4:1–22)

### What's Up with Lamentations?

1 *Lamentations tells us about the Jews' sadness.* These poems tell us how sad the Israelites were while in exile. They finally recognize their sins led to their present, pitiful state. Yet even in darkest despair there was a glimmer of hope.

2 *Lamentations reminds us to remain confident.* Did the Israelites benefit from being held captive for so long? Yes!

After their captivity the Israelites were never tempted into idolatry. While they were in exile the **synagogue** was invented. In the end the captivity proved to be a blessing, purifying God's people from many of the sins that had called for divine punishment.

**synagogue:** *the local meeting place of the Jewish people during New Testament times*

 ## DANIEL

### . . . a powerful captive

| WHO | Daniel, a young captive, |
|---|---|
| WHAT | delivers prophecies |
| WHERE | as a student in the king's school in Babylon |
| WHEN | around 605 B.C. |
| WHY | to tell people about the future history of the world. |

## IT TAKES GUTS TO BE DANIEL

Being a captive was hard. But it wasn't all bad. Most of the captives taken to Babylon settled in suburbs of the capital city; they owned their own homes and raised crops. Records recovered by archaeologists indicate many Jews went into business and prospered. Daniel was taken captive in an invasion around 605 B.C. He was enrolled in a school that trained administrators for the Babylonian Empire. He became a high official in both the Babylonian and Persian Empires, showing God's care of the faithful even in exile. Daniel was also a prophet, whose visions of the future told the captives that God was in control, and that one day he would bring his people home.

**GIMME THE BASICS**

101

**>>>CHECK IT OUT:**

Jeremiah 29:4–7;
 Ezekiel 8:1; 12:1–7

---

**Bible Summary: Daniel**

This incredible book is divided into two parts. The first half tells stories of Daniel and his relationships with world rulers. The second half is full of visions God gave Daniel to reassure his people that God was still in complete control of human history.

- Daniel's life and work (Daniel 1–6)
- Daniel's visions and prophecies (Daniel 7–12)

>>>CHECK IT OUT:
Daniel 8

*week:* seven years

*Messiah:* Jesus

>>>CHECK IT OUT:
Daniel 9:20–27;
   Matthew 21:1–11

GIMME THE BASICS

# What's Up with Daniel?

**1** *Daniel's life (Daniel 1–6).* Daniel developed a close relationship with the Babylonian ruler, Nebuchadnezzar, and other world rulers. Many believe that through Daniel's influence Nebuchadnezzar became a believer. The first six chapters tell us a lot of stuff about his life . . . stuff like:

Daniel's determination to follow God's laws (Daniel 1:1–21)
Daniel interprets Nebuchadnezzar's dream (Daniel 2:1–49)
Daniel's companions in the fiery furnace (Daniel 3:1–30)
Daniel and Nebuchadnezzar's conversion (Daniel 4:1–37)
Daniel and the handwriting on the wall (Daniel 5:1–31)
Daniel in the lions' den (Daniel 6:1–28)

**2** *Daniel's wild visions of the future (Daniel 7–12).* Daniel's visions showed that for centuries to come the promised land would be ruled by gentile world powers (definitely *not cool* if you were an Israelite). Yet the visions were reassuring. One day the promises given to Abraham and repeated by the prophets would be kept. The captivity did not mean God had abandoned his people.

**3** *Seventy long* **weeks** *(Daniel 9:20–27).* These chapters predict that the **Messiah** would enter Jerusalem around April 6, 32 A.D. And guess what, that's exactly what happened. You know, sometimes we look at prophecies in the Bible and say, "Yeah, well, that might come true." But look, this is just one of loads of prophecies that came true. When God's messengers make a prediction, you can count on them.

 **ESTHER**

*. . . born to be queen*

| | |
|---|---|
| WHO | An unnamed author |
| WHAT | wrote this book |
| WHERE | in Persia |
| WHEN | between 460 B.C. and 350 B.C. |
| WHY | to demonstrate that God was taking care of his captive people. |

## GOD IS WATCHING!

This is one of the most unusual books in the Bible. It's a poetic story about a young Jewish woman who became queen of Persia just in time to save God's people from being totally wiped out. Even though God is never mentioned in the book, it's clear he's at work. Even when they're exiled from their homeland, God hasn't forgotten his people.

### Bible Summary: Esther

When King Xerxes divorced his wife he chose a young girl, Esther, as his new wife. About the same time a high official in Xerxes's court, Haman, felt he'd been insulted by a lower official—a man named Mordecai who happened to be a Jew. Haman decided to wipe out the whole Jewish race as revenge, and Xerxes gave him permission! But then through a series of amazing "coincidences" (yeah, right!) Xerxes decided to honor Mordecai, Esther revealed she was a Jew, Haman angered the king and was executed, and the Jews were saved. Whew!

## What's Up with Esther?

1 *God provides for his children.* God does not need to work miracles to protect his people. He can influence, affect, and change the events in our world so that his will is accomplished. And we rarely notice!

2 *The book is awesome no matter what age you are.* You've got to read this book all at once, like a short story. Lots of people of all ages find the story fascinating, and are attracted to the brave young queen who risks her own life for her people.

 ## THE RETURN HOME

In 538 B.C. (see the time line on page 104) a radical and brave group of 42,360 Jews decided to reestablish a temple in Jerusalem. A second group, led by Ezra, returned later in 458 B.C., and a third group led by Nehemiah returned in 444 B.C. Once again there was a Jewish presence in the promised land. Yet in

the last five hundred years of Old Testament history, many more Jews lived scattered throughout Persia and subsequent eastern empires than in the land God had promised to Abraham.

 **EZRA**

*. . . homecoming!*

| | |
|---|---|
| WHO | Ezra |
| WHAT | wrote much of this book |
| WHERE | in Judah |
| WHEN | around 430 B.C. |
| WHY | to tell us about the Jews' return to Jerusa- lem. |

 **NEHEMIAH**

*. . . rebuilding Jerusalem*

| | |
|---|---|
| WHO | Nehemiah |
| WHAT | wrote much of this book |
| WHERE | in Judah |
| WHEN | around 430 B.C. |
| WHY | to tell us about the rebuilding of the city walls. |

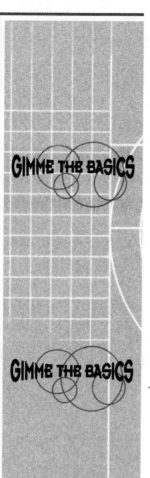

**GIMME THE BASICS**

**GIMME THE BASICS**

104

### Timeline for the Captivity and Return of the Jews

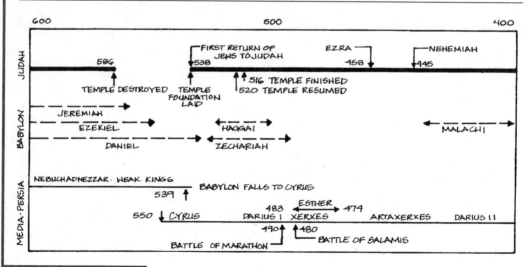

## WALL CONSTRUCTION 101

Ezra and Nehemiah tell us all about the difficulties and challenges the Jews faced, especially the Jews who chose to leave their captivity in Babylon and head for their homeland. Those who did return wanted to renew their relationships with God! They were fired up! They began rebuilding the temple. They began teaching God's law. And finally, they decided to restore Jerusalem's status as an important city by rebuilding the city's walls.

> ### Bible Summary: Ezra
> The first Jewish return took place shortly after Cyrus the Persian conquered Babylon. About forty-three thousand Jews returned, and went to work rebuilding the Jerusalem temple. Immediately they began laying the foundation. But opposition from the semipagan peoples in the land delayed its completion for eighteen years. The prophets Haggai and Zechariah got in on the action and encouraged them to get to work on the temple. They completed it in four years. Ezra led another group back to Judah, with authority to appoint **magistrates** and administer both Persian and God's laws. The book is organized by the two returns it describes.
> - The first return (Ezra 1–6)
> - The second return (Ezra 7–10)

*magistrates: a government official with administrative and judicial responsibilities*

### What's Up with Ezra?

**1** *Cyrus makes an important decree (Ezra 1).* About 150 years before the Persians overcame Babylon, God identified Cyrus as the ruler he would use to bring the Jewish exiles home. In the very first year of his reign, Cyrus fulfilled this prophecy. He issued a decree that permitted the Jews to return to the Holy Land! At the same time Cyrus permitted other captives to return to their homelands also. Many believe that Daniel influenced this reversal of policy.

>>>CHECK IT OUT:

Isaiah 44:24–45:7;
Ezra 1

**2** *Local opposition (Ezra 4–6).* When the Assyrians deported the people of Israel in 722 B.C., they had resettled the land with pagan people. The descendants of these people now of-

>>>CHECK IT OUT:

Ezra 5

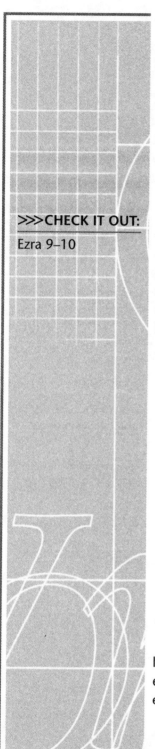

fered to help rebuild God's temple so they could worship there. The Jews refused. The locals were not members of the covenant community—they were pagans! Not a good group to surround yourself with if you want to rebuild something for God. These locals got really angry, so they began lying, spreading rumors about the Jews. Their efforts stopped work on the temple for eighteen years. Check out these chapters to see how King Darius settled the problems, raised cash for the temple's construction, and helped the Jews come out ahead.

>>>CHECK IT OUT:
Ezra 9–10

**3** *Ezra's reforms in Judah (Ezra 7–10).* Ezra arrived in Judah fifty-eight years after the temple was completed. He was shocked to discover that priests and other Jews had married pagan wives in direct violation of God's law. He confessed this sin in a prayer to God, which moved the people of Judah to repent. The foreign wives were divorced, and the people promised to observe God's law faithfully.

---

### Bible Summary: Nehemiah

Nehemiah gave up his position in the Persian court to become governor of Judah in 444 B.C. He rallied the Jews to rebuild the walls of Jerusalem and to repopulate the city. Nehemiah was also deeply concerned about the spiritual state of the Jews. He worked closely with Ezra to teach and enforce God's law, always setting a personal example as a godly leader. Nehemiah's book can be divided into three parts.

- The walls are rebuilt (Nehemiah 1–6)
- The covenant is renewed (Nehemiah 7–12)
- Judah's sins are purged (Nehemiah 13)

---

## What's Up with Nehemiah?

**1** *Nehemiah's morality (Nehemiah 5–6).* Nehemiah was the key to the successful rebuilding of the city walls. His selfless service was an example to all. And when the Jews' enemies threatened his life, Nehemiah's courage was also an example.

**2** *Nehemiah's final reforms (Nehemiah 13).* After a successful term as Judah's governor, Nehemiah returned to the Persian court. When Nehemiah returned to Judah in 431 B.C., he found that the people had slipped back into their old sinful ways. Once again Nehemiah was successful in introducing reforms. But it was clear that without strong, godly leaders, the people wouldn't remain faithful to the Lord.

 **HAGGAI**

### *. . . rebuild the temple!*

| | |
|---|---|
| WHO | The prophet Haggai |
| WHAT | preached four sermons |
| WHERE | to the people in Judah |
| WHEN | in 520 B.C. |
| WHY | urging them to complete the rebuilding of the temple. |

## GOD HAS A NEW HOUSE

The temple foundations had been laid, but no work had been done on it for years. Then, on August 29, 520 B.C., the prophet Haggai announced that material blessings had been withheld because God's people had failed to put him first. The little Jewish community took Haggai's words to heart and set out to finish building the temple.

> **Bible Summary: Haggai**
> Through a series of four messages the prophet moved the little Jewish community to completely rebuild the Jerusalem temple. Here are the messages and when Haggai gave them:
> - Put God first and finish the temple, August 29, 520 B.C.
> - God will provide needed finances, October 17, 520 B.C.
> - From this day I will bless you, December 18, 520 B.C.
> - David's throne will be established, December 18, 520 B.C.

### What's Up with Haggai?

1 *The new temple (Haggai 2:1–15).* The little Jewish community was almost nonexistent. Could they rebuild the temple or beautify it? Through Haggai God reminded the Jews that

>>> CHECK IT OUT:
Ezra 6:8–12; Haggai 2:1–15

**GIMME THE BASICS**

*"the silver is mine and the gold is mine"* (Haggai 2:8), so the Jews began rebuilding the temple. Ezra tells us how God provided. The Persian ruler diverted tax dollars from the Jews' enemies to pay for construction of the temple.

By the time of Christ, the temple constructed in the year 520 B.C. had been expanded and beautified to become one of the wonders of the ancient world.

**2** *Blessing follows obedience (Haggai 2:10–19).* Haggai made no promises when urging the Jews to finish the temple. But after they obeyed, and the work was begun, God did give them a promise: *"From this day on I will bless you."*

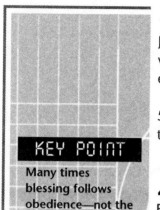

**KEY POINT**

Many times blessing follows obedience—not the other way around.

**OUTSIDE CONNECTION** **Martin Luther:** *Faith is a living, daring confidence in God's grace. It is so sure and certain that a man could stake his life on it a thousand times.*[1]

**GIMME THE BASICS**

## ➤➤ ZECHARIAH

### . . . the future of Israel

| WHO | Zechariah |
|---|---|
| WHAT | prophesied |
| WHERE | to the settlers in Judah |
| WHEN | at the same time as Haggai |
| WHY | to encourage them to rebuild the temple and look for the Messiah. |

## ➤➤ A TRIP ON A DONKEY

Talk about coincidences! On October 17, 520 B.C., the prophet Zechariah preached his first sermon and Haggai preached his second message. While Zechariah added his voice to Haggai's in urging the Jews to complete the temple, the bulk of Zechariah's message is filled with visions. He uses powerful images that focus on history's end. Many of Zechariah's images are incorporated in Revelation.

While Zechariah encouraged his own generation to rebuild the temple, he wanted every generation of God's people to know that God will fulfill the visions of the future that were given to earlier prophets. God's Messiah will come, and his rule will be established on the earth.

> **Bible Summary: Zechariah**
> This book is divided into two main parts. The first part of the book contains a series of visions about the future of the Jewish people and a response to questions about fasting by the returned exiles. The second part of the book describes God's intervention at history's end.
>
> *Part 1*
>   Eight visions (Zechariah 1:1–6:15)
>   Questions on **fasting** (Zechariah 7:1–8:23)
> *Part 2*
>   God's shepherd rejected (Zechariah 9:1–11:17)
>   God's final intervention (Zechariah 12:1–14)

**fasting:** *not eating; in Bible times people fasted to show sorrow for sin or passion in prayer*

## What's Up with Zechariah?

**1** *Eight cool visions (Zechariah 1:1–8:19).* On February 15, 519 B.C., Zechariah was given a series of visions. Each vision had to do with the future of the Jewish people. Although Gentile world powers would control the Holy Land, God would keep his ancient promises.

**2** *Questions about fasting (Zechariah 7–8).* During the captivity the Jews had observed two holidays commemorating the fall of the city and the destruction of the temple. When the temple is almost completed, the people ask Zechariah whether they should continue to observe these holidays, during which they fasted. God's answer? Basically he said, "Hey, people . . . you're fasting for all the wrong reasons! Instead of honoring an event, why not honor me with your lives!" (Check out God's *exact* response in Zechariah 7:9–10.) The same goes for us today. Are we attempting to honor God when we celebrate holidays (like Christmas) or are we out for the gifts? Do we remember God, or do we just like a day off? God's response to us would be the same as it was to the Jews.

**3** *God's plan at the end of time (Zechariah 9:1–14:20).* These chapters are full of clear prophecies about the Messiah.

**KEY POINT**

We should view holidays as opportunities to worship God.

**EXILE AND RETURN • ELEVEN**

 **MALACHI**

*. . . everything gets dark*

| | |
|---|---|
| WHO | The prophet Malachi |
| WHAT | wrote this last Old Testament book |
| WHERE | telling the people of Jerusalem |
| WHEN | around 400 B.C. |
| WHY | to examine their actions and respond to God's continuing love. |

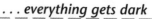 **WHA'D WE DO?**

Those who resettled in Jerusalem after the exile kept on sinning. Nehemiah 13 gives details about their repeated sins. Writing about thirty years later the prophet Malachi made it clear that within a few decades God's people had slid away from him again. This last book of the Old Testament serves as a reminder that throughout history God had been gracious to his people, but again and again they had strayed from him. God needed to do something drastic to get their attention and hearts.

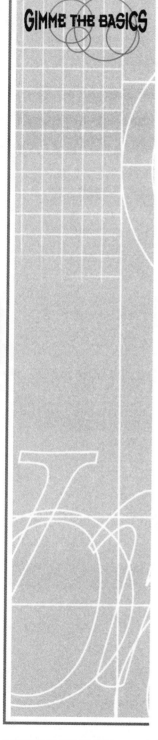

**GIMME THE BASICS**

---

**Bible Summary: Malachi**

The prophet challenges God's people to honor him, but they insist that they are already on good terms with God. In other words they're majorly confused! Malachi strips away their defenses, giving God's response to their pride. Malachi makes it clear that the people are:

- Neglecting God (Malachi 1:6–2:9)
- Breaking commitments (Malachi 2:10–16)
- Doubting God's presence (Malachi 2:17–3:5)
- Denying God's significance (Malachi 3:4–4:2)

The book concludes with a promise and a challenge. God will send his people a prophet to turn their hearts back to him, *"or else I will come and strike the land with a curse,"* God warned.

How has God cared for you throughout your life?_____

_____

 Your Move

When have you felt exiled from God? How did you "return from exile"?_____

_____

_____

What one word would you use to describe your history with God?_____

_____

_____

**GET REAL** This chapter has a lot of history in it. So, what makes history so important? Well, history is important because our history with God is our record of his interaction with us. It's all about him reaching into our time and our lives and doing wonderfully miraculous things. God's not ordinary, and his dealings with us are far from ordinary. If you were to write down all the things you've watched God do in your life, you'd have a modern-day example of the same sort of thing that's in these Bible books!

## What's Up with Malachi?

**1** *God's message of love (Malachi 1:2–5).* In ancient times God chose the <u>descendants</u> of Abraham, Isaac, and Jacob to be his own people, while rejecting any claim of the descendants of Esau to a special relationship with him. God has never backed away from his decision, and never will.

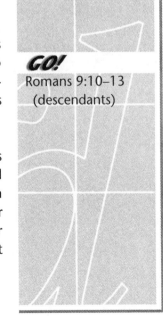

*GO!*
Romans 9:10–13
(descendants)

**2** *God's people don't seem to care (Malachi 1:6–2:16).* God's people still like to walk away from him. They offer God broken-down animals as sacrifices, the priests view serving in the temple as a burden, and the people are unfaithful to their spouses. If the people of Judah truly honored God in their hearts, their attitudes and actions would be very different indeed.

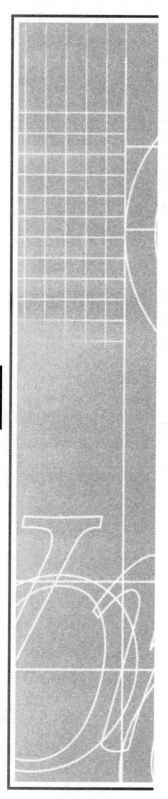

# CHAPTER cHECKUP

1. What Old Testament book expresses the sadness of the Jews taken captive to Babylon?
2. What book contains a specific prediction about the date on which the promised Messiah would enter Jerusalem as God's promised king?
3. Who were the two leaders whose books tell of the exiles' return to Judah?
4. What book of the Bible teaches by example that God is in control of our lives?
5. What two prophets encouraged people who returned to finish building God's temple?

## CRASH COURSE

▶ The experiences of Daniel and Esther showed that God continued to care for his people even though they had been kicked out of the promised land.
▶ Cyrus the Persian fulfilled Isaiah's prediction by permitting the Jews to return to their homeland and rebuild the Jerusalem temple.
▶ The prophets Haggai and Zechariah moved the Jews to finish the temple after construction had been halted for eighteen years.
▶ Ezra was appointed by the Persian king to oversee the administration of Persian law and God's law in Judah. Nehemiah served as governor of Judah. He rebuilt the walls of Jerusalem and kept the people of Judah focused on keeping God's laws.
▶ The last book of the Old Testament, Malachi, shows how difficult it was for God's Old Testament people to maintain their zeal for the Lord. To effectively deal with sin, God would have to do something new.

# PART 2

# THE NEW TESTAMENT

"HOME SCHOOLING ISN'T AS GREAT AS I THOUGHT IT WOULD BE. FOR CHEMISTRY CLASS, I HAVE TO TEST THE CHEMICAL REACTION BETWEEN LIQUID SOAP AND A PILE OF DIRTY DISHES. FOR MATH, I HAVE TO SUBTRACT DIRT FROM THE CARPET AND ADD POLISH TO THE FURNITURE. FOR PHYS ED, IT'S A GRUELING LAWN CARE TRIATHLON...."

 ## SO, WHAT'S THE NEW TESTAMENT?

The New Testament is a collection of twenty-seven books written in the first century A.D. These books tell the story of Jesus—the Messiah whose coming is predicted in the Old Testament. These twenty-seven books are "new" in the sense that when Jesus died on the cross and rose from the dead, he made possible a new relationship with God for everyone who believes in him.

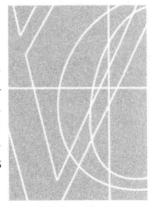

## GETTING TO KNOW GOD PERSONALLY

The Old Testament helps us understand what God is like. The New Testament shows us how we can have a personal relationship with God right now. When we have a personal relationship with Jesus, we can find fulfillment by loving God and other people.

 ## WHAT'S IN THE NEW TESTAMENT?

The books of the New Testament are divided into four different kinds of writings: the Gospels (biographies about Jesus), the Book of Acts (a book of history), letters of correspondence (written by Paul and other apostles), and the Book of Revelation (a book of prophecy). All of these books tell about Jesus Christ and what it means to be a follower of Jesus. The most important questions a person can ask are answered in these writings.

### THE GOSPELS

| Matthew, Mark, Luke, John | Who is Jesus? |
| | What did Jesus' miracles prove? |
| | What did Jesus teach about God? |
| | Why did Jesus have to die? |
| | Did Jesus really rise from the dead? |

### ACTS

| Acts | What happened to Jesus' followers after he rose from the dead? |
| | How did the Christian movement spread? |
| | Who did early Christians believe Jesus was? |

### LETTERS WRITTEN BY THE APOSTLE PAUL

| Romans, I, II Corinthians, Galations, Ephesians, Philippians, Colossians, I, II Thessalonians, I, II Timothy, Titus, Philemon | What does it mean to be "saved"? |
| | What special powers has God given to Christians? |
| | What will happen when Jesus comes back? |

### LETTERS WRITTEN BY OTHER APOSTLES

| Hebrews, James, I Peter, II Peter, I, II, III John, Jude | How are followers of Jesus different? |
| | Does God talk to believers today? |
| | Where is Jesus and what is he doing right now? |

### REVELATION

| Revelation | How will the world end? |
| | What will happen to people who have not trusted Jesus as Savior? |
| | What will heaven be like? |

# Jesus: The Real Deal

## 🔹🔹 LET'S DIVE IN!

Who's the most important person in the New Testament? Give up? It's Jesus! Most people have heard the story of his birth in Bethlehem and know that we celebrate Christmas as his birthday. In fact, every time we look at a calendar, we acknowledge that Jesus is the most important person who ever lived. The way we count time itself is by the days, months, and years before and after Jesus' birth!

## 🔹🔹 WHO'S JESUS?

Everyone admits that Jesus was a real person. He wasn't just a myth or fictional hero. But people do have different ideas about him. Some say he was an ordinary but an especially good person. Some say he was an extraordinary person, who was close to God, much like other great religious leaders. Some people believe Jesus was a little wacko, that he thought of himself as a divine messenger who went too far and got himself killed. Christians have a totally different idea about Jesus. For almost two thousand years Christians have said that Jesus is actually God. Christians believe that God chose to become a human being and live among us.

**KEY POINT**

Christians believe Jesus was and is God in human form.

# He's in the Old Testament Too!

There are hundreds of prophecies in the Old Testament that speak of an "Anointed One" whom God will send to deliver his people. In Hebrew "Anointed One" is translated "Messiah." In Greek "Anointed One" is translated "Christ." So the name Jesus Christ really means Jesus the Anointed One, or Jesus the Messiah.

Many Old Testament prophecies describe what the coming Messiah will do. But there are other prophecies that say who the Messiah will be. Check out these prophecies and you'll discover the Old Testament teaches the Messiah would be God himself!

>>>CHECK IT OUT:

Jeremiah 31:1–2
Luke 1:29–35

**KEY POINT**

The Old Testament contains lots of prophecies about Jesus.

1 *Psalm 2 describes the revolt of people against God (Psalm 2:1–3).* Psalm 2 even describes God's response to the revolt (Psalm 2:4–6), and tells of the future reign of Christ the Messiah (Psalm 2:7–9).

2 *Three things are really cool about the prophecy (Isaiah 7:14).* The first is that it talks about the child of a virgin, conceived without a human father. The second is that the child is to be named Immanuel. The name in Hebrew means "God with us." The third is that Isaiah made this prophecy seven hundred years before Jesus was born!

**OUTSIDE CONNECTION**

**John F. MacArthur, Jr.:** *The virgin birth is an underlying assumption of everything the Bible says about Jesus. To throw out the virgin birth is to reject Christ's deity, the accuracy and authority of Scripture, and a host of other related doctrines that are the heart of the Christian faith. No issue is more important than the virgin birth to our understanding of who Jesus is. If we deny that Jesus is God, we have denied the very essence of Christianity.*[1]

3 *Malachi 5:2 is a famous prophecy that says Bethlehem would be the Messiah's birthplace* (check out the map on page 132 to see where Bethlehem is located). About seven hundred years after Micah made this prediction, Jesus was born . . . in Bethlehem!

**4** *"Where is the God of justice?"* That's what people in Malachi's day were asking each other. God used Malachi to warn them that God was coming back for them. In Malachi's prophecy about the Messiah he is identified in Hebrew as the Lord—God himself—who comes to his own temple. *"'Then suddenly the Lord you are seeking will come to his temple; the messenger of the covenant whom you desire will come,' says the LORD Almighty"* (Malachi 3:1).

 ## HOW COULD HE CLAIM THAT?

The Old Testament teaches that the promised Christ was to be God as well as man. Some people have said that Jesus never claimed to be God. But when you read the Gospels, which tell all about Jesus' life on earth, we find that he really did say he was God—and that his listeners understood what he said! Here are four reasons we should believe Jesus was God.

**1** *Jesus claimed equality with God.* Through some of the things Jesus said and did, Jesus was actually claiming equality with God! (See John 10:30 and Luke 7:48–49.) The religious leaders either had to accept Jesus' claim and worship him as God, or reject Jesus' claim. They refused to believe that Jesus was God's Son, and instead tried to kill him!

**2** *Jesus said, "I am" (John 8:58).* When God revealed his personal name to Moses, he identified himself as "I am" (Exodus 3:14). John 8 records a debate Jesus had with some of the Jewish religious leaders. Jesus not only claimed God as his Father but told them, *"Your father Abraham rejoiced at the thought of seeing my day; he saw it and was glad"* (John 8:56).

The leaders got ticked. Why? Because Jesus, not even fifty years old, claimed to know what Abraham knew. Jesus' response was to claim that he existed long before Abraham was born—because Jesus was himself the "I am," the Jehovah, of the Old Testament! This made the church leaders even more upset. How'd they react? They tried to stone him. Why? Because they didn't believe what he said.

**KEY POINT**

Jesus claimed to be God.

117

**disciples:** *twelve men whom Jesus chose to teach and nurture*

**3** *Jesus' **disciples** confirmed his divinity.* How did he do this? He sent his disciples to circulate among the crowds and listen to what they were saying about him. The disciples reported that everyone knew he was someone special. So Jesus asked the disciples who they thought he was. Peter said Jesus was the Messiah, the Son of God.

Jesus replied, "Blessed are you . . . for this was not revealed to you by man, but by my Father in heaven," which makes it very clear that Peter was right. Jesus was far greater than any prophet; he was the Son of God.

**Sanhedrin:** *the Jewish supreme court*

**4** *Jesus told the **Sanhedrin** he was the Son of God (Matthew 26:63–64).* Finally the high priest ordered Jesus to tell them whether he was the Christ. What's especially interesting is that the high priest used the words "the Son of God." Jesus told them yes. He was the Christ, and he was God the Son. Jesus knew who he was. What'd they do? The religious leaders refused to believe him.

**C. S. Lewis:** *Christians believe that Jesus Christ is the Son of God because he said so. The other evidence about him has convinced them that he was neither a lunatic nor a quack.*[2]

### The Ultimate Proof

>>>**CHECK IT OUT:**

Acts 2:14–36; Psalm 16:9–10; Isaiah 53:9, 11

After Jesus was crucified and raised from the dead, the apostle Peter preached a powerful sermon in Jerusalem. You can check out that sermon in Acts, chapter 2. In it Peter talked about Jesus. He reminded people about how he was killed for them. He even quoted Old Testament prophecies that talked about the Messiah's death and resurrection. He said that this proved that the Messiah was God himself. The resurrection of Jesus was the ultimate proof. Jesus was both Lord (God) and Christ (the promised Messiah). With the resurrection of Jesus all doubt of Jesus' identity was put to rest.

**Max Lucado:** *When times get hard, remember Jesus. When people don't listen, remember Jesus. When tears come, remember Jesus. When disappointment is your bed partner, remember Jesus. When fear pitches his tent in your front yard. When death looms, when anger singes, when shame weighs heavily. Remember Jesus.*[3]

## SO WHY DID HE COME?

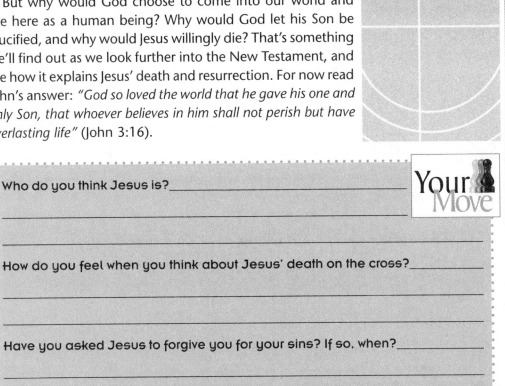

When we look at the evidence, it's clear who Jesus is. Jesus is God the Son. The Old Testament Messiah promised by the prophets was to be God himself. Jesus himself claimed to be the Son of God, and the resurrection of Jesus is proof that he was telling the truth. The New Testament writers identify Jesus as the very God who created the universe (John 1:3). So the testimony of the Bible is consistent and clear.

But why would God choose to come into our world and live here as a human being? Why would God let his Son be crucified, and why would Jesus willingly die? That's something we'll find out as we look further into the New Testament, and see how it explains Jesus' death and resurrection. For now read John's answer: *"God so loved the world that he gave his one and only Son, that whoever believes in him shall not perish but have everlasting life"* (John 3:16).

Who do you think Jesus is?_____

_____

_____

How do you feel when you think about Jesus' death on the cross?_____

_____

_____

Have you asked Jesus to forgive you for your sins? If so, when?_____

_____

_____

 God died for you. How do those words hit you? Think about it. All of the rotten stuff you've done. All of the crazy sinful stunts you've pulled. You built a wall between you and God. And despite all that, God breaks down the wall and looks at you as if you've never done anything wrong. God loves you so much he's willing to forget all that stupid stuff you've done. Pretty awesome, huh?

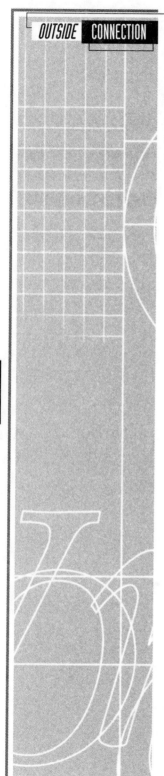

*Toby McKeehan:* Seek out God's love. Discover it. Read the Bible and learn about how much he loves you. I think once you know how much he loves you then you can't help but love him in return. But until you understand his love I don't think you can love him. Also, learn to serve each other despite the fact that our world is so self-serving in what kind of car you buy, what you wear, etc. . . . Our generation has forgotten that we are called to serve others.[4]

## CHAPTER CHECKUP

1. Who is the most important person in the New Testament?
2. Name two of the four Old Testament passages that say the Messiah will be God.
3. Name two of the four passages that report Jesus' claim to be God.
4. What New Testament passage teaches specifically that even though Jesus was God, he became a real human being?
5. What event proved that Jesus really was and is God?

### CRASH COURSE

▶ The prophet Isaiah predicted that a virgin would have a child, and he would be "God with us." (Isaiah 7:14)
▶ The prophet Micah predicted that the Christ would be born in Bethlehem but that his origins would be "from days of eternity." (Micah 5:2)
▶ Jesus claimed to be the "I am"—the God of the Old Testament. (John 8:58)
▶ The resurrection of Jesus proved that he really was the Son of God. (Romans 1:3)
▶ Hebrews says that Jesus is the exact representation of God's being. (Hebrews 1:3)
▶ Jesus said that love motivated God to send his Son to save the world. (John 3:16)

# The Life of Christ: Part 1

## MATTHEW • MARK • LUKE • JOHN

 **LET'S DIVE IN!**

Beginnings are always really cool. The New Testament begins with the ultimate beginning—four books about the life of Jesus on earth—also called the four **Gospels**. The first three Gospels are called **synoptic** Gospels, because each is organized chronologically. In this chapter we'll look briefly at each of the four Gospels and begin to trace the story of Jesus' life on earth.

**Gospels:** *means "good news"*

**synoptic:** *a summary, telling the life of Christ in chronological order*

 **ALL ABOUT JESUS**

Each Gospel tells the same story and sometimes uses the same words to describe the same events. Why are their four accounts of Jesus' life in the New Testament? The reason is that each of the Gospel writers shapes his account of Christ's life for a *different* group of people. Matthew shaped his account for the Jewish reader, emphasizing how Jesus fulfilled the Old Testament's prophecies about the Messiah. Mark shaped his account for the Romans, to show that Jesus was a man of action. Luke shaped his account for the Greeks, to show that

Christ was the ideal human being. John's Gospel emphasizes Christ's deity and was written to stimulate saving faith in Jesus, the Son of God.

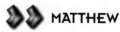 ## MATTHEW

*. . . good news for the Jews*

| | |
|---|---|
| WHO | The disciple Matthew |
| WHAT | wrote this account of Jesus' life |
| WHERE | in the **Holy Land** |
| WHEN | around A.D. 60 |
| WHY | to prove to the Jews that Jesus is the promised Messiah. |

### What's Up with Matthew's Gospel?

Over and over again Matthew quotes or refers to the Old Testament to show how Jesus fulfilled its prophecies concerning the Messiah. Here are some of the best parts of Matthew:

- Jesus' Sermon on the Mount (Matthew 5–7)
- Jesus' parables of the kingdom (Matthew 11–13)
- Jesus' teaching about the future (Matthew 24–25)

 ## MARK

*. . . good news for the Romans*

| | |
|---|---|
| WHO | Mark |
| WHAT | wrote this account of Jesus' life |
| WHERE | in Rome |
| WHEN | around A.D. 55 |
| WHY | to present Jesus to the Romans as a man of authority and action. |

### What's Up with Mark's Gospel?

Mark is the shortest of the Gospels. It focuses on Jesus' actions to show his authority, which appealed to the Romans. Generally, Romans were more interested in powerful action than philosophy. About a third of the book is about Jesus' last week on earth, ending with Christ's death and resurrection.

**GIMME THE BASICS**

**Holy Land:** *modern-day Israel and Palestine*

**GIMME THE BASICS**

122

 **LUKE**

*. . . good news for the Greek*

| | |
|---|---|
| WHO | The physician Luke |
| WHAT | wrote this account of Jesus' life |
| WHERE | in Caesarea |
| WHEN | around A.D. 58 |
| WHY | to present Jesus as an ideal human being who came to save the lost. |

## What's Up with Luke's Gospel?

Luke is the longest of the Gospels, written after he carefully investigated everything by interviewing people who actually saw Jesus. Luke was interested in showing Jesus' concern for women, the poor, and the oppressed. While Luke follows the same chronological plan of Matthew and Mark, Luke includes six miracles and nineteen parables that are not found in the other Gospels.

 **JOHN**

*. . . good news for all!\*

| | |
|---|---|
| WHO | The apostle John |
| WHAT | wrote this theological account of Jesus' acts and teachings |
| WHERE | in Ephesus of Asia Minor |
| WHEN | from A.D. 80 to 90 |
| WHY | to encourage people to have faith in Jesus. |

## What's Up with the Gospel of John?

How does John organize his book? John selects miracles and teachings of Jesus that emphasize key theological themes, such as Everlasting Life (John 5), Truth (John 8), and Belief and Unbelief (John 4; 7; 12). Also, all of the events John reported took place in Judea and Jerusalem.

**GIMME THE BASICS**

**>>>CHECK IT OUT:**

Luke 7:36–50; 10:25–42

**GIMME THE BASICS**

 **AWAY IN A MANGER**

**Bible Summary: Jesus' Birth**
When Jesus was born, the Roman Empire dominated the Mediterranean world. Judea, the province where Jesus was born, was governed by King Herod the Great, who ruled for Rome. Angels began to visit ordinary people, like Joseph and Mary, and their visits signified that the Messiah was about to come.

>>>CHECK IT OUT:

Matthew 1–2; Luke 1–3

WHO'S WHO

WHO'S WHO

WHO'S WHO

>>>CHECK IT OUT:

John 1:1–3

>>>CHECK IT OUT:

Luke 1:5–23; 1:26–38; 2:8–19; Matthew 1:18–25

**MARY:** At the time Jesus was born Mary was an average teenage girl. She was engaged to a carpenter named Joseph; it was common for teenage girls to get married back then. Mary was a descendant of King David. She had total faith in God. You'd think she would freak out when God told her that she was going to be the Messiah's mother, but she didn't.

**JOSEPH:** Joseph the carpenter was engaged to Mary and was also a descendant of King David. When he heard she was pregnant, he planned to break the engagement, but was he visited by an angel who told him that Mary had not been unfaithful.

**HEROD THE GREAT:** The powerful king over the Jews was old and dying when Jesus was born. Yet when he heard that a *"king of the Jews"* had been born, Herod tried to murder the young child.

### What's Up with Jesus' Birth?

**1** *Jesus really did descend from David (Matthew 1:2–17; Luke 3:23–37).* The Old Testament says the Messiah would be a descendant of David. Both Matthew and Luke trace Jesus' ancestry back to David.

**2** *Angelic visitations are associated with Jesus' birth!* While every child's birth is special, they are not normally announced by angels! The Gospels record six angelic visitations linked with the birth and infancy of Jesus! Jesus was totally special.

**3** *Witnesses confirm the identity of Jesus (Matthew 2:1–12; Luke 2:12–38).* Matthew and Luke found witnesses who confirmed who Jesus was. Two of the witnesses, Anna and Simeon, gave their testimony publicly when Mary came to the temple with Jesus to offer a sacrifice for her purification. The other witnesses appeared when Jesus was about two years old.

**R. C. Sproul:** *If you are covered by Jesus, your life is to be defined by a pursuit of the knowledge of God. The work just starts when you're converted. If the first question you should ask is how to finish the sentence, "I believe . . .," there is a second question: "Do I have an intense, vivid, powerful sense of the presence of God?"*[1]

*OUTSIDE* CONNECTION

**4** *Jesus lived and grew up as an ordinary child (Luke 2:40–51).* The Bible records only one event in Jesus' childhood. At age 12 he showed an understanding of God and his ways that amazed adult teachers when he talked to them in the temple.

 **REPENT!**

> **Bible Summary: John the Baptist**
> John the Baptist was Jesus' cousin. His birth and mission had also been announced by an angel. When Jesus was about thirty years old, John the Baptist began to preach in the Jordan River valley. He told Israel to repent, because the promised Messiah was coming.

### What's Up with John the Baptist's Mission?

**1** *John's ministry was predicted by Old Testament prophets (Luke 3:4–6).* The Gospel writers quote Isaiah 40:3–5 to describe John's role in preparing the way for Jesus: *"A voice of one calling in the desert, 'Prepare the way for the Lord, make straight paths for him'"* (Luke 3:4).

>>> CHECK IT OUT:

Luke 3:1–6

**2** *John's message was, "Repent!" (Luke 3:7–14; Matthew 3:4–10; Mark 1:2–6).* John urged people to repent, stop sinning, and seek forgiveness. He baptized those who confessed their sins and promised to change.

>>> CHECK IT OUT:

Luke 3:7–14

**3** *John's promise of the coming Savior (Matthew 3:11–12; Mark 1:7–8; Luke 3:15–18).* When people asked if John was the

>>> CHECK IT OUT:

Luke 3:15–18

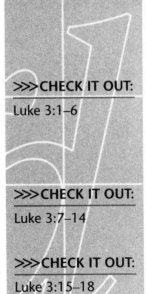

Messiah, he told them Christ was coming. He also told them the Messiah was far greater than he and would baptize with the **Holy Spirit** and fire.

**Holy Spirit:** *God, the third person of the trinity*

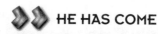 **HE HAS COME**

**Bible Summary: Jesus' Baptism**

One day Jesus came to the riverside and asked John to baptize him. When Jesus was baptized, John heard God speak from heaven identifying Jesus as *"my beloved Son,"* and the Holy Spirit settled on Christ in the form of a dove. John realized Jesus was the Messiah he had been sent to announce, and told some of his own followers that Jesus was the one.

## What's Up with Jesus' Baptism?

**1** *Jesus was identified as the Messiah (John 1:29–34).* God had told John that the Holy Spirit would descend visibly on the Messiah. The voice from heaven and the dove marked Jesus as the promised Messiah.

**2** *John pointed Jesus out as the Messiah (John 1:35).* John made it clear to others that Jesus was the man they were waiting for.

>>>**CHECK IT OUT:**
Matthew 3:13–17; Mark 1:9–11; Luke 3:21–23; John 1:19–34

*OUTSIDE* **CONNECTION**

**messianic:** *having to do with the Messiah*

**J. Dwight Pentecost:** *John had prepared the people for this momentous event. The Father had confirmed the appointment of the Son to the* **messianic** *work. Now the Son was officially presented by the designated forerunner to the nation Israel with God's full approval of his person and work.*[2]

>>>**CHECK IT OUT:**
John 1:29–35

 **I DARE YOU**

**Bible Summary: Jesus' Temptation**

After Jesus was baptized he was led by the Holy Spirit into the wilderness. He went without eating for forty days. When he was physically weak, Satan appeared and tempted Jesus three times. Jesus resisted each temptation. By doing this Jesus proved that he was sinless and had the right to be mankind's Savior. Only a sinless person could die for the sins of others.

## What's Up with Jesus' Temptation?

**1** *First came the temptation to turn stones to bread (Matthew 4:1–4).* We all get tempted to give in to physical needs and desires. When Jesus was hungry, Satan challenged him to turn stones into bread. Jesus refused, quoting Deuteronomy 8:3, which teaches that human beings are not to live by bread alone, *"but by every word that comes from the mouth of God."*

**2** *Second was the temptation to prove God is present (Matthew 4:5–7).* Satan took Jesus to the highest point of the temple and challenged him to jump. Satan quoted Psalm 91:11–12 to show that God would intervene and prevent Jesus from getting hurt. Jesus quoted Deuteronomy 6:16, which says people shouldn't test God. Human beings are to live by faith, not by trying to make God prove he is there for us.

**3** *Third was the temptation to have lots of power (Matthew 4:8–11).* Satan then offered Jesus immediate control of all the kingdoms of the world—if only Jesus would worship him. In the end Jesus would rule over the universe, but this would only happen after he went to the cross. Jesus refused to avoid the suffering that was coming.

>>>**CHECK IT OUT:**
Matthew 4:1–11;
Mark 1:12–13;
Luke 4:1–13

127

**Your Move**

What's the significance of Jesus' temptations?_____

_____

Have you ever been tempted? Write down what happened, and what you did.

_____

_____

Why do you think God allows us to be tempted?_____

_____

It's like this. God loves you *so much* that he allows you to be tempted. Every time you're tempted, and every time you resist temptation, you grow a little stronger. After a while you're like a tower covered with steel. Okay, not exactly like that, but kinda. Hey, Jesus was tempted and he survived. You'll survive too.

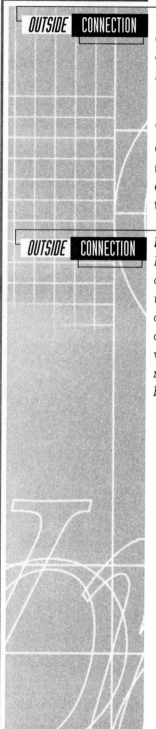

***Tony Campolo:*** *It's hard for us to accept that the Bible actually teaches that Jesus was tempted in all ways even as we are tempted, but it does. The difference between Jesus and us is that He never sinned.*[3]

**4** *Jesus used Scripture in meeting each temptation.* Jesus found an answer to each of Satan's temptations in God's Word. God's Word can help us overcome our temptations too, but we must use the Bible the same way Jesus did. Christ did not just quote a Bible verse, he acted on it. It's important to *know* what the Bible says, but it's equally important to *do* what it says.

***Duffy Robbins:*** *There is nothing abnormal or immoral about hunger. God gave us the desire to eat. We need to eat to stay alive. But, this same healthy desire for food can become an unhealthy desire that will kill us if we don't keep it under control. Just because we feel hunger doesn't mean we can go around scarfing every Twinkie, Dorito and cheeseburger within 100 miles. However, Satan's strategy is to take this normal desire and con us to the point where we are consumed by it.*[4]

## CHAPTER CHECKUP

1. Which Gospel does not tell the story of Jesus' life in chronological order?
2. Why are the two genealogies of Jesus different?
3. What marked Jesus' birth as special and unusual?
4. What was the message of John the Baptist?
5. What happened at Jesus' baptism that showed he was the promised Messiah?
6. Why was it important that Jesus not surrender to Satan's temptations?

### CRASH COURSE

▶ The four Gospel accounts of Jesus' life on earth were shaped to appeal to the major groups of people in the first-century Roman Empire.
▶ Jesus' birth was unique because: it was announced several times by angels, it was a fulfillment of several Old

Testament prophecies, and he was born of a virgin without a human father. (Matthew 1–2; Luke 1–3)

- John the Baptist fulfilled the prophecy of Isaiah that a prophet would announce the Messiah's appearance. God identified Jesus as the Messiah when he was baptized by John. (Isaiah 40:1–3; Matthew 3; Luke 3)
- Jesus proved that he was morally pure and had the right to be the Savior by overcoming Satan's temptations. (Matthew 4; Luke 4)

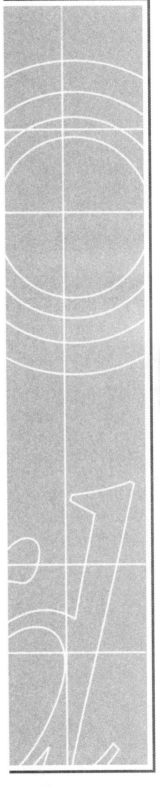

# The Life of Christ: Part 2

## MATTHEW • MARK • LUKE • JOHN

 **LET'S DIVE IN!**

After Jesus beat Satan in the wilderness he began to instruct and preach in Galilee and Judea (check out the map on page 132 to see where these places are). Everyone knew Jesus was different from other teachers. He did **miracles**! He taught with authority. Religious leaders felt threatened by him, so they opposed him.

*miracles: events supernaturally caused by God*

**WHO'S WHO** ?

**THE DISCIPLES:** Several groups appear in stories about Jesus. The most important are Jesus' disciples and the religious leaders who opposed him.

Jesus chose twelve men to travel with him, and he trained them to continue his work after his death. They are Peter, Andrew, Matthew, Thaddaeus, James, Philip, Thomas, Simon, John, Bartholomew, James (the less), and Judas.

*rabbi: a teacher of Old Testament law*

**WHO'S WHO** ?

**THE PHARISEES:** The Pharisees were a small but influential group of men who said they followed every detail of God's law. They believed that both the Scriptures and the **rabbis'**

## Map of Judea and Galilee

*Jesus taught and performed miracles in Galilee and in Judea for about three years. Almost everyone in the small Jewish homeland would have had a chance to hear him and see the miracles he performed.*

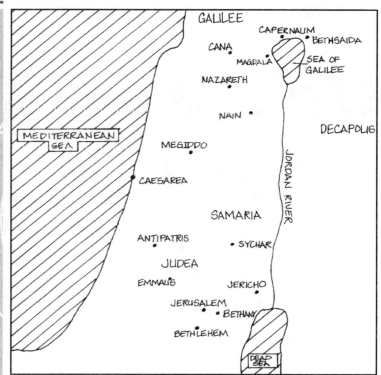

GALILEE
CAPERNAUM
BETHSAIDA
CANA
MAGDALA
SEA OF GALILEE
NAZARETH
NAIN
DECAPOLIS
MEDITERRANEAN SEA
MEGIDDO
JORDAN RIVER
CAESAREA
SAMARIA
ANTIPATRIS
SYCHAR
JUDEA
EMMAUS
JERICHO
JERUSALEM
BETHANY
BETHLEHEM
DEAD SEA

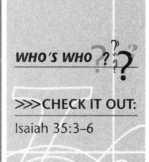

*WHO'S WHO*

>>> **CHECK IT OUT:**

Isaiah 35:3–6

interpretations of Scripture were equally important. Jesus followed the Scripture but ignored the interpretations of the rabbis. These dudes were Jesus' enemies.

**THE SADDUCEES:** The Sadducees were wealthy men who controlled the priesthood. They were rivals of the Pharisees, and recognized only the first five books of the Old Testament as Scripture. But they joined the Pharisees in opposing Jesus. They thought Jesus was a threat to their wealth and power.

## MIRACLES!

### Bible Summary: Miracles

The Gospels contain tons of miracles Jesus did. These miracles proved that Jesus was God's Son. A man who had been blind from birth said, *"If this man were not from God, he could do nothing"* (John 9:33). The healing miracles that Jesus did had never been done before, and the Old Testament identified them as miracles that would be done by the promised Messiah. The miracles of Jesus were evidence of his authority.

## What's Up with the Miracles in the Gospels?

**1** *They produced faith (John 2:1–11).* After Jesus was baptized he returned to Galilee with five of the men who later became his disciples. They stopped off at a wedding in Cana. And when the wine ran out, Jesus turned water into wine. When they saw what Jesus did, they put their faith in him.

**2** *They showed his authority over nature (Matthew 4:18–22; Mark 1:16–20; Luke 5:1–11).* One day Jesus told several fishermen to go out in their boats and cast their nets. Fishing was done at night, so Peter (the one with experience) thought it would be useless. He did it anyway. Guess what! A huge school of fish swam into their nets until their nets began to break. Their boats began to sink. Peter was astonished. He begged Jesus to go away because Peter felt ashamed of his doubt. Jesus didn't go away. He invited Peter to follow him. Jesus' miracles were amazing, but they were intended to draw people to him.

**3** *They showed his power over* **demons** *(Mark 1:21–28; Luke 4:31–37).* The Gospels frequently mention individuals who were possessed by demons. Mark 1:21–28 and Luke 4:31–37 describe a situation where a demon had seized and tormented the victim by simulating a painful disease or handicap.

The demons who came into contact with Jesus recognized him as *"the Holy One of God"* (Luke 5:34). Jesus ordered demons to leave their victims. And the demons were forced to obey him.

**4** *They showed his authority over sickness (Matthew 8:14–17; Mark 1:29–34; Luke 4:42–44).* The Bible records many times when Jesus healed people. Jesus' compassion led him to heal people right and left.

**Charles C. Ryrie:** *Why was she [Simon's mother-in-law] miraculously cured? So she might serve the Lord. Here is the clue to why God permitted her to be sick as well as many others of his children: so that we might learn that life and health and strength are given to us that we might serve. Sickness can be used to teach us what we should do with our health.*[1]

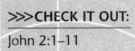

>>>CHECK IT OUT:
John 2:1–11

>>>CHECK IT OUT:
Luke 5:1–11

**KEY POINT**

Jesus' miracles demonstrated his power over nature, demons, sickness, and death.

*demons: fallen angels who follow Satan*

>>>CHECK IT OUT:
Luke 4:31–37

133

*OUTSIDE* CONNECTION

*Max Lucado: It isn't the circumstance that matters; it is God in the circumstance. It isn't the words; it is God speaking them. It wasn't the mud that healed the eyes of the blind man; it was the finger of God in the mud.*[2]

**5** *They showed his authority over death (Mark 5:35–43; Matthew 9:18–26; Luke 8:41–56).* Jesus was called to the home of a religious leader whose daughter was sick. Before he arrived the girl died. People began gathering for the funeral immediately (that's the way they did it back then). When they saw Jesus trying to heal the girl, they made fun of him. Jesus raised the girl to life. The Gospels report two other persons whom Jesus raised from the dead. The most significant was Lazarus, who had been dead for three days when Jesus called him back to life.

**6** *They showed his authority to forgive sin (Matthew 9:1–8; Mark 2:1–12; Luke 5:17–26).* Imagine this. You're in a house, listening to Jesus teach, and suddenly the roof opens and a paralyzed man is lowered through the roof. Does Jesus say, "You're healed"? Nope. He says, "Your sins are forgiven." This really upset the religious leaders. Only God could forgive sins. And there was no way they were going to accept that Jesus was really God.

Jesus knew what they were thinking and challenged them. Was it easier to pronounce sins forgiven, or to tell a paralyzed man to get up and walk? It is of course easier to say, "Your sins are forgiven." If a person tells a paralytic to "get up and walk," everyone will know for sure he possesses the power to heal! So Jesus, to prove he had authority to forgive sins, told the paralyzed man to get up and walk. And he did!

*J. Dwight Pentecost: Christ demonstrated by this miracle of healing that he was God and had the authority to forgive sin. The miracle silenced the Pharisees and the teachers of the law, who had resisted Christ's claim that he was God and could forgive sin.*[3]

 **THE HEART FIRST**

**Bible Summary: Sermon on the Mount**

As Jesus performed miracles he also taught the crowds that gathered to see him. We have two of Jesus' sermons. He spoke about the same subjects in what is called the Sermon on the Mount, recorded by Matthew, and the Sermon on the Plain, recorded by Luke. Jesus must have preached these sermons often as he traveled and spoke to crowds in Galilee and in Judea. Jesus' Sermon on the Mount highlights important truths that Christ emphasized to his first-century listeners.

## What's Up with Jesus' Sermon on the Mount?

**1** *Values (Matthew 5:3–10).* The **Beatitudes** present a set of values by which Jesus expects his followers to live. And these aren't the values most people think are important. Have a look at them and ask yourself, "Can I live by Jesus' values?"

**Beatitudes:** *Jesus' statements that begin "blessed are . . ."*

>>>**CHECK IT OUT:**

Matthew 5:1–7:29;
Luke 6:17–42

**2** *Jesus explained the true intent of Old Testament law (Matthew 5:17–47).* Jesus told his listeners that he had not come to abolish the **law and the prophets** but to *fulfill* them. In the first century a teacher who fulfilled the law explained its deepest and true meaning. Jesus explained what God intended people to understand from the laws God had given to Israel.

    When Jesus did this, it became clear why he called for a lifestyle that was different than what the Pharisees and Sadducees were leading (see Matthew 5:20). The Pharisees focused on the behavior the law described. But Jesus made it clear God is concerned with the heart, not just with behavior.

**law and the prophets:** *a phrase referring to all of the Old Testament*

>>>**CHECK IT OUT:**

Matthew 5:21–48

**Warren Wiersbe:** *Jesus made it clear that he had come to honor the law and help God's people love it, learn it, and live it. He would not accept the artificial righteousness of the religious leaders. . . . It made them proud, not humble; it led to bondage, not liberty.*[4]

 OUTSIDE CONNECTION

**3** *Jesus emphasized a personal relationship with God (Matthew 6:1–8).* Jesus went on to compare those who truly love God with those whose real love is their good reputation. In reality a relationship with God is sometimes a secret thing.

Read the Beatitudes. Which do you think is the most difficult to follow? Why?_____

_____

When have you felt "poor in spirit"? What did you do?_____

_____

After reading the beatitudes, what do you think Jesus' point is?_____

_____

Imagine this. You're there, on the "mount," and you're listening to Jesus give this awesome sermon and you're thinking to yourself, "This is cool, but no one can really live up to Jesus' standards, can they? Well, the answer is yes. You *can* live up to Jesus' standards. You can be humble, meek, poor in spirit, and you can still gain great things through God's power. You don't have to be a wimp . . . you *can* stand strong for God!

**hypocrite:** *an actor putting on a show to impress others*

**alms:** *money given to the needy*

Both the **hypocrite** and the true believer will give **alms** and pray, but the motive and nature of their actions will differ (see Matthew 6:2–4).

**Cris Carter:** *I now have a purpose in life, and it is to use the platform I have been given so that God's name might be glorified. God calls me to be truthful, to be frank and to step out in faith. I am responsible to use my influence and my resources for His glory.*[5]

**Warren Wiersbe:** *A hypocrite deliberately uses religion to cover up his sins and promote his own gains. True righteousness must come first from within. We should test ourselves to see whether we are sincere and honest in our Christian commitment.*[6]

**4** *Jesus taught how to pray (Matthew 6:9–13).* What we call the Lord's Prayer is found in Jesus' Sermon on the Mount. What is significant is not merely the words, but the attitudes that the words express.

**5** *Jesus taught trust in God as a loving Father (Matthew 6:25–34).* While the rabbis spoke of God as the Father, they did not think of an individual's relationship with God as being like that between a child and his own daddy. Jesus taught that God is by nature a heavenly Father, and that he has a father's love for human beings. Anyone who has a personal relationship with God has God for a father, and this means that God is committed to caring for him or her. (Where'd he say all this? Check out Matthew 6:25–34.)

**6** *Jesus taught life building (Matthew 7:24–27).* When Jesus' sermon drew to a close, he summed up the choice each hearer would have to make. As Christ often did, he used a story to emphasize his point. In Matthew 7:24–27 it was the story of two men who were building houses. The one built on a foundation of solid rock; the other built on a foundation of sand.

>>>**CHECK IT OUT:**

Matthew 12:22–29

*Michael Tait: Make every moment count because life is short and one day an answer to the way you live is going to be required of you. There's a reason why you live the way you live, so make it count. Only what is done for Christ will last.*[7]

OUTSIDE CONNECTION

137

 **TROUBLE ON THE WAY**

**Bible Summary: Controversy**

Jesus' miracles and teaching brought the issue facing Israel into clear focus. Would God's people accept Christ as the Messiah and Son of God? At first it seemed they might. But the religious leaders, who could not and did not deny Christ's miracles, began to challenge Christ and to oppose him publicly. Both Matthew and Mark describe a major confrontation they had.

### What's Up with All This Controversy?

Here's a passage that describes the sort of thing Jesus was up against: *"Then they brought him a demon-possessed man who was blind and mute, and Jesus healed him, so that he could both hear and see. And all the people were astonished and said, 'Could this be the Son of David?'*

*"But when the Pharisees heard this, they said, 'It is only by Beelzebub, the prince of demons, that this fellow drives out demons'"* (Matthew 12:22–24).

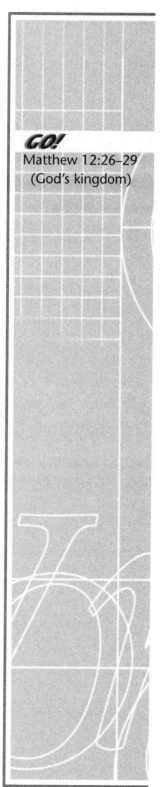

**GO!**
Matthew 12:26–29
(God's kingdom)

Jesus responded to the Pharisees by pointing out the foolishness of their theory. If his powers were demonic, that would mean Satan was fighting against himself. Such a spiritual civil war would lead to the destruction of Satan's kingdom. It was far more reasonable to assume that Jesus drove out demons by the power of God, in which case Jesus was greater than Satan, and God's kingdom really was at hand.

The issue was clear. But the people, who were used to following their religious leaders, were confused. As the controversy over Jesus grew, the story of the wise and foolish builder became more and more significant. Would God's Old Testament people build their future on the solid foundation of Jesus' words, or would they turn from him and build on sand?

## CHAPTER CHECKUP

1. Who were Jesus' disciples, how many of them were there, and why were they special?
2. Who were the Pharisees and Sadducees?
3. Jesus' miracles proved he spoke with divine authority. What kinds of miracles did Jesus perform?
4. What are the Beatitudes about?
5. How did Jesus fulfill the law and the prophets?
6. Why was Jesus' insistence that God is a Father so important?
7. Why weren't the people convinced by Jesus' miracles and teaching that he really was the Christ?

### CRASH COURSE

▶ Jesus performed many miracles in Galilee and Judea. They demonstrated his authority over nature, demons, sickness, death, and his authority to forgive sin.
▶ Jesus taught the people and performed miracles. He tried to help them understand the meaning of a personal relationship with God.
▶ Jesus taught about God's values, the real meaning of God's law, how to pray, and how to trust God as a loving Father.
▶ In all that Jesus did and said, he showed himself to have authority.

# The Life of Christ: Part 3

## MATTHEW • MARK • LUKE • JOHN

**CHAPTER CAPTURE**

- Religious Leaders Attack
- The Kingdom of Heaven
- Private Instruction

 LET'S DIVE IN!

The religious leaders got in Jesus' face all the time. The more miracles he did, the more they got upset. So Jesus changed his teaching style to be a little softer. He used parables to give instruction to the disciples.

 WE'LL GET YOU SOMEHOW

The Pharisees had accused Jesus of using Satan's power to perform miracles. As their opposition to Jesus got more intense, the religious leaders took every opportunity to challenge Jesus.

Chapters 7 through 9 of John's Gospel describe what happened one year during the **Feast of Tabernacles**. John sets the scene for us, describing the tension as everyone waited for Jesus to appear in Jerusalem. Here's how his story begins: *"Now at the Feast the Jews were watching for him and asking, 'Where is that man?' Among the crowds there was widespread whispering about him. Some said 'He is a good man.' Others replied,*

>>>CHECK IT OUT:

John 7–9; Luke 11

***Feast of Tabernacles:*** *the greatest Hebrew feast, which commemorated the Jews' forty years of wandering in Numbers 32:13*

'No, he deceives the people.' But no one would say anything about him for fear of the [religious leaders]" (John 7:11–13).

## What Happened When Jesus Arrived at the Festival?

**1** *The leaders attacked Jesus' authority (John 7:11–15).* Watch what happens when Jesus starts to teach: "Not until half-way through the Feast did Jesus go up to the temple courts and begin to teach. The Jews were amazed and asked, 'How did this man get such learning without having studied?'

"Jesus answered, 'My teaching is not my own. It comes from him who sent me. If anyone chooses to do God's will, he will find out whether my teaching comes from God or whether I speak on my own'" (John 7:14–17).

In order to be recognized as a teacher of religion you had to study for years alongside a Rabbi. People thought Jesus was speaking without authority. Jesus answered that his teaching came directly from God. Anyone who was committed to do God's will would realize he was teaching the true Word of God.

**2** *The leaders attacked Jesus' person (John 7:25–29).* It gets even more interesting in these verses: "At that point some of the people of Jerusalem began to ask, 'Isn't this the man they are trying to kill? Here he is, speaking publicly, and they are not saying a word to him. Have the authorities really concluded that he is the Christ? But we know where this man is from; when the Christ comes, no one will know where he is from.'

"Then Jesus, still teaching in the temple courts, cried out, 'Yes, you know me, and you know where I am from. I am not here on my own, but he who sent me is true. You do not know him, but I know him because I am from him and he sent me.'

"At this they tried to seize him, but no one laid a hand on him, because his time had not yet come" (John 7:25–29).

Everybody knew the religious leaders didn't like Jesus and wanted him dead, so they didn't understand why the leaders hadn't arrested him yet.

For some reason people thought the Messiah would come out of nowhere. They believed no one would "know where he is from." But if they had done their homework, they would have known from Micah 5:2 that the Messiah was to come "out of" Bethlehem.

Jesus focused on the most important point. He had come directly from God! The Israelites were not ready to accept this.

*Max Lucado: There is a direct correlation between the accuracy of our memory and the effectiveness of our mission. If we are not teaching people how to be saved, it is perhaps because we have forgotten the tragedy of being lost! If we are not teaching the message of forgiveness, it may be because we don't remember what it was like to be guilty. And, if we're not preaching the cross, it could be that we've subconsciously decided that—God forbid—somehow we don't need it.*[1]

**3** *The leaders attempted to trap Jesus (John 8:3–11).* Now religious leaders really get nasty: *"The teachers of the law and the Pharisees brought in a woman caught in adultery. They made her stand before the group and said to Jesus, 'Teacher, this woman was caught in the act of adultery. In the law Moses commanded us to stone such women. Now what do you say?' They were using this question as a trap, in order to have a basis for accusing him"* (John 8:3–6).

Jesus got bold. "Let the one who is without sin throw the first stone," he said, and one by one the woman's accusers left. Jesus said to her, *"Then neither do I condemn you. Go now and leave your life of sin"* (John 8:11). Jesus brought a forgiveness to the world so transforming that those who accepted him would be able to leave their life of sin.

**4** *The leaders rejected evidence of Jesus' authority (John 9:1–41).* Jesus gave sight to a man who was born blind. When the miracle is brought to the attention of the Pharisees, at first they try to deny the miracle. When several witnesses come forward to testify that the man really was born blind, the Pharisees try to prove that Jesus doesn't really have any power.

When they hear *how* Jesus healed the man (he made mud and put it on the man's eyes on the Sabbath), they got upset. According to them Jesus had worked on the Sabbath, and no one who works on the Sabbath is from God. But if Jesus wasn't from God, how could he heal the blind man? The Pharisees were caught! The Pharisees openly rejected the evidence before them, and insulted the man Jesus had healed: *"Then they hurled insults at him and said, 'You are this fellow's disciple! We* are disciples of Moses! We know that God spoke to Moses, but as for this fellow, we don't even know where he comes from.'

"The man answered, 'Now that is remarkable! You don't know where he comes from, yet he opened my eyes. We know that God does not listen to sinners. He listens to the godly man who does his will. Nobody has ever heard of opening the eyes of a man born blind. If this man were not from God, he could do nothing.'

"To this they replied, 'You were steeped in sin at birth; how dare you lecture us!' And they threw him out" (John 9:28–34).

After this incident the religious leaders were really ready to kill Jesus. It became increasingly clear that the religious leaders had succeeded in preventing the nation from acclaiming Jesus as Messiah and Lord.

## ⟫⟫ YOU WON'T UNDERSTAND

>>>CHECK IT OUT:
Matthew 13; Mark 4

When Jesus' disciples asked why he spoke to the crowds in parables, Jesus gave a surprising answer: *"The knowledge of the secrets of the kingdom of heaven has been given to you, but not to them. . . . This is why I speak to them in parables: 'Though seeing, they do not see: though hearing they do not hear or understand.'"* (Matthew 13:11, 13).

*J. Dwight Pentecost: The leaders had already indicated their purpose to reject the person of Christ and to discount his miracles because they believed his miracles were done by Satan's power. On the other hand, some had believed his word and accepted his person, and these needed instruction. Christ did not attempt to separate the unbelievers from the believers and then instruct only the believers. He constructed his teaching in such a way that those who had believed would understand, and those who had rejected, even though they heard, would not understand.*[2]

### What's Up with Jesus' Parables?

*GO!*
Matthew 13:11
(kingdom of heaven)

1 *They tell us about the kingdom of heaven.* Jesus said that his parables were about the secrets of the kingdom of heaven. The phrase *"kingdom of heaven"* means the rule of heaven, and defines how God exercises his authority in our world. What

142

143

Jesus revealed in his parables were secrets—stuff that had never
been revealed before.

**Kevin Johnson:** *Here's why heaven is so great. It ain't home to
princely hunks or fairy princesses. The magic kingdom is
real. God's people live happily ever after. It's a paradisal
place. It's re-made people. It's living in the light of the party,
God himself.*[3]

OUTSIDE CONNECTION

2 *The parables deal with God's kingdom on earth (Matthew
13:1–50).* The Old Testament prophets were expecting a
visible kingdom of God on earth. That kingdom will exist one
day, but because Israel rejected her Messiah, God introduced
an unexpected form of his kingdom. When Jesus came to earth,
he established God's kingdom (the church) in that he redeemed
people from sin and taught them how to live according to
God's values. Most Christians believe God's kingdom has not
fully materialized, but when Jesus returns to earth, God's kingdom will be the only kingdom.

**FOR YOU ALONE**

Eventually Jesus asked his disciples the question of all questions. Here's the passage: *"When Jesus came to the region of Caesarea Philippi, he asked his disciples, 'Who do people say the Son of Man is?'*

*"They replied, 'Some say John the Baptist, others say Elijah; and still others, Jeremiah or one of the prophets.'*

*"'But what about you,' he asked, 'Who do you say that I am?'*

*"Simon Peter answered, 'You are the Christ, the Son of the living God'"* (Matthew 16:13–16).

This was a turning point in Jesus' ministry. Although the people recognized Jesus as a prophet, they failed to accept him as the Messiah. However, as Peter's answer indicated in Matthew 16:16, the disciples did recognize Jesus as both the Christ and the Son of God. From this point on Jesus focused on instructing his disciples.

There's a ton of stuff in each Gospel about the private teaching Jesus gave to those who believed in him. Now we'll look at some of these teachings.

### What's Up with Jesus' Instruction of His Disciples?

1 *It's for those who believe in Jesus.* In our time we define a disciple or follower of Jesus by his or her trust in Jesus as *"the Christ, the Son of the living God."* Jesus' private instruction in the Gospels is addressed to people who did the same.

**Warren Wiersbe:** *Jesus Christ is the foundation rock on which the church is built. The Old Testament prophets said so (Psalm 118:22; Isaiah 28:16). Jesus himself said this (Matthew 21:42), and so did Peter and the other apostles (Acts 4:10–12). Paul also stated that the foundation for the church is Jesus Christ (1 Corinthians 3:11).*[4]

2 *Jesus began to speak of his coming crucifixion.* Until there was clear evidence that the nation would reject Jesus as the Messiah, Christ had not mentioned the cross. When it was clear the people would not accept him, Jesus began to tell his followers of his coming **crucifixion** and **resurrection**: *"From*

>>>**CHECK IT OUT:**

Matthew 16; Luke 15; John 13–16

**crucifixion:** *form of punishment where the convicted person was tied or nailed to a cross*

**resurrection:** *being brought from death to everlasting life*

144

that time on Jesus began to explain to his disciples that he must go to Jerusalem and suffer many things at the hands of the elders, chief priests and teachers of the law, and that he must be killed and on the third day be raised to life" (Matthew 16:21).

**3** Jesus taught his disciples what it would mean to follow him. In Scripture the cross represents Jesus' crucifixion, but it also represents God's will for Jesus. "Jesus said to his disciples, 'If anyone would come after me, he must deny himself and take up his cross and follow me. For whoever wants to save his life will lose it, but whoever loses his life for me will find it. What good will it be for a man if he gains the whole world, yet forfeits his soul? Or what can a man give in exchange for his soul?'" (Matthew 16:24–26) Jesus expects his disciples to do God's will, even when that means denying something they would rather do. The life that the disciple loses is his or her old life, lived apart from God. The life that the disciple gains is the new life that Jesus gives to his followers—a life of love, joy, and fulfillment—that lasts eternally.

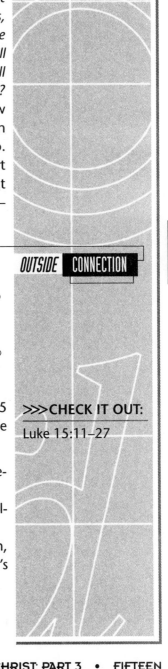

*Trent Dilfer: My focus has gradually changed from pleasing myself to pleasing God. God has also changed the way I view people. I used to look at people for how they could help me but now my perspective is how I can help them and love them. Since trusting Christ, my view of football has also changed. I now see playing in the NFL as a chance for me to influence people for Him.*[5]

**OUTSIDE CONNECTION**

**4** Jesus taught about God's attitude toward sinners. Luke 15 records three stories Jesus told to illustrate God's attitude toward sinners:

**>>>CHECK IT OUT:**
Luke 15:11–27

- God is like a shepherd who seeks a lost sheep and rejoices when it is found.
- God is like a woman who loses a valuable coin and celebrates when it is found.
- God is like a father who rejoices at the return of a son, even though the son has sinned and abused his father's love.

**OUTSIDE CONNECTION** *J. Dwight Pentecost:* Jesus taught that God loves sinners and searches for them; all heaven rejoices with God at the return of the lost. This teaching was in stark contrast to the attitude of the Pharisees, who in self-righteousness hated sinners and did not rejoice when tax collectors and sinners came to Christ and were restored to fellowship with God.[6]

**5** *Jesus taught about servanthood.* Shortly after Jesus had said he was going to die and live again, James and John, two of the disciples, had their mother ask Christ for the two most important posts in his future kingdom. When the other disciples heard this, they were upset and angry. Jesus used the opportunity to teach them about greatness. Here's what he said: *"You know that the rulers of the Gentiles lord it over them, and their high officials exercise authority over them. Not so with you. Instead, whoever wants to become great among you must be your servant, and whoever wants to be first must be your slave—just as the Son of Man did not come to be served, but to serve, and to give his life as a ransom for many"* (Matthew 20:25–28).

**OUTSIDE CONNECTION** *John Wesley:* Do all the good you can, by all the means you can, in all the ways you can, in all the places you can, at all the times you can, to all the people you can and as long as you can.[7]

**6** *Jesus taught his disciples to love each other.* One of the most intimate and private of Christ's times with his disciples is described in John 13–16, when the disciples shared a meal with Jesus the evening before he was crucified. Jesus began that evening's teaching by giving his disciples what he called a *"new commandment."* Here it is: *"A new command I give you: Love one another. As I have loved you, so you must love one another. By this all men will know that you are my disciples, if you love one another"* (John 13:34–35).

**7** *Jesus taught he's the only way to God (John 14:6).* It's popular today to believe "all religions lead to God," but Jesus made it clear that he's the only way to heaven. Before you go saying that Jesus is totally exclusive, think for a minute. Because Jesus is the way, the truth, and the life, any person who wants to can come to the Father through him! This makes Jesus' teaching inclusive. The disciples needed to grasp this truth firmly, not just for themselves, but to motivate them to share Christ with others.

**Max Lucado:** *When everyone else rejects you, Christ accepts you. When everyone else leaves you, Christ finds you. When no one else wants you, Christ claims you. When no one else will give you the time of day, Jesus will give you the words of eternity.*[8]

**Thomas à Kempis:** *"Follow thou me [Christ]. I am the way and the truth and the life. Without the way there is no going; without the truth there is no knowing; without the life there is no living. I am the way which thou must follow; the truth which thou must believe; the life for which thou must hope. I am the inviolable way; the infallible truth; the never-ending life. I am the straightest way; the sovereign truth; life true, life blessed, life uncreated."*[9]

**8** *Jesus taught that only love can motivate true obedience.* The rabbis of Christ's day taught that a person gained God's favor and earned a place in heaven by obeying his law. Jesus offered eternal life to sinners as a free gift. Obedience is a result of salvation, not a means to it.

**9** *Jesus taught that they must stay close to him.* One of the New Testament letters describes the fruit that God produces in the believer's life as *"love, joy, peace, patience, kindness, goodness, faithfulness, gentleness and self-control"* (Galatians 5:22–23). But Jesus warned his followers that these gifts would be theirs only if they stayed close to him.

**10** *Jesus told his disciples to **testify** about him.* He said, *"You also must testify, for you have been with me from the beginning"* (John 15:27).

**testify:** *to bear witness to what they saw and heard*

The private instruction Jesus gave his disciples is recorded in Scripture to guide us today. Christians build their lives on the truth that Jesus is the Christ, the Son of the Living God. Following Jesus means submitting to God's will, having compassion for people who don't know God, and seeking to serve others.

If we're committed to Jesus we'll love each other as he commanded, be moved by love to obey God, maintain our intimate relationship with Jesus, which is required for fruitfulness, and tell others about the love and grace of God expressed in Jesus Christ.

## CHApTeR cHeCkUp

1. Who said that Satan was behind the miracles Jesus performed?
2. Why was the charge that Jesus had not "studied" important?
3. Why did Jesus begin to use parables in speaking to the crowds?
4. What was the subject of the parables of Jesus?
5. What belief marks a person as a true disciple of Jesus?
6. What is the key to greatness for a disciple of Jesus?
7. What was Jesus' *new commandment* to his disciples?

### CRASH COURSE

▶ The Pharisees and other religious leaders openly attacked Jesus.
▶ When it became clear that the nation would not accept Jesus as the Messiah and Son of God, Jesus began to teach in parables.
▶ Jesus' parables were about a form of God's rule that wasn't known about in the Old Testament.
▶ Jesus gave private instruction to the disciples who believed he was the Christ. He taught them to choose God's will, to love each other, and to serve others.
▶ Jesus taught that love for him would produce obedience, and that disciples who obey him will live fruitful, productive lives.

# The Life of Christ: Part 4

## MATTHEW • MARK • LUKE • JOHN

CHAPTER CAPTURE
- Triumphal Entry
- Gethsemane
- The Cross
- Victory over Death

149

 **LET'S DIVE IN!**

During the last week of his life, Jesus went to Jerusalem for the Passover festival. When he entered the city, many people began calling him the Messiah. But within a few days he was arrested, tried before religious and Roman courts, condemned to death, and executed. The hopes of his followers were trashed. But within three days Jesus rose from the grave!

**A KING ON A DONKEY?**

### Bible Summary: Final Week

The week began when Jesus entered Jerusalem riding on a donkey. People called to him from the crowd and referred to him as the Son of David. The leaders got upset and began to react. They tried to trap him. Jesus condemned them and began instructing his disciples about what to expect in the future.

>>>**CHECK IT OUT:**

Matthew 21–25; Mark 11–13; Luke 19–21; John 12

## What's Up with Jesus' Last Week on Earth?

**1** *The homecoming (Matthew 21:1–17; Mark 11:1–11; Luke 19:28–44).* About four hundred years earlier the prophet Zechariah announced that Israel's king would enter Jerusalem riding a donkey (see Zechariah 9:9). Matthew describes the scene in Jerusalem on what we call Palm Sunday. It's an exciting account, and you can read it in Matthew 21:7–11.

**2** *Jesus drove merchants out of the temple (Matthew 21:12–17; Mark 11:12–17).* Jewish pilgrims who came to worship God at the temple could only use "temple money" to pay a tax that Old Testament law required. Guys called "money changers" set up tables in the temple where the correct coins could be purchased at an outrageous price. Other salesmen sold sacrificial animals that had been certified by the priests as being without blemish, and they charged way too much for these too! The chief priests received a percentage of the income. So, Jesus enters the city and heads for the temple. Guess what happens . . . *"Jesus entered the temple area and drove out all who were buying and selling there. He overturned the tables of the money changers and the benches of those selling doves. 'It is written,' he said to them, "My house shall be called a house of prayer," but you have made it a "den of robbers"'"* (Matthew 21:12–13).

**>>>CHECK IT OUT:**

Mark 11:27–12:12

**3** *Jesus exposed the motives of the religious leaders (Matthew 21:22–27; 33–45; Mark 11:27–12:12).* When he drove the merchants from the temple, Jesus directly challenged the chief priests. A group of priests demanded that Jesus tell them who gave him the authority to do what he had done. Jesus refused, and told a story about tenants who were left to tend their owner's vineyard. When the owner sent servants to collect his share, the tenants beat some and killed others. Finally the owner sent his son. Jesus concluded, *"But the tenants said to one another, 'This is the heir. Come, let's kill him and the inheritance will be ours.' So they took him and killed him and threw him out of the vineyard. What then will the owner of the vineyard do? He will come and kill those tenants and give the vineyard to others"* (Mark 12:7–9).

The religious leaders realized that Jesus was speaking about them. They were the tenants, left in charge of God's vineyards.

The servants were the prophets God had sent their forefathers; Jesus was the son. They were really upset! They wanted desperately to arrest Jesus, but they feared the reaction of the crowd.

At about midnight they found Jesus in a garden. They arrested him, and by dawn they had sentenced him to death.

**4** *Jesus exposed the hypocrisy of the religious leaders (Matthew 22:41–46; Mark 12:35–37; Luke 20:41–44).* Jesus exposed the hypocrisy of the leaders when he asked the Pharisees a question about Old Testament teaching on the Christ. Check out their argument in Matthew 22:42–45. Their argument proved that the Pharisees knew who Jesus really was, and hated him anyway. The religious leaders who claimed the right to interpret God's Word were rebellious tenants. They'd grab hold of any excuse to kill God's Son before even considering obedience to him. Jesus openly condemned the *"teachers of the law and Pharisees"* as hypocrites.

**5** *Jesus taught his disciples about the future (Matthew 24–25; Mark 13; Luke 21:5–36).* Jesus knew the religious leaders were determined to kill him. The last week of his life he took the time to tell his disciples what would happen after his death and resurrection. Included in Jesus' teaching were three key points:

>>>**CHECK IT OUT:**

Matthew 23:1–37

- First, Jesus would return to earth in power and glory. (Matthew 24:30–31)
- Second, no one would be able to predict when he would return. (Matthew 24:36)
- Third, until he does come, Jesus' followers are to watch for him and serve him faithfully. (Matthew 24:42–44)

## >> TOMORROW DOESN'T LOOK GOOD

Each of the Gospels gives a detailed account of Jesus' last day on earth. But not every Gospel describes each detail the same way. As evening approached several disciples made arrangements to share a meal with Jesus (the Last Supper), even as Judas arranged with the high priest to betray Jesus for thirty pieces of silver. John's Gospel describes the meal and conversation there; it also records a prayer that Jesus offered for all believers in John 17.

## What's Up with Jesus' Last Day?

**1** Jesus' prayer in Gethsemane (Matthew 26:36–46; Mark 14:32–42; Luke 22:39–42). Gethsemane was an olive grove that grew on a hill across the Kedron Valley from Jerusalem. The Bible reads, *"They went to a place called Gethsemane, and Jesus said to his disciples, 'Sit here while I pray.' He took Peter, James and John along with him, and he began to be deeply distressed and troubled. 'My soul is overwhelmed with sorrow to the point of death,' he said to them. 'Stay here and keep watch.'*

*"Going a little further, he fell to the ground and prayed that if possible the hour might pass from him. '**Abba**, Father,' he said, 'everything is possible for you. Take this cup from me. Yet not what I will, but what you will'"* (Mark 14:32–37).

**Abba:** *"Daddy" in Aramaic, the language Jesus spoke*

OUTSIDE CONNECTION

**J. Dwight Pentecost:** *Christ prayed that God might accept his death as full payment of the sin of sinners and bring him out of death and restore him to life again. Thus the prayer should be understood as a prayer for restoration to physical life by resurrection, and a restoration to full fellowship with his Father out of the spiritual death into which he would enter. The evidence that God answered Jesus' prayer is seen, first, in the fact that Christ was raised from the dead on the third day and given a glorified body. Second, it is seen in the fact that on the fortieth day he ascended to the Father to be seated at his right hand in glory.*[1]

**2** Jesus' arrest (Matthew 26:47–56; Mark 14:43–52; Luke 22:47–53; John 18:2–12). Judas led a mob sent by the high priest to seize Jesus. When one of the disciples tried to resist, Jesus said something that showed he remained in full control of the situation. It was majorly dramatic. Look at what Jesus said: *"Do you think I cannot call on my Father, and he will at once put at my disposal more than twelve **legions** of angels? But how then would the Scriptures be fulfilled that say it must happen this way?"* (Matthew 26:53–54)

**legions:** *military units usually comprising 4,000 to 6,000 soldiers.*

**3** Jesus was tried at night by three religious **tribunals** (Matthew 27:57–68; Mark 14:53–65; Luke 2:54–71; John 18:12–27). The critical point was reached near dawn when the high priest asked Jesus a question to which he knew Jesus' answer.

**tribunal:** *a court of justice.*

152

Here's their conversation: *"The high priest said to him, 'I charge you under oath by the living God: Tell us if you are the Christ, the Son of God.'*

*"'Yes, it is as you say,' Jesus replied. 'But I say to all of you: In the future you will see the Son of Man sitting at the right hand of the Mighty One and coming on the clouds of heaven.'*

*"Then the high priest tore his clothes and said, 'He has spoken* **blasphemy**! *Why do we need any more witnesses? Look, now you have heard the blasphemy. What do you think?'*

*"'He is worthy of death,' they answered"* (Matthew 26:63–66).

The problem was that no first-century Jewish court had the authority to impose a death sentence. That right belonged only to the Roman courts. While the charge of blasphemy might call for the death penalty in Judaism, it wasn't a capital crime to the Romans. In other words, they had to start making stuff up.

**4** *Jesus was accused of political crimes (Matthew 27:11–26; Mark 15:2–19; John 18:28–19:16).* John's Gospel describes in detail Jesus' trial before the Roman governor Pilate. The charge was political: in presenting himself as the Christ, Jesus was claiming to be the *King of the Jews.*

Pilate saw through their scheme, but finally gave in and ordered Christ to be crucified.

### 🔖🔖 NAILED TO A CROSS

Check out what *The Nelson Illustrated Bible Handbook* says about the crucifixion:

> Crucifixion was practiced as a method of torture and execution by the Persians before it was adopted by the Romans. Roman law allowed only slaves and criminals to be crucified. Roman citizens were not crucified. The victim's arms are stretched out above him, fastened to a cross bar fixed near the top of a stake slightly taller than a man. Suspended this way, blood is forced to the lower body. The pulse rate increases, and after days of agony the victim dies from lack of blood circulating to the brain and heart. The Romans often placed a **titulus** above the sufferer naming

**blasphemy:** *to speak of God in an irreverent way*

>>>**CHECK IT OUT:**

John 18:28–19:16

**153**

**titulus:** *Latin for "title," used here as a sign*

THE LIFE OF CHRIST: PART 4 • SIXTEEN

**scourging:** *to punish by whip or lash*

his crime. **Scourging** before crucifixion hastened death, as did breaking a victim's legs.

## What's the Significance of Jesus' Death on the Cross?

**1** *He was pierced for our transgressions.* Isaiah 53:4–6 gives an incredible account of what would happen to the Messiah seven hundred years before he was born. Take a moment, crack open your Bible, and read it.

*OUTSIDE* CONNECTION

**Josh McDowell:** *Christ's loneliest time on earth came at the cross. As he thought about the spiritual and physical pain that lay ahead, he shook in prayer. Remember in the garden of Gethsemane? He was heading toward the cross, and he cried out, "If it be possible, let this cup be taken from me. Let the crucifixion be taken from me. However, your will be done." See, more than not going through the suffering and pain was his desire to follow God's will.*[2]

## KEY POINT

Christ died for the forgiveness of your sins.

**2** *Christ died for us (Romans 5:8–9).* Writing to the Romans the apostle Paul explained the reason for Jesus' death in these words: *"God demonstrates his own love for us in this: While we were still sinners, Christ died for us. Since we have now been* **justified** *by his blood, how much more shall we be saved from wrath through him?" (Romans 5:8–9)*

**justified:** *declared not guilty*

*OUTSIDE* CONNECTION

**Max Lucado:** *The cross did what sacrificed lambs could not do. It erased our sins not for a year, but for eternity. The cross did what man cannot do. It granted us the right to talk with, love, and even live with God.*[3]

**3** *God made him . . . sin for us (2 Corinthians 5:21).* The apostle Paul explained further when writing a second letter to the Corinthians. At the cross an amazing transaction took place. Jesus took our sins on himself; his death was the penalty that we deserved. God then credited the righteousness of Jesus to us! With sin paid for, there was no longer a barrier between human beings and God. With Jesus' own righteousness credited to our account, we are welcome to enter God's presence.

What does Jesus' death mean to you?_____

What's the most difficult aspect of this story to communicate to others?_____

_____

If you had been present at the crucifixion, what would your reaction have been?

_____

_____

**GET REAL.** Jesus died for you. That's a fact. But here's the problem. A lot of us have taken that fact, held it inside, felt good about our eternal destination, and left it there. All too often Jesus' death for us doesn't make a real difference in the way we live. We accept what he did, then we go on sinning. Or, we never tell our friends about what Jesus did for them. Want your life to reflect what Jesus did? Live for him, and tell everyone you know!

**F. F. Bruce:** *If there is one sentence more than another which sums up the message of [John], it is this. The love of God is limitless; it embraces all mankind. No sacrifice was too great to bring its unmeasured intensity home to men and women; the best that God had to give, he gave—his only son, his well-beloved. The gospel of salvation and life has its source in the love of God. The essence of the saving message is made unmistakably plain.*[4]

**OUTSIDE CONNECTION**

 ## UP FROM THE GRAVE HE ROSE

Jesus was buried late Friday afternoon in the garden tomb of Joseph of Arimathea, and his body remained there all of Saturday. Early Sunday Jesus rose from the dead.

Looking back on the resurrection of Jesus from the dead, the apostle Paul sees it as God's powerful and ultimate declaration that he truly was and is the <u>Son of God</u>.

And what significance does the resurrection of Jesus have for you and me? The resurrection is both proof and promise that death is not the end for anyone.

>>>**CHECK IT OUT:**
Matthew 28; Mark 16; Luke 24; John 20–21

 *GO!*
Romans 1:3
(Son of God)

## CHApTeR cHeCkUp

1. What event began Jesus' last week on earth?
2. According to Matthew 23 what did Jesus say that the Pharisees and teachers of the law were?
3. What was Jesus charged with in the Jewish courts? What was Jesus charged with in Pilate's court?
4. What happened to Jesus' body after he was crucified?
5. How does the Bible explain the significance of Jesus' death?
6. What does the fact of Jesus' resurrection mean for us today?

### CRASH COURSE

▶ When Jesus entered Jerusalem on Palm Sunday, he was acclaimed as the Messiah. Jesus exposed the hypocrisy of the leaders and openly condemned them.

▶ The religious leaders determined to kill Jesus to maintain their own power and position. Jesus told his disciples that he would be crucified, but that afterward he would come to earth again to rule.

▶ Jesus was captured at night, tried in court, and condemned by the Jewish Sanhedrin for claiming to be the Son of God. Jesus was crucified by the Romans as *King of the Jews*.

▶ Jesus died and was buried, but on the third day he rose from the grave and was seen by many people.

# Church on Fire!

## ACTS

 **LET'S DIVE IN!**

What started Christianity? When did it begin? Simple. Christianity began when Jesus rose from the dead. The disciples began to proclaim Jesus Christ as resurrected Lord. Loads of people in Jerusalem believed their message, and a community of believers was formed. Acts traces the early growth of Christianity from its Jewish roots to a faith that spread throughout the Roman Empire (see map on page 158).

 **ACTS**

### . . . the spread of the gospel

**GIMME THE BASICS**

| | |
|---|---|
| WHO | Luke, a physician and friend of Paul, |
| WHAT | wrote this book of history about the early church |
| WHERE | in Rome |
| WHEN | about A.D. 63 |
| WHY | to record the spread of the gospel throughout the Roman world between A.D. 33 and 63. |

The first chapter of Acts presents three keys to understanding Christianity in the first century—and today!

## Key #1

*The promise of the Holy Spirit (Acts 1:8).* The first key to understanding Acts and the New Testament is to know that when Jesus returned to heaven, he sent the **Holy Spirit** to give us power for Christian living and Christian witness. The Book of Acts is the story of the works of the Holy Spirit in and through believers in Jesus.

## Key #2

*The work of Jesus (Acts 1:9–11).* Forty days after the resurrection Jesus was taken up into heaven. He will remain there until he comes back again.

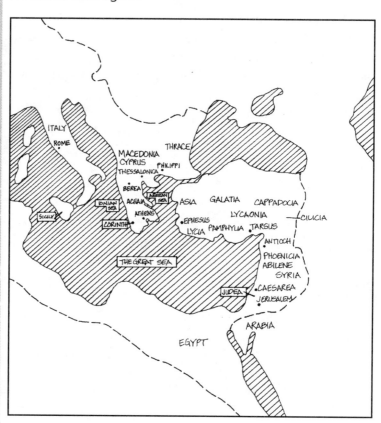

---

>>>**CHECK IT OUT:**

Acts 1

**Holy Spirit:** *God, the third person of the trinity*

**Map of the Roman Empire**

*Within thirty years of Jesus' resurrection the gospel had spread throughout the Roman empire. There were Christian groups in most of its major cities. The rapid spread was made possible because Rome maintained good roads and had wiped out the pirates who had made sea travel unsafe. Everyone spoke the same language, Greek, which made it possible to share the gospel in different countries. And the New Testament Epistles, written in Greek, could be read by everyone.*

158

## Key #3

*Christianity is spread by Jesus'* **witnesses** *(Acts 1:8)*. In Acts Jesus' disciples become his **apostles**; they testify to the reality of Jesus' resurrection. Although Acts emphasizes the ministry of two apostles, the privilege of being Jesus' witness is given to every believer.

 **WEIRD TONGUES**

### Bible Summary: The Church Grows

When the Holy Spirit came he gave the apostles power. Acts 2–7 records two powerful sermons of Peter, and it tells how the crowd responded. The leaders who killed Jesus threatened the apostles and even the unity of the Christian community. But guess what! The church in Jerusalem multiplied rapidly.

**PETER:** Peter was the head disciple and apostle. He preached the first sermon.

**STEPHEN:** Stephen was a **deacon** and Christian witness. He was stoned to death in Jerusalem for the things he said about Jesus, which were true.

### What's Up with Acts 2–7?

1 *The Holy Spirit came upon Jesus' followers (Acts 2:1–21).* Fifty days after the resurrection, the Holy Spirit came upon Jesus' followers, who had gathered for prayer. The appearance of the Holy Spirit for the first time came with a very visible sign—the sound of rushing wind, tongues of fire above the believers' heads, and the miraculous translation of what the believers said, so that each foreign visitor to Jerusalem *"heard them speaking in his own language"* (Acts 2:6).

Peter explained this weirdness by referring to an Old Testament prophecy in which God promised, *"I will pour out my Spirit on all people"* (Joel 2:28).

2 *The first two sermons (Acts 2:22–3:26).* Acts records two sermons that Peter preached to crowds gathered in Jerusalem (Acts 2:22–39; 3:12–26).

---

**witness:** *those who testify to what they have experienced*

**apostles:** *the twelve disciples plus Paul and other New Testmaent missionaries; they were sent out to spread the gospel*

### >>>CHECK IT OUT:

Acts 2–7

*WHO'S WHO* ??

*WHO'S WHO* ??

**deacon:** *a church officer; a servant*

159

**3** *People get psyched about Jesus (Acts 2:41; 6:7).* After Peter's first sermon, about three thousand people responded to the gospel and trusted Jesus as Savior.

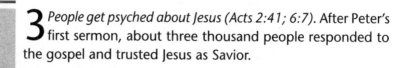

**F. F. Bruce:** *The disciples' public witness met with widespread acceptance in Jerusalem, and their following increased rapidly. They also won over a number of Pharisees, and even a considerable body of priests. The one group that showed direct hostility to the new community was the Sadducean party [the Sadducees], especially the chief priests and temple authorities.*[1]

**4** *The first church—lots of love! (Acts 2:42–47; 4:32–35).* These two passages are often quoted to illustrate an "ideal" church family. What should you look for when seeking a good church? Look for people devoted to God's Word, caring fellowship, and prayer.

*OUTSIDE* **CONNECTION**

**Paul Little:** *If we are serious about representing Christ, we need to think through how we can be the best friends possible to non-Christians. It takes effort for all of us to resist socializing exclusively with our Christian friends.*[2]

**5** *Good people don't always get along (Acts 4–7).* The Jerusalem church didn't always get along. They faced a lot of challenges.

 **GO TELL IT ON THE MOUNTAIN**

**Bible Summary: Expansion**

After Stephen was killed the Christians in Jerusalem were persecuted, and most were forced to leave the city. But as the new believers traveled, they shared the gospel with others. Soon the message spread to Judea and even to Samaria (see map on page 132), where Samaritans also accepted Christ as Savior. The great surprise for the early Jewish Christians took place when a retired Roman centurion named Cornelius was converted, and it dawned on all that the message of salvation was for all people, not just for God's covenant people, the Jews.

>>>**CHECK IT OUT:**

Acts 8–12

**PHILIP:** One of the first deacons, who launched a revival in Samaria.

WHO'S WHO ?

**SAUL:** A young Pharisee who after his conversion becomes famous (ever heard of the apostle Paul?).

WHO'S WHO ?

**BARNABAS:** An early convert who became a leader in the first Gentile church. He was also Paul's companion on his first missionary journey.

WHO'S WHO ?

### What's Up with Acts 8–12?

**1** *Philip preaches . . . people get saved! (Acts 8:1–25).* The Samaritans were foreigners who were forced to live in Israel back in Old Testament times. While they worshiped Israel's God, the Jews didn't like them and had nothing to do with them. But Philip's preaching and the miracles he performed in Jesus' name convinced many of the Samaritans to trust Christ.

>>> CHECK IT OUT:

Acts 8:1–25

*Tim Baker:* The real truth is that God is after our urgency. He wants us to be passionate about our lives with him. He wants us to feel compelled to tell others our story. He wants us to remember our experiences with him and walk wildly into the world hearts pumping, adrenaline flowing.[3]

OUTSIDE CONNECTION

**2** *Philip is sent to one (Acts 8:26–40).* The Holy Spirit took Philip from a ministry of thousands in Samaria to share the gospel with one individual, an Ethiopian **eunuch**, who was leaving Jerusalem. God is as concerned with the salvation of a single individual as he is with thousands. Kewl!

**eunuch:** by the first century this was the title of a high official in some lands

**3** *Saul's* **conversion** *(Acts 9).* The Jewish supreme court sent Saul to arrest Christian Jews in Damascus—another city in the empire. On the way Christ interrupted Saul's trip! He spoke to Saul, and Saul became a Christian. Saul became Paul, and the same dude who had worked very hard to persecute Christians was now someone who tried to plant churches and help people follow Christ.

**conversion:** turning to God

>>> CHECK IT OUT:

Acts 9:1–31

*Warren Wiersbe:* Saul of Tarsus became Paul the Apostle, and his life and ministry have influenced people and nations

OUTSIDE CONNECTION

161

How have you helped the church grow?_____

_____

What's the toughest part about telling others about your relationship with God?

_____

_____

What's your reaction when others tell you about their relationship with God?

_____

**GET REAL** It can be very easy to spend your teenage years waiting until you're an adult to serve. But guess what. God is calling you to serve right now. There's no waiting until you're older.

162

ever since. Even secular historians confess that Paul is one of the most significant figures in world history.[4]

**Gentiles:** *a non-Jews*

4 *Peter's vision (Acts 10:9–22).* The Jews considered **Gentiles** unclean. This meant that contact with a Gentile could disqualify a Jew from participating in worship at God's temple. God gave Peter a vision, and a voice from heaven told Peter to kill and eat <u>unclean animals</u>. Peter refused, saying, *"Surely not, Lord! I have never eaten anything impure or unclean."* God said Peter should not call something unclean that God had made clean, including Gentiles! Immediately afterward messengers came from Cornelius, a retired Roman officer (a Gentile), inviting Peter to his house. Peter realized that God wanted him to go.

*GO!*
Leviticus 11
(unclean animals)

>>>CHECK IT OUT:
Acts 10:9–22

5 *The conversion of Cornelius (Acts 10–11).* When Peter shared the gospel at the house of Cornelius, all who gathered there believed, and began to speak in tongues. Peter saw this as a sign that God had accepted Gentiles into the church.

>>>CHECK IT OUT:
Acts 11

**OUTSIDE CONNECTION**

*Craig S. Keener:* Until now no one had believed that Gentiles could be saved on the same terms as Jewish people, who had been chosen for salvation by God's sovereign grace.[5]

**6** *The first Gentile church is set up in Antioch (Acts 11:1–30).* News reached Jerusalem that a church made up of Gentiles existed in Antioch. Soon the apostles sent Barnabas to Antioch, where he became a leader. And Barnabas made Paul a member of the leadership team.

**7** *Peter is divinely freed (Acts 12).* King Herod Antipas, a grandson of Herod the Great, executed the apostle James. When he saw that this pleased the Jewish leaders, he arrested Peter. But an angel freed Peter from prison and later struck Herod with a fatal sickness. God was protecting his church!

In Acts this is the last we hear of Peter. Church history tells us Peter ministered primarily to Jewish Christians throughout the Roman Empire, and he was crucified in Rome under Emperor Nero around A.D. 66.

 **OFF WE GO (A.D. 46–57)**

---

**Bible Summary: Paul's Journey**

The apostle Paul went on three missionary journeys (see illustrations, page 164–165) to major cities of the Roman Empire. He and his companions set up churches in these population centers. The new Christians then spread the gospel to the surrounding villages and countryside. Later Paul revisited these churches to give them additional teaching. He also wrote letters of instruction to the young churches. His letters were collected and distributed to churches everywhere. Thirteen of Paul's letters are in the New Testament.

---

**PAUL:** Paul becomes the leader of the **missionary** team and starts the spread of the gospel throughout the Roman Empire.

**SILAS:** Silas was Paul's partner on the second and third journeys.

### What's Up with Acts 13–20?

**1** *Paul's missions strategy (Acts 13–14).* When he first entered a city, Paul went to the Jewish synagogue to teach about Jesus, which was where people, both Jews and non-Jews, who were interested in God usually hung out. Many of these people responded to the gospel and made up the core of the first Christian churches.

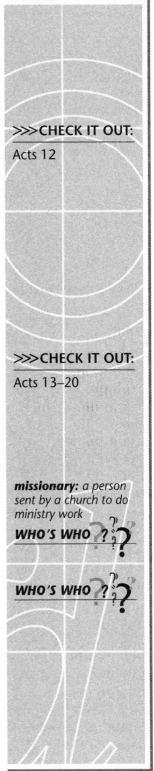

>>>**CHECK IT OUT:**
Acts 12

>>>**CHECK IT OUT:**
Acts 13–20

**163**

**missionary:** *a person sent by a church to do ministry work*

**WHO'S WHO** ??

**WHO'S WHO** ??

## Paul's First Missionary Journey (Acts 13:4–14:28)

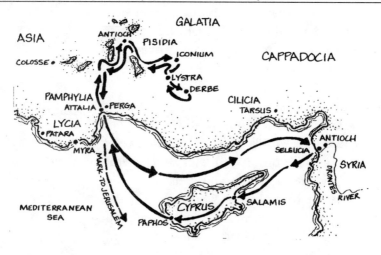

## Paul's Second Missionary Journey (Acts 15:39–18:22)

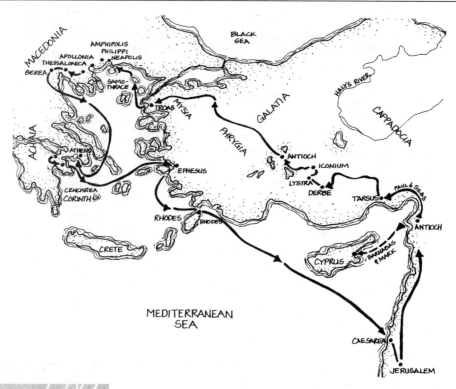

**Ron Luce:** The opportunity of a lifetime could be knocking at your door, but unless you see the signs of the times as God does you will not recognize the opportunity.[6]

**2** *The Jerusalem Council in A.D. 49 (Acts 15).* Paul was successful in starting Christian churches in a lot of the Roman Empire's major cities, which led to a problem. Some Jewish Christians thought the Gentile believers should believe in Jesus *and* follow Jewish customs at the same time.

To Paul this was a corruption of the gospel, which offers salvation to sinners solely on the basis of faith in Jesus, who died for humans' sins. Peter agreed, arguing that God saved Jew and Gentile alike who trusted in Christ. After a lengthy discussion, James, the brother of Jesus, summarized the council's conclusion, quoting the prophet Amos to show that Gentiles would be converted as Gentiles. All the council asked of the Gentiles was that they refrain from practices that would make it difficult for Jewish believers to fellowship with them.

**>>>CHECK IT OUT:**

Acts 15:1–21

**3** *The challenges of missionary life (2 Corinthians 11:23–28).* It's clear from Acts 16 and 19 Paul and his team faced many challenges and difficulties spreading the gospel throughout the Roman Empire. Paul sums up twenty years of missionary experience in 2 Corinthians 11:23–29. It reads like a diary entry. Have a look!

**>>>CHECK IT OUT:**

Acts 16:16–40;
19:1–51

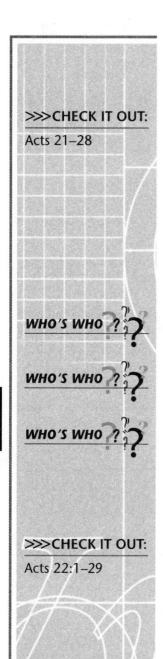

>>>CHECK IT OUT:

Acts 21–28

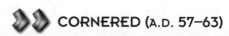 CORNERED (A.D. 57–63)

**Bible Summary: Paul's Trial**

In A.D. 57 Paul felt led to return to Jerusalem. When a riot broke out there, Roman soldiers rescued him and he claimed protection as a Roman citizen. The Jews claimed Paul was a political agitator and religious renegade. The Roman governor kept Paul in Caesarea (see illustration, page 158) for two years, hoping for a bribe. When a new governor was appointed, Paul again exercised his right as a Roman citizen. He appealed to Caesar to have his case decided in Rome. Acts tells the story of Paul's journey to Rome (see illustration, page 167) and even includes information about a shipwreck along the way, but the book concludes before Paul goes to trial.

WHO'S WHO ?

**FELIX:** The Roman governor of Palestine who hoped Paul would offer him a bribe.

WHO'S WHO ?

**FESTUS:** The new Roman governor who asked Paul to go to Jerusalem for trial.

WHO'S WHO ?

**KING AGRIPPA (Herod Agrippa II):** The administrator of Judea under the Romans, who heard Paul's defense with Festus.

### What's Up with Acts 21–28?

**1** *The Jerusalem riot and Paul's arrest (Acts 21:17–22:29).* Prominent signs were posted in the Jerusalem temple, warning Gentiles not to enter on pain of death. The riot broke out when Jews, who recognized Paul, falsely accused him of bringing Gentiles into the inner portion of the temple, where Gentiles were not allowed.

>>>CHECK IT OUT:

Acts 22:1–29

After being rescued, Paul asked to speak to the crowd. He recited his training under a famous rabbi and told the story of his conversion. But when Paul reported that the Lord told him to go to the Gentiles, the crowd rioted again.

*OUTSIDE* **CONNECTION**

*Warren Wiersbe: Paul was about to explain why he was involved with the Gentiles, but the Jews in the temple would not permit him to go on. No devout Jew would have anything to do with the Gentiles! Had Paul not uttered that one word, he might have later been released; and perhaps he knew*

**Paul's Journey to Rome (Acts 27:1–28:15)**

this. However, he had to be faithful in his witness, no matter what it cost him.[7]

**2** *The trial before Felix (Acts 24:1–27).* Luke describes Felix as "well acquainted with the Way," the early name of Christianity. Paul's bold witness frightened but also fascinated Felix, who kept Paul under house arrest for two years in hopes of getting a bribe.

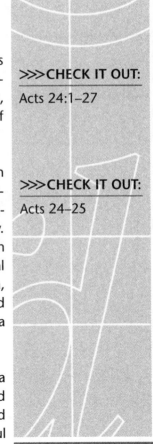

>>>**CHECK IT OUT:**

Acts 24:1–27

**3** *The trial before Festus (Acts 25–26).* Festus went to govern the province that included Judea and Jerusalem. On arriving he considered the Jews' request that Paul be sent to Jerusalem for trial. The Jews were hoping to kill him on the way. Rather than agree, Paul exercised his right as a Roman citizen to *"appeal to Caesar"*—to be tried in Rome by an imperial court. Later Festus discussed Paul's case with King Agrippa, who asked to hear Paul's defense. For the third time recorded in Acts, Paul tells the story of his conversion, this time to a room filled with high officials.

>>>**CHECK IT OUT:**

Acts 24–25

**4** *The voyage to Rome (Acts 27–28).* Acts concludes with a terrible storm that wrecked the ship on which Paul and other prisoners were being taken to Rome. When they arrived in Rome no charges had been forwarded from Jerusalem. Paul

167

CHURCH ON FIRE! • SEVENTEEN

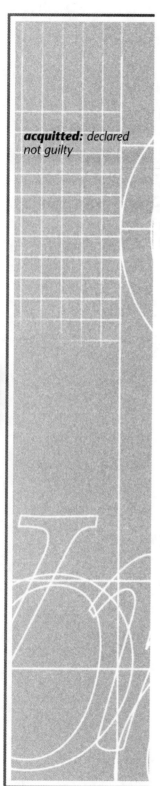

lived there under guard for two years, freely sharing the gospel with visitors and with the soldiers who guarded him.

## What Happened to Paul?

**acquitted:** declared not guilty

Acts ends before Paul goes to trial. Tradition tells us he was **acquitted** and continued his missionary work by going to Spain. Later, during the reign of Nero, again Paul was arrested. This time the faithful apostle, like Peter, was put to death in Rome. But the gospel message he had carried throughout the Roman Empire had taken root in the hearts and lives of many. Just a few centuries later, Justin Martyr, an early church father, would write that in Africa, Christians were "all but a majority in every city!"

# CHAPTER cHECKUP

1. What kind of literature is Acts?
2. What did the coming of the Holy Spirit provide the disciples?
3. What were two of the five basic truths emphasized in Peter's first two gospel sermons?
4. What was important about the conversion of Cornelius?
5. How many missionary journeys of Paul are reported in Acts?
6. Why was the Jerusalem Council significant?
7. When Acts ends, where is the apostle Paul?

### CRASH COURSE

▶ Acts is a history of the expansion of Christianity during the thirty years after Jesus' resurrection. Jesus sent the Holy Spirit to empower his disciples to be witnesses throughout the world.
▶ Peter was the first to preach the gospel message to the Jews and the Gentiles.
▶ After Paul's conversion he took the gospel to the Gentile world.
▶ In three missionary journeys over a span of eleven years the apostle Paul established churches in many of the major cities of the Roman Empire.
▶ Paul's arrest and trial gave him opportunities to present the gospel to important government officials in Palestine and in Rome itself.

# Explaining the Gospel

CHAPTER CAPTURE

- The Epistles
- Righteousness and Unrighteousness
- Divine Judgment
- God's Solution
- Rely on Grace

ROMANS • GALATIANS

## ▶▶ LET'S DIVE IN!

The last five chapters have covered Matthew through Acts—books of the Bible that consist of stories or "historical narrative" about Jesus and about Jesus' followers. This chapter will cover the first two books that are totally different. They're called epistles. The epistles are letters written by Jesus' apostles, sometimes to churches and sometimes to individuals. There are twenty-one of them in the New Testament, and each is designed to instruct believers on a variety of topics. The letters were so popular that everyone wanted copies, so they were copied and sent to other churches. Everyone considered them Scripture—transmitted through men, but **inspired** by the Holy Spirit.

*inspired: God-guided*

There are two major collections of letters: the *Pauline Epistles* and the *General Epistles*. The Pauline Epistles were written by Paul, and the General Epistles were written by Peter, John, Jude, James, and the unknown author of Hebrews.

GIMME THE BASICS

 **ROMANS**

*. . . God's gift of righteousness*

| | |
|---|---|
| WHO | The apostle Paul |
| WHAT | carefully explained the Christian gospel |
| WHERE | to Christians in Rome |
| WHEN | about A.D. 57 |
| WHY | so they would understand the relationship between grace and righteousness. |

 **RIGHTEOUS LIVING**

Remember the Old Testament? It revealed God as a moral being, whose law laid out standards of righteousness that God expected his people to maintain. Then the Christian gospel burst on the scene, and Jesus' apostles announced that because Christ died for our sins, God would forgive the sins of anyone who simply trusted in him. To some the gospel message seemed too unbelievable. What about righteousness? Isn't

### KEY POINT

The Book of Romans teaches the relationship between grace and righteousness.

What do you think it means to live righteously?_____ **Your Move**

_____

What struggles do you face in trying to live this way?_____

_____

_____

How can you encourage others to live righteously?_____

_____

**GET REAL**  What's so special about Paul? For starters, he knew all about living righteously. For years he was a really good Jew because he followed all the Jewish laws. But when he met Jesus he realized there wasn't anything *truly* righteous about how he lived. How about you? Are you following God on the outside, but abandoning him in your heart? Are you more attached to God's rules than you are to God?

a salvation won by faith inconsistent with the very nature of a God who is righteous and who, as the Old Testament reveals, expects righteousness from his people? Paul answers these questions in his letter to the Romans.

##  A SAMPLE OF ROMANS

Want a feel for this book? Let's check out some verses together. Paul talks a lot about human righteousness and points out that *no one* is righteous in God's sight. If salvation depends on our efforts to please God by doing what he requires, we're in huge trouble! And our trouble all begins with our alienation from God! It is this **alienation** that has brought all human beings under the wrath of God. I'll quote some verses for you and explain them.

*alienation: separation*

##  GOD'S WRATH FOR THE UNRIGHTEOUS

### Watch Yer Back!

Here's a verse about the wrath of God: *"The **wrath** of God is being revealed from heaven against all the **godlessness** and wickedness of men who suppress the truth by their wickedness"* (Romans 1:18). God isn't asleep—he's paying attention to our sin.

*wrath: God's intent to punish the sinner*

*godlessness: failure to show reverence to God*

God judges sin, both now and later. He judges sin now by allowing negative consequences. For example, if somebody steals something, often God allows that person to get caught and punished. That's one type of God's judgment. The other type will happen at the end of history when God will release *all* his punishment for everybody's sins. Anyone who has not trusted in Jesus will be in *big* trouble when that happens. Anyone who has trusted in Jesus will be allowed to enter heaven because Jesus already took the punishment for those who have trusted in him.

>>>CHECK IT OUT:
Romans 1:18–3:20

*Max Lucado: In living for today, the hut-building **hedonist** destroys his hope of living in a castle tomorrow. What was true in Paul's day is still true in ours, and we would do well to heed his warning. Otherwise, what is to keep us from destroying ourselves?*[1]

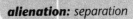

*hedonist: pleasure seeker*

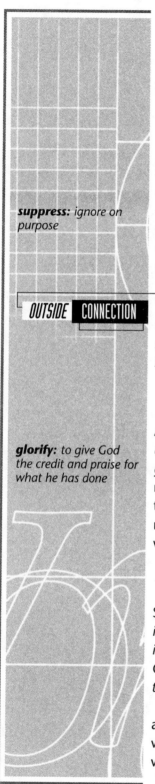

## It's Obvious God Exists!

Here's a passage about God's existence: *"Since what may be known about God is plain to them, because God has made it plain to them. For since the creation of the world God's invisible qualities—his eternal power and divine nature—have been clearly seen, being understood from what has been made, so that men are without excuse"* (Romans 1:19–20). What do humans deny? They deny that God exists. Paul's point is that creation is like a great radio transmitter; it proves God exists! Human beings who **suppress** the truth of God's existence are *"without excuse, "* because to reject or ignore God they must have willfully "turned down" their inner receiver. Human beings have willfully refused to accept the message God is broadcasting.

**suppress:** *ignore on purpose*

**OUTSIDE CONNECTION**

**Warren Wiersbe:** *Human history is not the story of a beast that worshiped idols, and then evolved into a man worshiping one God. Human history is just the opposite: man began knowing God, but turned from the truth and rejected God.*[2]

## Not Gonna Bow. Period.

**glorify:** *to give God the credit and praise for what he has done*

And here's a verse about humans' refusal to listen to God: *"For although they knew God, they neither **glorified** him as God nor gave thanks to him"* (Romans 1:21). What's the best way to respond to God? The best way is to give God credit for everything he's done and to thank him. Rather than do this, humans have ignored the truth that God exists and deserves our worship.

## Have It Your Way!

So God responded to human wickedness: *"God gave them over in the sinful desires of their hearts to sexual impurity for the degrading of their bodies with one another. They exchanged the truth of God for a lie, and worshiped and served created things rather than the Creator—who is forever praised. Amen"* (Romans 1:24–25).

The phrase *"gave them over"* is repeated in Romans 1:26 and 1:28. It means God allowed people to be as sinful as they wanted to be. He did not stop them. Paul has said that God's wrath *"is being"* revealed from heaven (Romans 1:18). The sexual impurity and the other sins he describes in this chapter are clear evidence that God's wrath is directed against those who have rejected him. Sin may look attractive, but it makes us miserable!

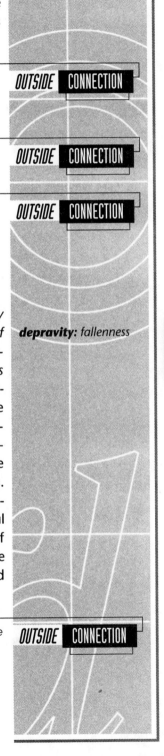

**Everett F. Harrison:** *Man is a religious being, and if he refuses to let God have the place of preeminence that is rightfully his, then he will put something or someone in God's place.*[3]

OUTSIDE CONNECTION

**Warren Wiersbe:** *The lie is that man is his own god, and he should worship and serve himself and not the Creator.*[4]

OUTSIDE CONNECTION

**Max Lucado:** *God's highest dream is not to make us rich, not to make us successful or popular or famous. God's dream is to make us right with him.*[5]

OUTSIDE CONNECTION

## Wake Up, I'm Here

In summary, Paul says humans *"have become filled with every kind of wickedness, evil, greed and **depravity**. They are full of envy, murder, strife, deceit and malice. They are gossips, slanderers, God-haters, insolent, arrogant and boastful; they invent ways of doing evil; they disobey their parents; they are senseless, faithless, heartless, ruthless"* (Romans 1:29–31). Genesis reveals the source of all that is good in human beings. God created humankind in his own image, with the capacity to love, to respond to love, to enjoy beauty and make beautiful things. The first part of Romans is about all that is evil in human beings. Why is there evil in human beings? Because humans have chosen to disobey God and do their own thing. How does Paul know this? Just look around you, and you'll see all sorts of evil—children without parents, dirty movies, women who are abused. All of this evil stuff proves that people have turned their backs on God and his Word.

**depravity:** *fallenness*

**Warren Wiersbe:** *Paul names 24 specific sins, all of which are with us today.*[6]

OUTSIDE CONNECTION

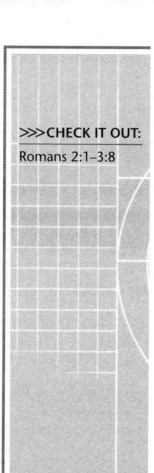

 **GOD'S PRINCIPLES OF DIVINE JUDGMENT**

### You're Gonna Get It!

>>> **CHECK IT OUT:**
Romans 2:1–3:8

Paul writes, *"All who sin apart from the law will also perish apart from the law, and all who sin under the law will be judged by the law"* (Romans 2:12). It'd be difficult to use the Ten Commandments to judge everyone's behavior—not everyone knows them! Jews understood the Ten Commandments, but Gentiles certainly didn't. Regardless, everyone will be judged for their wrongdoings, because even Gentiles know they do wrong.

### Everyone Knows "Right" and "Wrong"

Paul's focus turns to the Gentiles: *"Indeed, when the Gentiles who do not have the law, do by nature things required by the law, they are a law for themselves, even though they do not have the law, since they show that the requirements of the law are written on their hearts, their consciences also bearing witness, and their thoughts now accusing, now even defending them"* (Romans 2:14–15). Paul's point is that all people, regardless of whether they're Christian or not, recognize that some things are morally right and others are morally wrong. Every person's conscience bears witness to the fact that he or she has violated *his own standards,* if not God's!

Because God is totally just and fair, God won't judge those who do not know his law by that law. Instead, he will judge them by their own moral standards! And when that happens every person will be judged guilty!

 ***Max Lucado:*** *Before I knew the law, I was at peace. Now that I know the law, an insurrection has occurred. I'm a torn man. On one hand I know what to do, but I don't want to do it. My eyes read the sign, "Do Not Enter," but my body doesn't want to obey.*[7]

 ***Everett F. Harrison:*** *Despite the great differences in laws and customs among people around the world, what unites them in a common humanity is the recognition that some things are right and others are wrong.*[8]

174

## You and Your Conscience

The apostle Paul quotes the Old Testament as proof that all have sinned: *"We have already made the charge that Jews and Gentiles alike are all under sin. As it is written: There is no one righteous, not even one; there is no one who understands, no one who seeks God"* (Romans 3:9–11). Now Paul offers scriptural proof for his statements. God's Word says *"there is no one righteous, not even one."* When a human being stands before God to be judged by him, not one will be judged righteous.

*Warren Wiersbe: Measured by God's perfect righteousness, no human being is sinless.*[9]

OUTSIDE CONNECTION

## The Law Won't Get You to Heaven

God realized that no one could live up to the standard of righteousness expressed in the law. God intended the law to be a mirror, to show us how far short we fall of being what we ought to be! Through the law we become aware of sin. Romans 3:20 says, *"No one will be declared righteous in his sight by observing the law; rather, through the law we become conscious of sin."*

 BUT THERE'S HOPE!

Romans was written for those who assumed that in promising to forgive sins, God was acting against his own nature as a righteous God. Paul's response is totally cool. Those who assume such must first face a simple fact. No human being is or can become righteous. <u>All have sinned</u>. If salvation depends on human effort to do what is right, all are lost indeed!

*GO!*
Romans 3:23
(all have sinned)

Our problem? We reject God and we sin. God's solution? Jesus Christ died to pay the penalty for our sin. Through faith in God and the acceptance of Christ's death as a sacrifice people can be forgiven and reestablish a personal relationship with God! Just as our rejection of God produced sins in us and society, the restoration of a personal relationship with God will produce righteousness within us when we are joined to Jesus Christ!

Romans teaches us that the gospel is about righteousness! God declares those who believe in Jesus to be righteous in his sight. And then God works in the believer's life to produce a righteousness that we could never demonstrate apart from him.

**OUTSIDE CONNECTION**

*Max Lucado: Simply put: The cost of your sins is more than you can pay. The gift of your God is more than you can imagine. "A person is made right with God through faith," Paul explains, "not through obeying the law" (Romans 3:28).*[10]

 **GALATIANS**

**GIMME THE BASICS**

*. . . the law or the Spirit?*

| WHO | The apostle Paul |
|-----|------------------|
| WHAT | wrote this letter |
| WHERE | to Christians in the province of Galatia |
| WHEN | about A.D. 49 |
| WHY | to explain how freedom from the demands of Old Testament law promotes righteous living and true goodness. |

 **GET WITH THE GRACE**

Acts 15:1 tells us that after Paul and Barnabas completed their first missionary journey, some other guys followed them and told people that to be saved, they had to be circumcised. These **Judaizers** insisted that Gentile Christians be *"required to obey the law of Moses"* (Acts 15:5). Many new Christians were confused. After all, the Old Testament was God's Word. Shouldn't Christians be responsible to keep its laws as well as trust in Christ?

Paul saw this as a critical distortion of the gospel. He sent this letter to the Galatian churches to help them understand the limitations of the law and the secrets of depending on God's Holy Spirit.

*Judaizers: men who taught that Christians must keep Jewish laws*

176

**A SAMPLE OF GALATIANS**

### Be Led by the Spirit of God

Paul says, *"But if you are led by the Spirit, you are not under the law"* (Galatians 5:18). Life by the Spirit is neither **legalism** nor a **license** to sin. It is instead an openness to God's inner leading and a ready willingness to reach out to others in love.

**legalism:** *an ungodly attachment to rules*

**license:** *permission*

### We Know and Can See the Difference

Paul lists the characteristics of a sinful life and the characteristics of a life governed by the Spirit: *"The acts of the sinful nature are obvious: sexual immorality, impurity and debauchery; idolatry and witchcraft; hatred, discord, jealousy, fits of rage, selfish ambition, dissensions, factions and envy; drunkenness, orgies and the like. I warn you, as I did before, that those who live like this will not inherit the kingdom of God. But the fruit of the Spirit is love, joy, peace, patience, kindness, goodness, faithfulness, gentleness, and self-control. Against such things there is no law"* (Galatians 5:19–23). Laws are meant to keep evil from getting out of hand. Christians who live godly lives don't have to fear the law. They will be full of good attitudes and behavior because the Holy Spirit lives inside them, motivating them.

**Warren Wiersbe:** *The contrast between works and fruit is important. A machine in a factory works, and turns out a product, but it could never manufacture fruit. Fruit must grow out of life, and, in the case of the believer, it is the life of the Spirit. The old nature cannot produce fruit; only the new nature can do that.*[11]

*OUTSIDE* **CONNECTION**

### Wrapping It Up

Romans and Galatians find the key to both our despair and our hope in relationship with God. It is because of man's lost relationship with God that sin has gained its grip on individuals and society. And it is through a restored relationship with God offered to us in Jesus Christ that we have hope for living a truly good life.

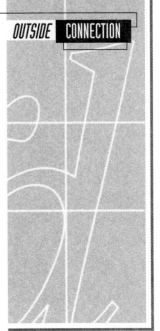

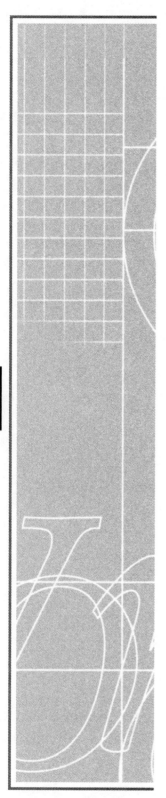

# CHApTeR cHeCkUp

1. What kind of literature is the New Testament epistles?
2. What is the theme of Paul's letter to the Romans?
3. What are three things Romans teaches about righteousness?
4. What is the root cause of sin?
5. How can God judge people who have never heard his law?
6. What is the true role of God's law?
7. What is the theme of Paul's letter to the Galatians?
8. What's the difference between being led by the law, and being led by the Spirit?

## CRASH COURSE

▶ Many books in the New Testament were originally letters written by apostles to teach Christians.
▶ The book of Romans was written to show how the gospel relates to righteousness.
▶ Romans teaches that no human being is righteous, but when someone is cleansed by Jesus, the Holy Spirit will help that believer to live a righteous life.
▶ Romans traces the root of human sin to humankind's alienation from God.
▶ Galatians emphasizes that both salvation and Christian living are experienced by reliance on the grace of God, not dependence on God's law.

# Letters on the Christian Life

**CHAPTER CAPTURE**

- Problem Solving
- Then and Now
- Spiritual Principles
- Encouragement
- Misunderstandings

## 1, 2 CORINTHIANS • 1, 2 THESSALONIANS

 **LET'S DIVE IN!**

Paul and his crew did a lot of traveling. They traveled from city to city spreading the gospel. In each city a young church was established. Paul and his companions would spend a few months or even a year with most congregations, teaching the basic truths of the gospel. The missionaries would then move on to another city and do the same thing again.

Even though Paul and his team revisited the newly established churches whenever possible, the young believers often had questions. When Paul heard about questions or problems in one of the churches he set up, he'd sit down and write them a letter. In this chapter we'll look at four letters of Paul that are clearly problem-solving epistles.

 **1 CORINTHIANS**

### GIMME THE BASICS

*. . . how to get back on track*

| | |
|---|---|
| WHO | The apostle Paul wrote this letter |
| WHAT | in response to fights that were tearing congregations apart |
| WHERE | in Corinth |
| WHEN | about A.D. 57 |
| WHY | to show them how to rebuild a loving community. |

 **SAME OLD STORY**

First-century Corinth was a busy city with a population of around 250,000. Its population included native Greeks, a large number of Jews, Asians, Roman settlers, government officials, and businessmen. Priestess-prostitutes in Corinth's temple to **Aphrodite** helped create a climate of immorality that was Corinth's claim to fame. Paul visited Corinth in A.D. 50 and stayed there for about eighteen months, establishing a large body of believers there with members from every part of society. About five years after the church was founded, messengers from Corinth told Paul about the fights that were tearing the congregation apart.

*Aphrodite: the Greek goddess of love and beauty*

>>> CHECK IT OUT:

Acts 18:1–18

**PAUL'S WAY OF THINKING**

The text of Paul's first letter to the Corinthians is easy to follow, because the apostle addresses the problems one by one. Rather than give a short answer to problems in the church, Paul typically reviews basic truths the Corinthians need to understand, and then applies these truths to solve the problem. We'll look at some of the arguments Paul makes to see what we can learn.

### My Leader Is Better than Yours (1 Corinthians 1–4)

- *The problem:* The unity of the church has been ripped apart by groups that fought over which leader they should be loyal to (1 Corinthians 1:10–17).

- *The truth:* Human wisdom, which relies on human reasoning, and God's wisdom, which is far above human reasoning, are different in nature (1 Corinthians 1:18–2:4). God's wisdom must be discerned by those who rely on the Spirit. The arguing in Corinth shows that the believers there are **worldly** (1 Corinthians 2:5–3:4).
- *The solution:* Human leaders are to be respected as servants entrusted with the secret things of God. Leaders should not be admired because they split off from a different group of Christians (1 Corinthians 4:1–21).

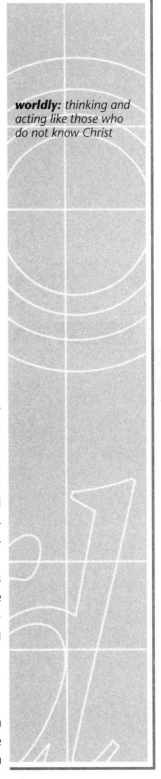

**worldly:** *thinking and acting like those who do not know Christ*

## The Wicked Must Go (1 Corinthians 5:1–6:20)

- *The problem:* Sexual immorality is outta control (1 Corinthians 5:1–2).
- *The truth:* Christians shouldn't associate with believers who practice sexual immorality (1 Corinthians 5:3–6:20).
- *The solution:* Expel the wicked man from among you (1 Corinthians 5:13).

## Stay Hitched (1 Corinthians 7:1–39)

- *The problem:* Believers were confused about marriage. A few of the married were refraining from sexual relations, others divorced, others hesitated to get married (1 Corinthians 7:1).
- *The truth:* One purpose of marriage is to meet the sexual needs of each partner. A person with a strong sex drive should marry (1 Corinthians 7:2–9). The married should not divorce, but if a non-Christian spouse leaves a believer, the Christian need not remain unmarried (1 Corinthians 7:10–14).
- *The solution:* The married should not give up sexual relations (1 Corinthians 7:5) or divorce (1 Corinthians 7:10). There are good reasons to remain single, but any unmarried person may wed without sinning (1 Corinthians 7:36) as long as he or she weds another believer (1 Corinthians 7:39).

## Don't Offend Your Brother (1 Corinthians 8:1–11:1)

- *The problem:* Most meat sold in the first century was from animals that had been sacrificed to pagan gods. Some Corinthian Christians shopped in markets associated with pagan temples, convinced *"that an idol is nothing at all."* Others thought it was downright awful for Christians to have anything at all to do with pagan idols. (1 Corinthians 8:1–7).

- *The truth:* There is some truth in each party's argument. But this is an issue that should be approached on the basis of love, with consideration for the *weaker* brother who sees eating such meat as participating in idolatry (1 Corinthians 8:7–10:22).

- *The solution:* Within the church, seek first the good of others. When eating with an unbeliever, don't ask whether the meat came from idol sacrifices. But if somebody tells you it came from idols and obviously thinks it's wrong for you to eat it, don't eat it. Why? Because even though it's true that you are free to eat it as a Christian, if other people think it isn't right and you go ahead and eat it, they will look down on your Christian freedom. It's more important for people to view Christian freedom as good than for you to exercise that freedom every chance you get (1 Corinthians 10:23–11:1).

## Pentecost (1 Corinthians 12:1–14:39)

- *The problem:* Young Christians in Corinth assumed that those who had the **gift of tongues** were especially spiritual and closer to God (1 Corinthians 12:1–3; 14:2–3).

- *The truth:* The Holy Spirit gives each believer a **spiritual gift**. The gifts differ, but every gift is a sign of the Holy Spirit's presence in the believer's life (1 Corinthians 12:1–11). Christians are like parts of a human body; the Spirit's gifts fit each person for his or her role in the **Body of Christ**, and every person has an important part to play (1 Corinthians 12:12–31). Don't overemphasize tongues; unlike tongues, the intelligible words spoken by a prophet instruct and build others up, so this gift is more important (1 Corinthians 14:1–25).

- *The solution:* When you meet together let everyone take turns contributing to the service in an orderly way. And if someone with the gift of **interpreting** tongues is present, those who speak in tongues can take part too (1 Corinthians 14:25–33).

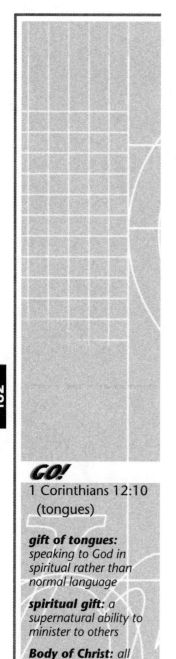

### GO!
1 Corinthians 12:10 (tongues)

**gift of tongues:** *speaking to God in spiritual rather than normal language*

**spiritual gift:** *a supernatural ability to minister to others*

**Body of Christ:** *all believers united to Jesus and each other*

**interpreting:** *translating*

**Billy Graham:** *According to the Bible, love is the dominant principle of life.*[1]

**OUTSIDE CONNECTION**

### Don't Worry about Tomorrow (1 Corinthians 15:1–58)

- *The problem:* Some are saying there is no resurrection (1 Corinthians 15:12).
- *The truth:* If there is no resurrection, Christ wasn't raised, and the gospel is a lie (1 Corinthians 15:12–19). But Christ has been raised from the dead, and in the end will destroy death itself (1 Corinthians 15:20–28). The resurrection body awaiting us will be glorious, powerful, and spiritual, and when we are clothed with immortality we will experience the victory Christ has won (1 Corinthians 15:29–57).
- *The solution:* Give yourselves fully to the work of the Lord, because you know that your labor in the Lord is not in vain (1 Corinthians 15:58).

 **2 CORINTHIANS**

*. . . secrets of ministry*

**GIMME THE BASICS**

| | |
|---|---|
| WHO | The apostle Paul wrote this letter |
| WHAT | sharing principles underlying his ministry |
| WHERE | to the Corinthian church |
| WHEN | about A.D. 58 |
| WHY | to encourage believers and to warn those who were still rebellious. |

 **PAUL WRITES ANOTHER ONE**

Paul's second letter to the Corinthians was written within a year of the first. He had heard encouraging reports that many responded to his blunt letter by facing their sins and working to resolve problems. But a hostile minority remained determined to reject Paul's guidance. In this warm and revealing letter Paul tells the Corinthians how much he loves them, and tells them his vision of Christian ministry. He also warns those who still rejected his authority as an apostle of Jesus Christ.

**183**

What are the top two causes of arguments between you and your friends?_____

_____

How do you show love for your friends?_____

_____

What's the best way to be honest with a friend?_____

_____

Sometimes fighting is easier than getting along. We get in a bad mood and a friend rubs us the wrong way and the whole thing snowballs. Paul could have left things alone with the Corinthian church, but he didn't. He valued friendship, so he was quick to comfort the people who were hurt by his first letter. Are you quick to comfort friends that you hurt?

184

 **A SAMPLE OF 2 CORINTHIANS**

### Paul's Weakness

**>>>CHECK IT OUT:**

2 Corinthians 12:7–10

A group of false "super-apostles" (2 Corinthians 11:5) bragged about their strengths and ridiculed Paul's weaknesses. (Paul wasn't a great speaker, and he wasn't very physically fit either.)

Paul's response is surprising. First he refers to a *"messenger of Satan"* that torments him. *"To keep me from becoming conceited, . . ."* Paul writes, *"there was given me a thorn in my flesh, a messenger of Satan, to torment me"* (2 Corinthians 12:7). Most believe this thorn in Paul's flesh was a disfiguring and debilitating eye disease that made Paul even more open to teasing by people who hated him.

**OUTSIDE CONNECTION**

**Warren Wiersbe:** *The Lord knows how to balance our lives. If we have only blessings, we may become proud; so he permits us to have burdens as well.*[2]

## Paul's Prayer

Paul's response to his pain was appropriate: *"Three times I pleaded with the Lord to take it away from me"* (2 Corinthians 12:8). Like others with an illness or disability, Paul prayed. Some people say healing is guaranteed to believers who have enough faith. Certainly Paul was a man of faith and prayed with utter confidence. But as the next verse tells us, God's answer was no: *"But he said to me, 'My grace is sufficient for you, for my power is made perfect in weakness'"* (2 Corinthians 12:9).

In Paul's case God permitted the illness for more than a while. First, the disability was to keep Paul from becoming conceited. Second, it was to make Paul a less cluttered channel through which God's power might flow. Paul understood God's message. His disability was a blessing, and it constantly reminded him to rely on God rather than on his own gifts and abilities.

He concluded, *"Therefore I will boast all the more gladly about my weaknesses, so that Christ's power may rest on me"* (2 Corinthians 12:9).

**185**

**OUTSIDE CONNECTION**

**Dwight L. Moody:** *When God delivered Israel out of Egypt he didn't send an army. God sent a man who had been in the desert for 40 years, and had an impediment in his speech. It is weakness that God wants. Nothing is small when God handles it.*[3]

**OUTSIDE CONNECTION**

**Martin Luther:** *Those whom God adorns with great gifts he plunges into the most severe trials in order that they may learn that they're nothing . . . and that he is all.*[4]

## 1 THESSALONIANS

### . . . live holy!

**GIMME THE BASICS**

| | |
|---|---|
| WHO | Paul wrote this letter |
| WHAT | to encourage further commitment |
| WHERE | from believers in Thessalonica, |
| WHEN | about A.D. 51 or 52, |
| WHY | toward holy living. |

## YOU'RE DOING A GRAND JOB!

The city of Thessalonica was the capital of the Roman province of Macedonia. Rome maintained a great naval base there. Paul and his team spent a short time there because some Jews became angry that Gentiles were accepting Christ as Lord. While Paul spent less than three months in Thessalonica, a flourishing church was planted there. This first letter to the church was written after Timothy visited the city and brought back a positive report to Paul.

 ## A SAMPLE OF 1 THESSALONIANS

### What about the Dead?

A few Thessalonian Christians had died, and some were devastated. They were certain the dead had missed the blessings that would come when Jesus returned. So, Paul wrote a famous passage to clarify what the future holds for all believers. You can read his encouragement in 1 Thessalonians 4:13–14.

Biological death closes the door on this world, but for the Christian it opens the door to heaven. Those living when Jesus returns have no special advantage over believers who have died! *"For the Lord himself will come down from heaven, with a loud command, with the voice of the archangel and with the trumpet call of God, and the **dead in Christ** will rise first"* (1 Thessalonians 4:16). When Jesus returns, the first event will be the resurrection of Christians who have died.

### Rapture!

Then something extraordinary will happen. *"We who are still alive and are left will be **caught up** with them in the clouds to meet the Lord in the air. And so we will be with the Lord forever. Therefore encourage each other with these words"* (1 Thessalonians 4:17–18). The living and those who have died, transformed and in resurrection bodies like his own, will be caught up to be with the Lord forever.

**dead in Christ:** Christians who have died

**caught up:** taken up to heaven in the **Rapture**

**Rapture:** when the church is removed from the earth

**OUTSIDE CONNECTION**

**Kevin Johnson:** *The rapture is a ride guaranteed to satisfy the most savage roller coaster animal. It'll be an up-to-the-*

186

sky-high faahwang—major bungee jump recoil. Like the great Christian writer Oswald Chambers once said, "I do not know how I am going to stay up 'in the air' with the Lord, but that is no business of mine."[5]

 **2 THESSALONIANS**

*. . . more info about Jesus' return*

WHO — The apostle Paul wrote this letter
WHAT — talking more about Jesus' return
WHERE — to the Thessalonians
WHEN — within a few months of his first letter
WHY — to encourage the persecuted and to set some people straight.

 **HOLD YER HORSES!**

Paul's first letter hadn't cleared up all the Thessalonians' confusion about the future. The Thessalonians thought that the persecution they were experiencing was part of the <u>Great Tribulation</u> (in other words . . . they thought the end of the world was coming). Paul explains that this can't be. He also reminds them about a **man of lawlessness** the prophet Daniel and Jesus himself said would appear before the end of the world.

This individual, whose appearance will mark the beginning of history's end and also called the Antichrist (Against- or Counterfeit-Christ), is described by Paul as *"one who will oppose and will exalt himself over everything that is called God or is worshiped, so that he sets himself up in God's temple, proclaiming himself to be God"* (2 Thessalonians 2:4).

**C. S. Lewis:** *In the long run the answer to all those who object to the doctrine of hell, is itself a question: "What are you asking God to do?" To wipe out all their past sins and, at all costs, to give them a fresh start, smoothing away every difficulty and offering every miraculous help? But he has done so, on Calvary. To forgive them? They will not be forgiven. To leave them alone? Alas, I am afraid that is what he does.*[6]

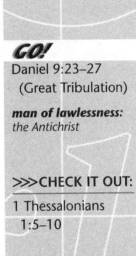

**GIMME THE BASICS**

**GO!**
Daniel 9:23–27
(Great Tribulation)

***man of lawlessness:***
*the Antichrist*

**>>>CHECK IT OUT:**

1 Thessalonians
1:5–10

**OUTSIDE CONNECTION**

# CHAPTER CHECKUP

1. Name Paul's four problem-solving epistles.
2. What solution did Paul give to the problem of immorality in the church?
3. What was wrong with the Corinthians' emphasis on the gift of tongues?
4. What are two reasons why Christians should be generous givers?
5. What were two reasons God did not answer Paul's prayers for healing?

## CRASH COURSE

▶ When Paul heard of problems in the churches, he wrote letters of instruction and encouragement.

▶ Many of the problems addressed in Paul's first letter to the Corinthians are common in churches today.

▶ Paul's second letter to the Corinthians explains concepts his ministry was based on.

▶ Paul wrote 1 Thessalonians to encourage the persecuted Christian community.

▶ In 2 Thessalonians Paul corrected misunderstandings about Christ's return to earth, and he urged holy living while they waited.

# Letters from Prison

## EPHESIANS • PHILIPPIANS • COLOSSIANS

CHAPTER CAPTURE

- The Living Church
- Working Out Salvation
- God Becomes Man
- Stuff for Daily Living

189

 LET'S DIVE IN!

Acts ends with Paul in a Roman prison waiting for his trial. For two years Paul lived there under guard, and he was free to receive visitors. Often the visitors were from churches Paul had started, so he would talk with the visitors about how things were going in their churches. He would send the visitors home with letters that he asked the visitors to deliver to everybody at their churches. The Books of Ephesians, Philippians, and Colossians are examples of these letters. They're called the "prison epistles."

 EPHESIANS

### ... the true church

GIMME THE BASICS

| | |
|---|---|
| WHO | The apostle Paul wrote this letter from prison |
| WHAT | exploring the true nature of Christ's church |
| WHERE | with the Christians in Ephesus |
| WHEN | about A.D. 62 |
| WHY | to contrast Christianity with the religion of that great temple city. |

**THE CHURCH IS YOU AND ME**

When the apostle Paul and his missionary team first reached Ephesus, it was the leading city in Asia Minor, made rich by the pilgrims who flocked to the city to visit the magnificent temple of Diana. Even though this cultic temple was successful, the population of the city was spiritually hungry. Paul's presentation of the gospel was so effective that it threatened the citizens who depended on the sales of religious trinkets and on feeding and housing visitors.

> **Bible Summary: Ephesians**
> The basic message of Ephesians is that Christ's church is alive—not a dead institution. Father, Son, and Holy Spirit were each intimately involved in forming the New Testament community of faith, which can be understood as a living temple, as the Body of Christ, and as the family of God the Father.

## Ephesians under a Microscope

I. Hello there! (Ephesians 1:1–2).
II. Let me tell what the church is (1:3–3:21).
   A. It's God's creation (1:4–23).
   B. It's really just one people (2:1–22).
   C. It's the family of God (3:1–21).
III. Now I want to tell you how to be an effective church (4:1–6:20).
   A. Be ministers (4:1–16).
   B. Be pure (4:17–5:20).
   C. Be righteous in every relationship (5:21–6:9).
   D. God will help you! (6:10–20).
IV. Bye for now! (6:21–24).

## What's Up with Ephesians?

**1** *God has done amazing things for believers (Ephesians 1:3–14).* Paul writes that God has blessed believers with *"every spiritual blessing in Christ."* He goes on to show how God has been actively involved in providing the blessings Christians now enjoy.

**>>>CHECK IT OUT:**
Ephesians 1:3–14

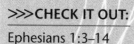

190

**2** *Paul's prayers for the Ephesians (Ephesians 1:15–22; 3:14–20).* Paul's prayers are a major feature of the prison epistles. In his first prayer for the Ephesians Paul prays for them to know God better, and to realize that his great power is at work in and for them. In his second prayer Paul asks God to help the Ephesians love each other.

**3** *Faith and* **works** *(Ephesians 2:1–10).* The raw material with which God constructed his church is human beings who are spiritually *"dead in* [their] **trespasses** *and sins."* By nature every human impulse is to satisfy the cravings of the sinful nature. To form Christ's church God made such persons *"alive in Christ."* The new life God provides is entirely a gift of divine **grace**—not something anyone can earn by doing good.

**works:** *good deeds*

**trespasses:** *sinful acts*

**grace:** *God's favor shown to those who have done nothing to merit it*

**Lewis Smedes:** *Realistic common sense tells you that you are too weak, too harassed, too human to change for the better; grace gives you the power to send you on your way a better person.*[1]

*OUTSIDE* **CONNECTION**

**4** *How to imitate Christ (Ephesians 4:20–5:7).* In Ephesians 2:10 Paul says Christians are *"God's workmanship, created in Christ Jesus."* Now Paul applies this truth. As God's workmanship, Christians are not supposed to be bitter or angry or mean. They're supposed to be kind and gentle and compassionate. Paul urges believers to imitate Jesus (Ephesians 5: 1–2).

**>>>CHECK IT OUT:** Ephesians 4:22–5:2

**5** *House head (Ephesians 5:21–32).* People had the wrong idea of what it means to be the head of the house. They thought the husband was supposed to be a dictator who demands his wife to **submit** by giving up her rights in order to serve him. But Paul didn't mean this at all. Paul said the Christian husband is to model himself on Jesus Christ—the head of the church. As Christ loved the church and gave himself for it, a husband is to love his wife. He's to care for her and help her achieve her full potential as a person. This kind of love makes it easy for a wife to respect her husband.

**submit:** *Christian submission is not giving in, but being responsive*

**GIMME THE BASICS**

 **PHILIPPIANS**

*. . . real joy*

| | |
|---|---|
| WHO | The apostle Paul wrote this letter from prison |
| WHAT | to share the joy he experienced |
| WHERE | with the Christians in Philippi |
| WHEN | about A.D. 62 |
| WHY | to comfort them. |

 **JOY IN TOUGH TIMES**

Paul's imprisonment in Rome upset many of the churches he had founded. The Christians in Philippi felt close to Paul and had often sent him cash to help with his mission. In this very personal epistle Paul shares his own feelings about being in jail. Rather than seeing his imprisonment as a setback for the gospel, Paul believes it will motivate believers throughout the empire to be even more bold in sharing the good news of Jesus Christ.

How have you suffered for being a Christian?_____ **Your Move**

_____

How does suffering bring us closer to God?_____

_____

When we're suffering, what things relieve our pain?_____

_____

_____

 **GET REAL**

Paul's point is simple. If you're a believer, you're going to suffer. Not easy to take? Well, check out how Paul handled it. He had it *really* tough, but he kept his eyes on God. Got friends who tease you because you trust Christ? Adults think you're a little loopy, and let you know it? Keep your eyes on Christ. If you can do that, you'll be okay.

One cool feature of Philippians is how often Paul expresses his own sense of joy and rejoicing. Paul is happy in prison—a place where most people would find it impossible to be happy.

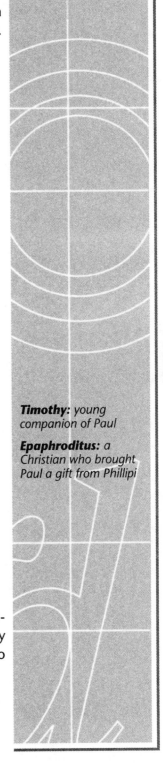

### Bible Summary: Philippians

The city of Philippi was a Roman colony, settled by old army veterans. It had no Jewish community, but it did have a strong gentile Christian church and Paul had close ties with it. One of the major features of this book is a powerful passage that describes the humility of Jesus, who surrendered the benefits of his divinity to become a human being and die for us. Christ is now with God, which is a reminder to believers everywhere that the way up is down, and the path of selfless giving leads to personal fulfillment.

## Philippians under a Microscope

I. Hello! (Philippians 1:1–11).
II. Things are going well for me and for the gospel (1:12–26).
III. Your attitude should be Christlike (1:27–2:18).
   A. Be stable! (1:27–30).
   B. Be humble! (2:1–11).
   C. Be obedient! (2:12–18).
IV. I hope to send **Timothy** and **Epaphroditus** to you (2:19–30).
V. Don't be fooled by false teachers (3:1–21).
   A. Beware of Judaizers (3:1–11).
   B. Beware of perfectionists (3:12–17).
   C. Beware of enemies (3:18–21).
VI. Follow God! (4:1–9).
VII. Thank You! (4:10–20).
VIII. Farewell! (4:21–23).

**Timothy:** *young companion of Paul*

**Epaphroditus:** *a Christian who brought Paul a gift from Phillipi*

## What's Up with Philippians?

**1** *The source of Paul's joy.* In Philippians Paul identifies a number of sources for his joy—sources which can provide joy for us as well. Try reading one or two of the following verses to get a feel for the different sources of Christian joy.

| Paul Finds Joy | Philippians |
|---|---|
| in partnering with others to share the gospel | 1:4 |
| in stimulating others to share the gospel | 1:18 |
| in the prayers of others for him | 1:19 |
| in the unity and love of the Philippians | 2:2 |
| in the privilege of suffering for others | 2:17 |
| in the Lord himself | 3:1; 4:4 |
| in fellow believers he loves | 4:1 |
| in the love others show him | 4:10 |

**2** *Paul's inner conflict over dying (Philippians 1:23).* If the Roman court were to rule against Paul, he would be executed. In facing this reality Paul's inner conflict was not motivated by a fear of death. His inner conflict was between wanting to be with Christ (in heaven) on the one hand, and wanting to be of service to the churches he had planted, on the other.

**3** *Working out salvation isn't easy (Philippians 2:12–13).* Paul encourages the Philippians to *"work out their salvation."* What did Paul mean by this? He meant that people who are saved should act like they're saved. They should do the things required by the God who saved them.

**KEY POINT**

People who are saved should act like it.

**OUTSIDE CONNECTION**

**Pope John Paul III:** *Every Christian—as he explores the historical record of Scripture and tradition and comes to a deep, abiding faith—experiences that Christ is the risen one and that he is therefore the eternally living one. It is a deep, life-changing experience. No true Christian can keep it hidden as a personal matter. For such an encounter with the Living God cries out to be shared—like the light that shines, like the yeast that leavens the whole mass of dough.*[2]

**4** *A description of the confident Christian (Philippians 3:2–11).* Paul warns the Philippians against false Jewish teachers who brag about all they've done for God. Paul quotes his own qualifications and then calls his credentials worthless! What counts is knowing Christ. Paul's confidence is based on the fact that Christ's resurrection power can be experienced right now by believers who want to know Jesus better.

**5** *Freedom from anxiety is ours to claim (Philippians 4:6–7).* Paul's obvious sense of joy seems strangely out of place. Most of us in a similar situation would be worried and anxious. But Paul shares his secret with us: in everything, and with thanksgiving, he presents his requests to God. God floods his heart with indescribable peace. Paul has turned his problems over to the Lord, and he doesn't think about them anymore.

How can this be? Paul says *"I can do everything through him who gives me strength"* (Philippians 4:13). Circumstances have no power over Paul. God gives the strength needed to do whatever needs to be done. Guess what . . . we can be just like Paul!

 **COLOSSIANS**

### . . . God in daily life

| WHO | The apostle Paul |
| WHERE | wrote this letter |
| WHERE | from prison to Christians in Colosse |
| WHEN | about A.D. 62 |
| WHY | to clear up their confusion created by false teachers. |

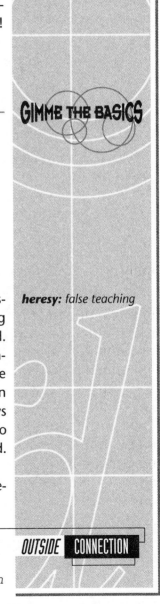

GIMME THE BASICS

 **GOD IS HERE**

Part of Colossians is about a **heresy** that confused early Christians. Some people argued that all physical matter—anything you could touch—was evil. Only what was spiritual was good. Paul pointed out that if this were true, God could have nothing to do with the whole universe. What's more, it would be impossible for God to come in human form, which would mean Jesus was not God. According to this heresy, it also follows that what Christians do in their daily lives has nothing to do with spirituality, for daily life is conducted in the material world. In short, these people were mixed up!

Paul's letter to the Colossians confronts this heresy and presents Jesus Christ as God come in the flesh.

**heresy:** *false teaching*

**Duffy Robbins:** *When we don't have any set standard, we tend to get squeezed into the world's mold—we start to conform to whatever people around us say is right. We begin*

OUTSIDE CONNECTION

to have our path directed by whoever is the most persuasive at any given time.[3]

> **Bible Summary: Colossians**
>
> Curtis Vaughn gives some cool insight into the false teachings that Paul attacks in Colossians. Here's a breakdown of what he says:
>
> - These theories "professed to be a 'philosophy,' but Paul, refusing to recognize it as genuine, called it a 'hollow and deceptive philosophy' (Colossians 2:8)."
> - These theories "placed too much emphasis on ritual circumcision, dietary laws, and the observance of holy days." Read Colossians 2:11, 14, 16–17.
> - According to the false teachers, Christ was only one of many unseen powers that needed to be "placated and worshiped." See Colossians 2:15, 18–19.
>
> To counter this false teaching, Paul presents a powerful portrait of Jesus Christ and his work on our behalf. He also offers an appealing description of the life by which Christians can honor him.

## What's Up with Colossians?

**1** *Paul shows them how to grow (Colossians 1:9–11).* Paul's prayer outlines a step-by-step plan for anyone who wants to grow spiritually and deepen his or her personal relationship with God. It's awesome, and you might want to read it for yourself and see how it applies to your life.

**Edmund P. Clowney:** *Wisdom starts in heaven but works at street level, where we bump shoulders with others. It isn't satisfied with information retrieval: You can't access wisdom by the megabyte. Wisdom is concerned with how we relate to people, to the world, and to God.*[4]

**2** *The real Jesus (Colossians 1:15–23).* The Bible makes absolutely clear who Jesus is. Colossians 1:15–23 is one of the clearest in Scripture. It gives a detailed account of Jesus and his purpose.

**Warren Wiersbe:** *To many people, Jesus Christ is only one of several great religious teachers, with no more authority than*

196

they. He may be prominent, but he is definitely not preeminent. They may not be denying him, but they are dethroning him and robbing him of his rightful place.[5]

**3** *Jesus makes all the difference (Colossians 1:22).* Paul writes, "Now [God] has **reconciled** you by Christ's physical body through death to present you holy in his sight" (Colossians 1:22). God the Son took on a flesh-and-blood human body, and in that body Christ died on the cross. In that act of self-sacrifice, Jesus paid for all our sins, bringing us back into conformity with God by making us holy in his sight.

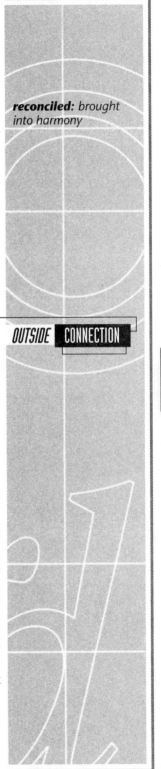

**reconciled:** brought into harmony

**4** *Will the real Christian please stand up? (Colossians 2:20–23; 3:12–17).* Some people have a peculiar idea about what real Christians are like. Colossians 2:20–23 and Colossians 3:12–17 contrast the fake and the real Christian lifestyle.

**Warren Wiersbe:** *People who religiously observe diets and days give an outward semblance of spirituality, but these practices cannot change hearts. Legalism is a popular thing because you can 'measure' your spiritual life—and even brag about it. But this is a far cry from measuring up to Christ.*[6]

OUTSIDE CONNECTION

197

## CHAPTER CHECKUP

1. What is the theme of Ephesians?
2. According to Ephesians 2, what is the relationship between faith and works?
3. What are responsibilities of the husband as "head of the house?"
4. What can a Christian do to gain freedom from anxiety?
5. What heresy is Paul combating in Colossians?
6. What passage in Colossians makes it absolutely clear that Jesus is God?
7. What are two characteristics of "fake" Christians? What are two characteristics of "real" Christians?

## CRASH COURSE

▶ While imprisoned in Rome the apostle Paul wrote letters of instruction to several churches he founded.

▶ In Paul's letter to the Ephesians he contrasts Christianity with "religion," and Christ's living church with buildings.

▶ To create the church God gave spiritual life to persons who were dead to God because of their sins.

▶ Paul urged the Philippians to work out the salvation that God had given them in Christ. Philippians 2 shows how Christ surrendered the benefits of his divine nature to become a human being and die on the cross.

▶ Paul's letter to the Colossians emphasizes the fact that Jesus Christ is God, who took on a real human body. Colossians reminds us that the way we live our daily lives is important to God, and that what we do daily glorifies him.

# Letters to Friends

## 1, 2 TIMOTHY • TITUS • PHILEMON

- Be an Example
- Godly Leaders
- False Teachers
- Good Works
- Slavery

 **LET'S DIVE IN!**

Most of the New Testament letters of Paul were written to churches, but four were written to individuals.

Timothy and Titus were both young leaders who traveled from church to church. Their ministry was to correct false teaching and help people live godly lives. The letters Paul wrote to them are filled with practical advice. The two letters to Timothy and the one letter to Titus are called the "pastoral epistles." The short letter to Philemon has another purpose entirely. In it Paul encourages a well-to-do Christian to welcome back a runaway slave who had become a Christian through Paul's witness.

 **1 TIMOTHY**

### . . . the healthy local church

| | |
|---|---|
| WHO | The apostle Paul |
| WHAT | wrote this letter of advice |
| WHERE | to Timothy, who was on a mission for Paul in Ephesus, |
| WHEN | around A.D. 64 |
| WHY | to correct problems in the church and to restore spiritual health. |

**GIMME THE BASICS**

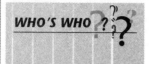
**TIMOTHY:** Timothy had been a member of Paul's missionary team. He was a young man whose father was Greek and whose mother was Jewish. Paul had sent him on several missions (1 Corinthians 4:17; 16:10; Acts 19:22; 2 Corinthians 1:1, 19), and he had not always been successful.

##  LOOKING FOR A CHURCH?

Timothy was shy and unassertive. Despite this Paul treated Timothy as a son and recognized his potential as a leader of the next generation of Christians. At the time Paul wrote, Timothy was in Ephesus, sent there to resolve problems that had emerged in the church and to establish stronger local leadership. It was a challenging mission, and Paul outlines many of the steps Timothy would need to take. Paul's instructions to Timothy paint a picture of the ideal church.

> **Bible Summary: 1 Timothy**
> In this letter Paul describes the strong and healthy church that he expects Timothy to help establish in Ephesus. In addition Paul gives Timothy guidelines to follow.

### What's Up with 1 Timothy?

**sound doctrine:** correct teaching

**1** **Sound doctrine** *(1 Timothy 1:3–11).* Paul states an important reason for why Timothy should confront those who teach false doctrine. God's truth will produce *"love, which comes from a pure heart and a good conscience and a sincere faith"* (1 Timothy 1:5). False doctrine promotes controversy and ungodliness.

In the next paragraphs (1 Timothy 1:12–17) Paul points out that he himself was once the worst of sinners, a persecutor, and a violent man. But the gospel message of the love and grace of God transformed Paul completely.

**Duffy Robbins:** *We live in a culture that has managed to blur the line between falsehood and truth. Whether it's politicians or educators or ministers or bankers or athletes or the kid who sits next to you in English—it's hard to know whom you can trust anymore.*[1]

**2** *One God and one **mediator** between God and man (1 Timothy 2:1–5).* The Bible never apologizes for presenting faith in Christ as the only way that a person can establish a personal relationship with God. The common notion that all religions lead to the same God is dead wrong. Jesus Christ died to pay the price of sin for all human beings, and trust in him is the only avenue that leads to God.

**mediator:** *a go-between who brings parties together*

>>>**CHECK IT OUT:**

1 Timothy 3:1–7

**3** *How to be a leader (1 Timothy 3:1–16).* The list that Timothy makes is interesting. It notes character qualities and not spiritual gifts. The reason is that leaders are to be mature Christians who model the godly Christian character that the Holy Spirit seeks to produce in all believers. We see this clearly when we compare the words Paul used to describe the Christian way of life with those he used to describe the qualifications of a leader.

**4** *Advice for every young believer (1 Timothy 4:12).* Paul's advice to Timothy is ideal for any believer, whether young in years or young in the faith: *"Don't let anyone look down on you because you are young, but set an example for the believers in speech, in life, in love, in faith, and in purity"* (1 Timothy 4:12).

**5** *The widows' corps (1 Timothy 5:3–16).* The New Testament church demonstrated a real concern for widows and the fatherless by providing support for them. Widows couldn't get a job, so Paul advised younger widows to remarry. Those widows with adult children should be supported by their families (1 Timothy 5:16).

The church also entrusted a special ministry to older widows who had demonstrated solid Christian character (1 Timothy 5:9–10). That ministry, described in Titus 2:4–5, was to *"train the younger women to love their husbands and children, to be self-controlled and pure, to be busy at home, to be kind, and to be subject to their husbands, so that no one will malign the Word of God."*

**6** *Don't love money! (1 Timothy 6:3–10, 17–19).* We often hear it said, "money is the root of all evil." That's wrong. Paul wrote *"for the love of money is a root of all kinds of evil"* (1 Timothy 6:10). The person who develops a passion for wealth is vulnerable to *"foolish and harmful desires that plunge men into ruin and destruction"* (1 Timothy 6:9).

Having money can be a good thing—if the wealthy person

Why do you think it's so easy to love possessions instead of loving God?_____

_____

What happens to our relationship with God when we put possessions above him?_____

_____

What is the best way to put money or possessions in their right place?_____

_____

It's so easy to love "stuff," isn't it? It's easy to love your favorite pair of shoes a little too much. It's totally easy to go crazy about your music, too. God doesn't force us to live totally for him. He allows us to learn from our mistakes. So, when we choose to love "things" over loving him, he lovingly watches our mistakes. And he continues to stand watching for when we realize how wrong we are and reach out to him. Got your priorities mixed up? Loving a possession over the giver? Let go and cling to God.

is eager to be rich in good deeds, generous, and willing to share with others. But all too often the rich depend on their money rather than on God, and they become arrogant. Paul's solution is for everyone to develop a passion for godliness, and to be content with having just the basic necessities. A good conscience and a good reputation are worth more than millions.

> **Warren Wiersbe:** *There is always more spiritual wealth to claim from the Lord as we walk with him. As we search the Word of God, we discover more and more of the riches we have in Christ.*[5]

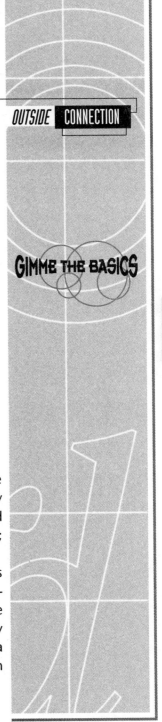

 ## 2 TIMOTHY

### . . . *warning! warning! warning!*

| | |
|---|---|
| WHO | The apostle Paul |
| WHAT | wrote this letter to Timothy |
| WHERE | from prison in Rome |
| WHEN | about A.D. 67 |
| WHY | to warn him about the danger of false teachers who were infiltrating the church. |

 ## LIARS!

Acts ended with Paul under house arrest in Rome. He was there for two years. After being released Paul went on a missionary journey to Spain. However, within five years Paul was arrested again and imprisoned in Rome. This time Paul did not survive; he was executed under the Roman Emperor Nero.

Most believe this was the last letter Paul wrote before his execution. While the Christian community had begun to experience governmental persecution, the apostle was more concerned about those who were corrupting the church by false teaching. In this letter Paul urges Timothy to serve as a good soldier of Jesus Christ and remain committed to the truth revealed by God.

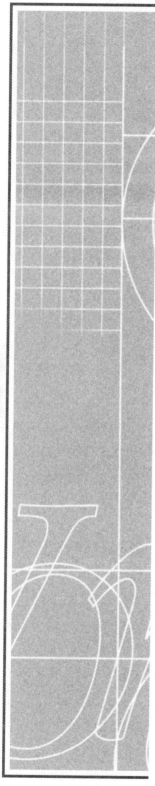

Bible Summary: 2 Timothy

This book is a call to remain faithful to Christ and to sound teaching. It was really important because of the threat posed by false teachers. Highlights of Paul's letter are (1) his statement about the confidence we can have in Scripture, and (2) his description of the attitude we should have when sharing God's truth with others.

## 2 Timothy under a Microscope

   I. Howdy! (2 Timothy 1:1–2).
  II. Be faithful!(1:3–2:13).
     A. Remain true to what you learned as a child (1:3–7).
     B. Be faithful as I have been faithful (1:8–15).
     C. Be faithful as others have been faithful (1:16–18).
     D. Carry with you the faithfulness of noble people (2:1–7).
     E. Be like soldiers (2:4).
     F. Be like athletes (2:5).
     G. Be like hard-working farmers (2:6).
     H. Show Christ the same faithfulness he showed us (2:8–13).
  III. Cling to God's Word (2:14–26).
     A. Handle it correctly (2:8–19).
     B. Prepare yourself (2:20–23).
  IV. Present God's Word the right way (2:24–26).
   V. Get ready for difficult times (3:1–4:8).
     A. There will be people who don't care (3:1–5).
     B. And there will be people who trust false teachers (3:6–9).
  VI. Lead a godly life (3:10–13)
     A. Use the scriptures as your guide (3:14–17).
     B. Keep on preaching! (4:1–5).
     C. I'm outta here! (4:6–8).
  VII. See you soon, I hope (4:9–18).
 VIII. Say hi to my buddies for me (4:19–22).

## What's Up with 2 Timothy?

**1** *The parental role (2 Timothy 1:5).* The apostle Paul traces Timothy's faith back to his mother and grandmother, who passed the flame of faith on to young Timothy when he was a child.

**2** *Opposition to God's truth (2 Timothy 2:24–26).* Paul describes the approach Timothy should take in addressing opposition. He warns against quarreling and prescribes an attitude of kindness that leads to gentle instruction. Why not rely on forceful argument and debate? Paul makes it clear that the real problem is spiritual, not intellectual. God alone can lead those who oppose the gospel to a knowledge of truth.

**3** *Some churches ain't cool (2 Timothy 3:1–5).* Paul looks ahead to terrible times and describes people who are evil and active in the church. He says they will have a *"form of godliness."* They'll go to church, sing the hymns, and congratulate the preacher on his sermon. But true godliness is exhibited in lives that Jesus Christ has transformed. Paul has something definite to say in reference to people who go through the motions without exhibiting God's work in their hearts: *"Have nothing to do with them."*

**4** *The importance of knowing and living Scripture (2 Timothy 3:15–17).* Paul focuses our attention on the holy Scriptures, *"which are able to make you wise for salvation through faith in Christ Jesus."* If we expect God's Word to get into our lives, we must commit ourselves to get into God's Word— regularly!

 **TITUS**

*. . . how to be God's people*

| | |
|---|---|
| WHO | The apostle Paul |
| WHAT | wrote this letter |
| WHERE | to Titus, who was in Crete, |
| WHEN | about A.D. 65 or 66 |
| WHY | to correct problems in the church. |

**TITUS:** Titus was a young leader who instructed the churches once the apostles were gone. Titus successfully completed several missions for Paul, and the apostle had great confidence in his abilities.

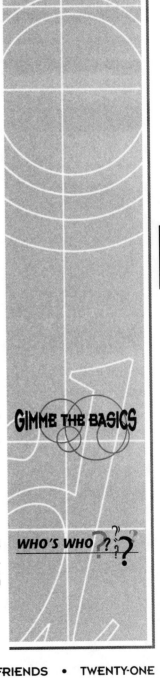

GIMME THE BASICS

WHO'S WHO ???

 **BE EAGER TO DO GOOD**

The Cretans had a questionable reputation. Titus' mission to Crete was to motivate the Christians who had received the gospel to be transformed by God's grace into a people who were eager to *"devote themselves to doing what is good"* (Titus 3:8). When Paul wrote to Titus, he probably had less than two years to live.

> **Bible Summary: Titus**
> Paul's advice to Titus is similar to the advice he gave in his first letter to Timothy. Both were to work to establish a strong local leadership for the church. Both were to concentrate on teaching sound doctrine, with a goal toward producing godly persons whose lives would glorify God. Particularly significant is Paul's emphasis on the importance of good works, to be done by those who have experienced the grace of God.

206

### What's Up with Paul's Letter to Titus?

>>>**CHECK IT OUT:**

Titus 1:5–9;
  1 Timothy 3:1–13

**1** *Appointing elders (Titus 1:5–9).* It was and is vital to the health of a local congregation to be led by a team of godly leaders. Paul charged Titus with appointing these leaders, which are called elders, overseers, or bishops interchangeably throughout the New Testament.

**2** *Teaching that jives with sound doctrine (Titus 2:1–15).* Titus 2 says teaching is encouraging a lifestyle that fits with the truth contained in God's Word.

How should committed people live? Paul says they should live with self-control, reverence, integrity, and uprightness, while warning against slander, addiction to alcohol, and anything that would give others anything bad to say about believers. When Christians show that they can be fully trusted, they *"will make the teaching about God our Savior"* attractive.

**3** *Emphasizing the transforming moral power of grace (Titus 2:11–14).* These verses are among the most powerful in the New Testament: *"For the grace of God that brings salvation has appeared to all men. It teaches us to say 'No' to ungodliness*

LEARN THE WORD • THE BIBLE FOR TEENS

and worldly passions, and to live self-controlled, upright and godly lives in this present age, while we wait for the blessed hope—the glorious appearing of our great God and Savior, Jesus Christ, who gave himself for us to redeem us from all wickedness and to purify for himself a people that are his very own, eager to do what is good" (Titus 2:11–14).

**4** *Gettin' renewed (Titus 3:3–8).* Paul reminds Titus that God has given his Spirit to those who have been **justified** by faith in Christ. Paul urges Titus to stress this truth because the Spirit's presence is the basis for all Christian living, and those who recognize his presence are to be *"careful to devote themselves to doing what is good."* Faith in Jesus changes human beings—and that change is to be expressed in our daily lives.

 **PHILEMON**

### . . . pleading for a runaway slave

| | |
|---|---|
| WHO | The apostle Paul |
| WHAT | wrote this letter to Philemon |
| WHERE | in Rome |
| WHEN | during his first imprisonment |
| WHY | to plead the case of a runaway slave who had been converted. |

**OUTSIDE CONNECTION**

**justified:** *pronounced "not guilty" of sins which Jesus' death paid for*

**>>>CHECK IT OUT:**

Ephesians 2:1–10

**OUTSIDE CONNECTION**

**GIMME THE BASICS**

207

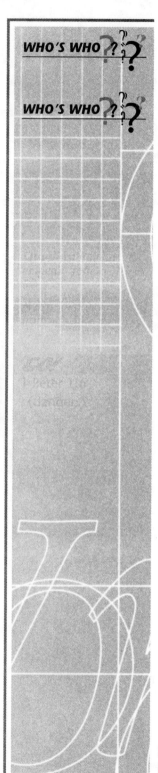

**WHO'S WHO**

**PHILEMON:** Philemon was a wealthy Christian who had been converted under Paul's ministry. Like other wealthy men in the Roman Empire, Philemon owned slaves.

**WHO'S WHO**

**ONESIMUS:** Onesimus had been a slave of Philemon. Apparently he stole from his master and ran away to Rome, where he met Paul and became a Christian. Tradition reports that Onesimus became the bishop of Ephesus in the second century.

 **FORGIVE AND PRESS ON**

Onesimus stole money from his master, Philemon, and ran away to Rome, where he met Paul and became a Christian. Paul sent him back with this letter that reminds Philemon of their close friendship and urges him to welcome Onesimus back. Paul offers to pay Philemon back for any loss due to Onesimus's past actions and delicately reminds Philemon that he owes his salvation to Paul's ministry.

> **Bible Summary: Philemon**
> This one-chapter letter is the briefest of the New Testament epistles. After a typical greeting and prayer Paul pleads for his new "son" in the faith, Onesimus.

### Philemon under the Microscope

I. Greetings! (Philemon 1–3).
II. I've been praying for you (4–7).
III. I have a request for you concerning Onesimus (8).
   A. He's a new Christian (9–11).
   B. I'm sending Onesimus back to you (12–14).
   C. He is a slave, but he is also a brother in Christ (15–16).
IV. *Puuuulease* welcome Onesimus!
V. Welcome him as you would welcome me (17–21).
VI. I hope to visit soon (22).
VII. Farewell, my friend (23–25).

### Brothers in Christ

In the first-century Roman Empire, over 20 percent of the population were slaves.

The New Testament does not launch a crusade against the evil of slavery. But Christianity did introduce a new principle, reflected in this letter and others. Slaves and masters alike became believers, and each was urged to show love and concern for the other. In a household where both were believers, they were to treat each other as brothers in Christ.

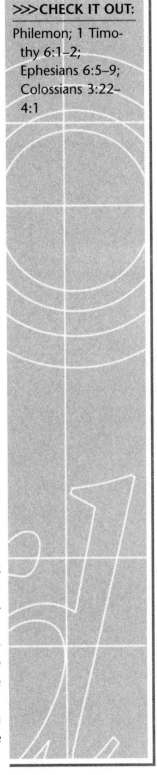

>>>CHECK IT OUT:

Philemon; 1 Timothy 6:1–2;
Ephesians 6:5–9;
Colossians 3:22–4:1

## CHApTeR cHeCkUp

1. Which three of Paul's four personal letters are called pastoral letters?
2. What ministry did the early church have for widows?
3. How would you correct the quote, "Money is the root of all evil?"
4. What is involved in Christian teaching besides communicating biblical truths?
5. The one who has been justified by faith will express that by devoting oneself to what?
6. What was the change in the relationship between Philemon and Onesimus that Paul relied on to move Philemon to welcome back his runaway slave?

### CRASH COURSE

▶ Paul wrote four personal letters to individuals rather than to churches.
▶ Paul's first letter to Timothy urged him to be an example of the truths he taught. One of the most important tasks in strengthening a church was to see to it that the congregation had godly leaders.
▶ Paul's second letter to Timothy is probably the last of his epistles, written just before his execution. In it Paul warns Timothy against false teachers, and stresses the importance of teaching and living God's Word.
▶ Paul's letter to Titus emphasizes the importance of performing good works. Paul reminds Titus that God's grace brings personal rebirth and renewal. Good works are the product of saving grace.
▶ Paul's letter to Philemon illustrates how Christian faith bridged the gap between slave and slave owner in the Roman world.

# Defining Jesus

## HEBREWS

CHAPTER CAPTURE

- New Covenant
- God's Son
- High Priest
- Perfect Sacrifice
- Faith and Discipline

 **LET'S DIVE IN!**

Most of the New Testament epistles were written to gentile churches. But the letter called *Hebrews* was written specifically to Jews who had accepted Jesus as Lord and Savior. They often felt a deep affection for the way of life they had known from birth, and sometimes wondered if they had been right in committing themselves to Christ. The writer of this powerful letter understands their feelings, and tries to show them how everything in the Old Testament points toward Christ.

 **HEBREWS**

*. . . Christ is the best!*

| | |
|---|---|
| WHO | An unknown author |
| WHAT | compared Old and New Testament revelations |
| WHERE | to Hebrew Christians everywhere |
| WHEN | before A.D. 70 |
| WHY | to demonstrate the superiority of Christ. |

**GIMME THE BASICS**

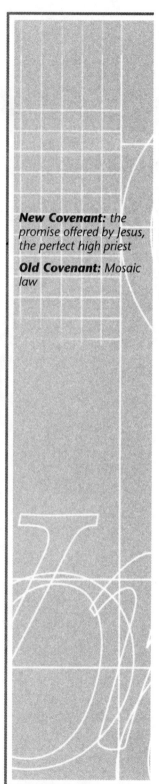

 ## A NEW COVENANT FOR ALL

In the beginning Christianity was a Jewish movement. But within a few decades the church became mostly gentile, and Jews who believed in Christ were cut off from the synagogue and the temple (the places they worshiped). These and other pressures led some Jewish Christians to wonder whether they should return to their roots.

The writer of Hebrews tried to resolve their doubts. He saw clearly that Jesus was the fulfillment of all the Old Testament promises. He saw that the **New Covenant** Christ instituted on the cross is tons better than the **Old Covenant** Moses introduced at Mount Sinai. The writer of Hebrews tries to show the superiority of Jesus and the awesome benefits of a personal relationship with the living Savior.

**New Covenant:** *the promise offered by Jesus, the perfect high priest*

**Old Covenant:** *Mosaic law*

> ### Bible Summary: Hebrews
> Hebrews compares Old and New Testament revelations point by point. The Old Testament is divine revelation, which offered great benefits to Israel as God's special people. But the New Testament is a superior revelation, and its benefits are not only superior; they are available to all who believe in Jesus.

### Hebrews under a Microscope

I. Jesus is the Living Word (Hebrews 1:1–4:13).
   A. He's the ultimate revelation (1:1–14).
   B. So, don't run from him, okay? (2:1–4).
   C. He's the source of salvation (2:5–18).
   D. He's superior to Moses (3:1–6).
   E. You *need* to respond to him (3:7–4:13).
II. Jesus is our high priest (4:14–8:13).
   A. Jesus can relate to us because he was human (4:14–5:10).
   B. Grow up! (5:11–6:20).
   C. Jesus is the greatest priest ever! (7:1–28).
   D. The New Covenant replaces the Old Covenant (8:1–13).
III. Jesus was the perfect sacrifice (9:1–10:39).
   A. His sacrifice cleanses us (9:1–28).
   B. His sacrifice removes sin (10:1–18).
   C. Don't turn from him, okay? Really! (10:19–39).
IV. Be a part of Jesus' ministry (11:1–12:29).

A. Faith has always been important and still is (11:1–40).

B. Hardship is God's discipline (12:1–13).

C. Don't miss God's grace (12:14–29).

V. Hang in there! (13:1–21).

VI. Farewell! (13:22–25).

 HE'S GOD'S SON

**Bible Summary: Hebrews 1:1–4:13**

In the past God's revelation was transmitted in various ways, but now he has spoken through his Son. The Son, Jesus, is fully God and thus even greater than angels. It would be dumb to drift away from truth that is revealed by Jesus. Our destiny depends on our link with Jesus, who became human to die for our sins, to free us from Satan's power, and to lift us with him far above the angels!

>>>CHECK IT OUT:

Hebrews 1:1–4:13

### What's Up with Hebrews 1–4?

**1** *Jesus' I.D.? (1:1–3).* The writer begins by affirming Jesus' identity as God's Son, and by making it clear what this title means. Jesus is identical with God, so that when we see Jesus, we see exactly what God is like. It is important to be completely clear about the identity of Jesus. The fact that Jesus Christ is **God incarnate** is the central and foundational truth on which the New Testament rests.

*God incarnate: God in human form*

**2** *Jesus' superiority to angels (Hebrews 1:5–14).* The writer quotes seven Old Testament passages that establish the superiority of Jesus to angels. Jewish tradition held that angels served as mediators when God gave the law to Moses. The active involvement of angels made the law even more binding. But the new revelation was given personally by God's Son, who is superior to angels.

**3** *Warning against drifting (Hebrews 2:1–4).* To warn of the danger involved in drifting back to Judaism, the writer presents the image of a ship drifting away from its **moorings**. His readers were familiar with the danger of disobeying God's

*moorings: places where boats are anchored*

213

law. It was much more dangerous to ignore a salvation announced by the Lord himself!

**Billy Graham:** *I have in many ways failed ... I haven't lived a life of devotion, meditation, and prayer. I've allowed the world to creep into my life way too much.*[1]

**atonement:** satisfying God's demand that sin be paid for

**4** *Jesus is the source of man's salvation (Hebrews 2:5–18).* Jesus *"shared our humanity"* to save us in the only way possible—by making **atonement** for our sins. Jesus not only reveals God, but through his suffering he brings many people into the kingdom of God (Hebrews 2:10).

**5** *Jesus is greater than Moses (Hebrews 3:1–6).* No one was more revered than Moses in Judaism. Demonstrating that Christ is greater than Moses was a powerful argument for the superiority of Christianity.

**innate:** existing within someone from birth

**Leon Morris:** *Moses was no more than a member—even though a very distinguished member—of the household. He was essentially one with all the others. Christ has an innate superiority. He is the Son and as such is 'over' the household.*[2]

>>> **CHECK IT OUT:**

Numbers 13:26–14:35

**6** *Warning against unbelief (Hebrews 3:7–4:13).* The writer looks back to an incident recorded in Numbers. Through Moses God told the Israelites to enter Canaan, but the people refused. As a result, the whole generation was doomed to wander in the wilderness for forty years until all its adult members had died. This was all because when God spoke to the people, they hardened their hearts, refused to trust him, and disobeyed.

>>> **CHECK IT OUT:**

Hebrews 4:1–13

**7** *Take a break! (Hebrews 4:1–13).* The writer talks a lot about the importance of rest in the life of the believer. When a person fully trusts Jesus, he or she discovers that Christ has, and in fact is, the answer for all the needs of the heart. Knowing this, the believer is free to rest in God's loving care.

**F. F. Bruce:** *The moral must have been plain enough to the recipients of the epistle. For they too had experienced the redeeming power of God; they too had the promise of the* *homeland of the faithful to look forward to; but one thing could prevent them from realizing the promise, just as it had prevented the mass of the Israelites who left Egypt from entering Canaan—and that one thing was unbelief.*[2]

## HE'S OUR HIGH PRIEST

**Bible Summary: Hebrews 4:14–8:43**

The priests of the Old Testament era were **intermediaries** between God and man, offering the sacrifices which enabled worshipers to approach Israel's holy God. But the high priest alone had the privilege of making the annual sacrifice that atoned for all the people's sins. Jesus is the ideal high priest. After pausing to warn his readers again, the writer continues to explore the superiority of Jesus' priesthood.

### What's Up with Hebrews 4:14–8:43?

**MELCHIZEDEK:** At the time of Abraham, Melchizedek was both king of Jerusalem and a priest. Psalm 110:4 announced that God's Son would be a priest like Melchizedek. After Abraham's victory over some marauding kings (Genesis 14), Melchizedek blessed Abraham, and Abraham gave a tenth of what he had to this priest and king.

**1** *Jesus cares (Hebrews 4:14–5:10).* Jesus lived among us as a human being and experienced the weaknesses that we experience. We can appeal to Jesus with complete confidence that he will hear us. While Jesus was ordained to his priesthood by God, it was his obedient life as a human being that **perfected** him for his high priestly role.

**2** *Grow up! (Hebrews 5:11–6:12).* The Hebrew Christians' failure to commit fully to Jesus had stunted their spiritual growth. The foundation had been laid, and they were to build their lives on that foundation, but they failed to do so.

*Josh McDowell: Becoming a Christian without living your faith every moment of every day is, well, absurd. It's ludicrous. It's like getting married and not accompanying your*

**intermediaries:** *go-betweens or mediators*

>>>**CHECK IT OUT:**
Hebrews 4:14–8:13

**WHO'S WHO ???**

>>>**CHECK IT OUT:**
Hebrews 5:1–10

**perfected:** *not made him better, but equipped him*

>>>**CHECK IT OUT:**
Hebrews 6:1–12

*OUTSIDE* **CONNECTION**

spouse on the honeymoon. Love isn't supposed to happen like that. You are designed to enjoy your identity as a newly-wed. Faith isn't supposed to happen like that. You are designed to enjoy your identity as God's child.[4]

**3** *God's promises are an anchor for the soul (Hebrews 6:13–20).* The writer reminds his readers that God has done everything possible to make his purpose clear. Because there is nothing greater to swear by, God swore by himself. Therefore we can believe his promise to take care of us Christians. *"We have this hope as an anchor for the soul, firm and secure"* (Hebrews 6:19).

**4** *The superiority of Jesus' priesthood (Hebrews 7:1–28).* Returning to the theme of Christ's priesthood, the writer points out the differences between Jesus as high priest with the priests of the Old Testament. Jesus' priesthood is superior to that of Old Testament priests.

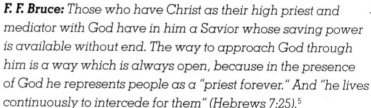

**F. F. Bruce:** *Those who have Christ as their high priest and mediator with God have in him a Savior whose saving power is available without end. The way to approach God through him is a way which is always open, because in the presence of God he represents people as a "priest forever." And "he lives continuously to intercede for them"* (Hebrews 7:25).[5]

**5** *Jesus' priesthood (Hebrews 8:1–13).* Earlier the writer of Hebrews noted that *"where there is a change of the priesthood there must also be a change of the law"* (Hebrews 7:12). Each element of Old Testament religion—law, sacrifices, priesthood, worship—was linked to form a balanced whole. Jesus was the destination to which Old Testament religion pointed.

The Old Testament contains the promise that God would one day replace the Old Covenant with a New Covenant. With the death and resurrection of Christ, God formed the New Covenant with Christ as our high priest; the New Covenant is now in effect. The law God wrote in stone is now being written on the living hearts of believers. In other words, the Holy Spirit guides and directs us.

This doesn't mean we should throw all of Old Testament

law in the trash. For example, we definitely should keep the Ten Commandments. But the New Covenant did put an end to the laws that had to do with rituals and made other laws more clear.

**Kay Arthur:** *Man can be right with God! Righteousness is more than goodness; it is right standing with God. Righteous means to be straight. It is to do what God says is right, to live according to his standards. But righteousness in man requires a new heart. And man can have a new heart! "I will put my law within them, and on their heart I will write it . . . for I will forgive their iniquity, and their sin I will remember no more" (Jeremiah 32:40).[6]*

*OUTSIDE* CONNECTION

 ## THE PERFECT SACRIFICE

**Bible Summary: Hebrews 9:1–10:39**

The Old Testament tells about an earthly sanctuary where priests offered sacrifices. While these sacrifices indicated cleansing was necessary, they were not by themselves capable of purifying people totally. God commanded them to be repeated over and over again, which shows how ineffective they really were. But Jesus offered himself as a sacrifice, not in an earthly temple but in heaven itself.

The sacrifices of the Old Covenant were reminders of the fact that human beings are sinners. The once-and-for-all sacrifice of Jesus is evidence that our sins truly have been forgiven. Because of Jesus there is no longer any sacrifice for sin.

>>>CHECK IT OUT:

Hebrews 9:1–10:39

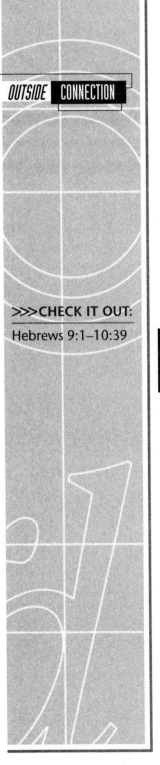

### What's Up with Hebrews 9:1–10:39?

1 *Significance of the earthly sanctuary (Hebrews 9:1–10).* The writer points out that every aspect of Old Testament religion had symbolic significance. For instance, the fact that the high priest could only enter the inner room of the tabernacle or temple, the Holy of Holies, once a year, and then only with a sacrifice, showed that people had no direct access to God under the old system. The sacrifices offered there were unable to *"clear the conscience"* of the worshiper.

>>>CHECK IT OUT:

Hebrews 9:11–28

**2** *The power of the blood of Christ (Hebrews 9:11–14).* Unlike Old Testament animal sacrifices, Christ's blood can *"cleanse our consciences from dead works, so that we may serve the living God"* (Hebrews 9:14). Christians are no longer held in the deadly grip of past sins; forgiveness sets the believer free to serve God.

**3** *Predicting Christ's death (Hebrews 9:15–28).* The Old Covenant required blood to be shed if sins were to be forgiven and if people were to be purified. All of the Old Testament sacrifices pointed toward the one ultimate sacrifice Jesus would make on Calvary, shedding his blood to take away our sins.

**4** *The finality of Christ's sacrifice (Hebrews 10:1–18).* The writer keeps the focus on the fact that Jesus needed to offer only the one sacrifice, for *"we have been made holy through the sacrifice of the body of Jesus Christ once for all"* (Hebrews 10:10). The fact that Jesus offered only one sacrifice is proof that we have been forgiven.

**5** *A warning against turning away from God (Hebrews 10:19–39).* The writer showed what a wonderful salvation God provided in Christ. The appropriate response to this is to accept him and encourage other believers to do good things (Hebrews 10:24). To deliberately turn one's back on Jesus would be treating Christ's blood as an *"unholy thing"* and would be an insult to the Holy Spirit.

---

**Bible Summary: Hebrews 11–13**

By this point in the epistle, the readers understand why life under the New Covenant is superior to life under the Old; at every point the salvation Jesus provides is superior! The writer then goes on to show that New Covenant blessings are accessed by faith, and that God will continue to discipline his children that they might share his holiness.

---

>>>CHECK IT OUT:

Hebrews 11:1–12:29

**faith:** *a trust in God that moves a person to respond to his Word*

**Old Testament saints:** *true believers in God who lived before the death of Christ*

### What's Up with Hebrews 11–13?

**1** *The importance of faith (Hebrews 11:1–40).* It was **faith**— the conviction that God exists and that he rewards those who seek him—that enabled **Old Testament saints** to accomplish the things for which we honor them.

**Michael Yaconelli:** *Curiosity requires courage. You must be willing to ask questions even when they threaten everyone around you. Faith is more than believing; it is an act of courage, a bold grasping of God's truth. Faith is a wrestling match with God, an intense struggle with truth in an attempt to squeeze every bit of knowledge out of it.*[7]

*OUTSIDE* **CONNECTION**

>>>**CHECK IT OUT:**

Hebrews 11:1–31

**2** *Jesus is our example (Hebrews 12:1–3).* Jesus is not only the object of our faith. Because he is the supreme example of one who lived by faith, he is also our inspiration.

**3** *Living through tough times (Hebrews 12:4–13).* The writer encourages his readers—including us—to maintain a healthy perspective on difficult times. These are experiences provided by God himself as discipline. They're examples of how much God loves us.

**4** *Don't miss the grace! (Hebrews 12:14–28).* The writer contrasts Mount Sinai, representing the Old Covenant of law, with Mount Zion, representing the gospel of grace.

**219**

---

Do you feel it's possible to accomplish great things for God at your age? Explain._____

**Your Move**

_____

What prevents you from doing awesome things for God?_____

_____

Why is it important to be a person who has great faith?_____

_____

You want to accomplish great things for God, right? It feels impossible sometimes, doesn't it? Maybe you fight messages like "You're too young" or "You're not talented enough." But look, God has called you to do something for him. His call might be to discover a cure for a fatal disease. Or, it might be to be a pastor. What's the secret? Obey God. When you hear him call, do what he says. That's the secret to great faith.

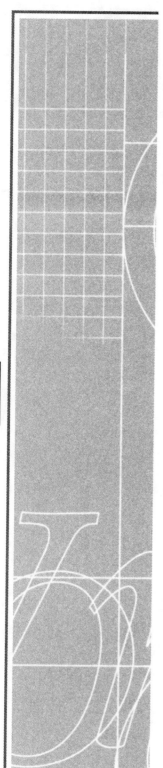

The sight at Mount Sinai was terrifying and it spoke of judgment. The view at Mount Zion is one of blessing. If anyone refuses God's offer of grace and instead turns back to the law, he will not escape the wrath of God.

**5** *Concluding encouragement (Hebrews 13:1–21).* The Book of Hebrews closes with a variety of brief encouragements to godly living, and with one of the most beautiful benedictions to be found in Scripture.

## CHAPTER cHECKUp

1. Who was Hebrews written to?
2. Why did the author write this book?
3. In what ways is Jesus the best high priest?
4. What does the New Covenant do for believers that the Old Covenant could not do?
5. Why is it significant that Jesus offered only one sacrifice for sins?
6. What does Hebrews 11 explore the significance of?
7. How are hardships evidence of the love of God?

### CRASH COURSE

▶ Jesus, the Son of God, brought humankind God's final revelation.
▶ As God's Son, Jesus is superior to angels and to Moses, so the revelation he brought deserves our fullest attention.
▶ Jesus has been ordained by God as our high priest. Because he lives forever he can save everyone who comes to God through him.
▶ Jesus offered his own blood to God as a sacrifice for sins.
▶ Jesus' one sacrifice cleanses believers and guarantees their forgiveness.
▶ Jesus' death initiated the promised New Covenant, not only promising forgiveness but also the inner transformation of believers.
▶ Believers need faith; it helps them accomplish great things.

# Practical Stuff

## JAMES • 1, 2 PETER
## 1, 2 AND 3 JOHN • JUDE

**CHAPTER CAPTURE**

- Practical Advice
- Suffering and Persecution
- False Teachers
- Importance of Love

221

 **LET'S DIVE IN!**

In the past few chapters we've learned a lot about Paul's letters. Other people wrote letters to some of the first-century churches too—people like Peter and John, who were apostles, and Jesus' half brothers James and Jude, who were leaders in the church. Each writer had a special reason for writing, and each letter makes a definite contribution to our understanding of Christian faith and life.

 **JAMES**

### . . . got faith?

| | |
|---|---|
| WHO | James |
| WHAT | wrote this letter to Jewish Christians in the Middle East |
| WHERE | in Jerusalem |
| WHEN | around A.D. 48 |
| WHY | to encourage believers to have faith in Christ. |

**GIMME THE BASICS**

**>>> CHECK IT OUT:**

Acts 15:13–21;
Galatians 1:19

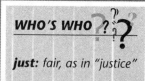

WHO'S WHO

**just:** *fair, as in "justice"*

>>> CHECK IT OUT:

James 2:14–26

**superficial:** *shallow, fake*

**creed:** *an accepted system of religious or other belief*

222

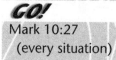

**GO!**
Mark 10:27
(every situation)

**JAMES:** James was a half brother of Jesus. He became a leader of the church in Jerusalem. Tradition portrays him as a man of prayer, whose nickname was "the **Just**."

 YOU GOTTA HAVE FAITH

James is probably the earliest of the New Testament epistles. James, a pastor, was very concerned that Christians put their faith into practice in their daily lives. James pointed out the differences between **superficial** faith and faith that involves both trust in and commitment to Jesus as Lord. James knew how important it is that Christians live out their faith in actions.

> **Bible Summary: James**
> This letter urges readers to pay attention to how faith is expressed in daily life. Writing within fifteen years or so of Christ's resurrection, James is concerned that people see the difference between **creeds** and faith that is lived out day to day. This brief letter mentions faith even more than Paul's letter to the Galatians!

### What's Up with the Book of James?

James is filled with insights for Christians who want to honor the Lord by the way they live. Here are some highlights.

**1** *The source of temptation (James 1:13–15).* Do you ever feel like blaming God when you're tempted? Give it up. James says God never tempts anyone. The pull we feel toward sin comes from within us, not from the situation. In fact, God only gives good gifts. James's point is that <u>every situation</u> in which God places us is intended to bless us, not to trip us up. Harm comes only when we give into the inner pull toward sin. When we respond in a godly way, we're blessed, which is what God intended all along.

**2** *Faith that counts (James 2:14–26).* James says faith that does not produce right actions is false . . . and dead!
James teaches that Abraham's faith did produce right actions. We call Abraham righteous because he was obedient. He did

right because God had actually worked within him to make him righteous! James is speaking of two kinds of faith: superficial faith that doesn't produce right actions and saving faith, the kind Abraham had, that does produce right actions. James teaches that we should not claim to have saving faith unless we back up our claim with actions that naturally come from such faith. Saving faith is not completed until it is acted out.

**Leon Morris:** *The kind of faith [James] objects to is the kind of faith the devils have (James 2:19). They believe in God, but that does nothing more than produce a shudder. A faith that does not transform the believer so that his life is given over to doing good works is not faith as James understands it. That is dead faith.*[1]

**3** *All about prayer (James 4:1–3).* James has a practical approach to life, and it's revealed in two statements about prayer. He says that some people go about getting what they want the wrong way. He writes *"you do not have, because you do not ask God" (James 4:2).* The Christian life is to be one of dependence on the Lord. But we shouldn't approach prayer as a magic lamp. The person who prays in Jesus' name should seek from God what Jesus sought—the Father's will, and the privilege of serving others.

**C. S. Lewis:** *When the event you prayed for occurs your prayer has always contributed to it. When the opposite event occurs your prayer has never been ignored; it has been considered and refused, for your ultimate good and the good of the whole universe.*[2]

God answers each prayer, but sometimes he says no.

 **1 PETER**

*. . . following Jesus' example*

| | |
|---|---|
| WHO | The apostle Peter |
| WHAT | wrote this letter |
| WHERE | from Rome to Christians everywhere |
| WHEN | about A.D. 64 or 65 |
| WHY | urging Christians to follow Jesus' example and live holy lives. |

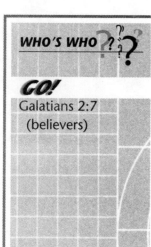

## WHO'S WHO

**GO!**
Galatians 2:7
(believers)

*Claudius: Roman emperor from* A.D. *41–54*

*Nero: Roman emperor from* A.D. *54–68*

**GO!**
1 Peter 1:6
(dangers)

**PETER:** The apostle Peter had been Jesus' leading disciple from the beginning. After Jesus' resurrection, Peter preached the first gospel sermons and developed a special ministry to Jewish <u>believers</u>. He and Paul were both executed in Rome under the Emperor Nero.

 ## AND YOU THINK YOU HAVE IT BAD!

Thirty years after the resurrection of Jesus, Christianity had spread throughout the Roman Empire. By this time it was seen as distinct from Judaism, so the Roman government viewed it as a foreign, illegal religion. Emperor **Claudius** had been intent on restoring traditional Roman religion, and now a half-mad **Nero** was in power. Nero would torture and kill thousands of believers in the city of Rome, and the decades ahead would hold great suffering for those who identified themselves with Jesus and his people.

Peter was well aware of the <u>dangers</u> that lay ahead and his letter, sent to all Christians scattered throughout the empire, was a call to holiness as well as an attempt to help his readers better understand the purpose of suffering in the believer's life.

> **Bible Summary: 1 Peter**
> This letter of Peter provides Christians with encouragement in the face of persecution, and reminds them that believers are called to both holiness and suffering. Peter wants his readers to see that God allows suffering. Whether it's a blessing or not depends on how we respond to it.

### What's Up with Peter's First Epistle?

1 *Total joy (1 Peter 1:3–9).* Peter writes about the joy a believer can experience even while suffering *"in all kinds of trials."* He compares our trials to the hot furnaces in which goldsmiths melt precious metal to rid it of impurities. The salvation God provides is real, now and for eternity, which enables us to feel joy despite pain, and this is proof that God truly has saved us!

224

**2** *The significance of Jesus' example (1 Peter 3:8–18).* What about situations where Christians suffer unfairly? Peter says this isn't abnormal. When bad stuff happens, Peter says we should not be scared, remember that Christ is still Lord, and remain positive. When people are amazed that we can remain positive despite being treated unfairly, we're to tell people what the basis for our hope is (see 1 Peter 3:16).

**3** *Suffering as a Christian (1 Peter 4:12–19).* Peter reminds his readers that Christians should not be surprised when hard times come. In a sense suffering enables us to draw closer to Christ. Peter's final word on the topic is good advice. *"So then, those who suffer according to God's will,"* he writes, *"should commit themselves to their faithful Creator and continue to do good"* (1 Peter 4:19).

 **2 PETER**

*. . . watch out for false teachers*

| | |
|---|---|
| WHO | The apostle Peter wrote this letter |
| WHAT | both warning and encouraging Christians |
| WHERE | while in Rome |
| WHEN | just before his death in A.D. 67 or 68 |
| WHY | in view of emerging dangers from false teachers. |

 **EVIL FROM WITHIN**

Near the end of his life Peter became deeply concerned about the future of Christ's church. In his first epistle he wrote about dangers from outsiders who would persecute Christians. In his second epistle Peter writes about dangers from the inside.

**Bible Summary: 2 Peter**
In this short letter Peter addresses two issues that most concerned him.
- He urges believers to concentrate on living productive lives.
- He describes false teachers and what God will do to them eventually.

GIMME THE BASICS

>>>CHECK IT OUT:
2 Peter 1:3–9

## What's Up with 2 Peter?

**1** *The Christian experience (2 Peter 1:3–9).* God has done all that's needed to equip us for life and godliness, by giving us promises that permit us to share in the divine nature itself. But we've got to be active and focus on developing godly character.

**Ron Luce:** *What happened to those days when we did not care how long a worship service lasted? When did we hunger for righteousness more than anything else? What happened to the radical abandonment that characterized our early days in Christ? When was the last time we read our Bible cover to cover. Have we ever done it? Are we giving from the overflow of the well, or are we scraping the bottom to see if there is anything left to give?*[3]

**2** *What's a false teacher? (2 Peter 2:1–22).* Peter emphasizes the fact that God will deal with false teachers. *"The Lord knows how . . . to hold the unrighteous for the day of judgment, while continuing their punishment"* (2 Peter 2:9). Second Peter 2:1–22 is one of three Bible passages that specifies the signs by which false teachers can be recognized.

>>>**CHECK IT OUT:**
2 Peter 3:10–13

**3** *The end motivation (2 Peter 3:1–14).* Peter describes two attitudes that people adopt in response to Christ's promise to come again. The unbeliever makes fun of Christ's return and ignores the history recorded in Scripture. The believer lives a holy and godly life and looks forward to heaven.

**William Law:** *If you attempt to talk with a dying man about sports or business, he is no longer interested. He now sees other things as more important. People who are dying recognize what we often forget, that we are standing on the brink of another world.*[4]

**Kevin Johnson:** *Peter is talking about an attitude of confident faith: You can look forward to the final overthrow of evil—and to an eternal home where God's sweet will is done every day in every way. Faith in those facts should burst from*

226

*your brain into your life: You can live a holy and godly life—spotless, blameless and at peace with God.[5]*

 **1, 2, 3 JOHN**

### . . . how to love and obey

| | |
|---|---|
| WHO | The apostle John |
| WHAT | wrote these letters |
| WHERE | while living in Ephesus |
| WHEN | near the end of the first century |
| WHY | to encourage love for others and obedience to God. |

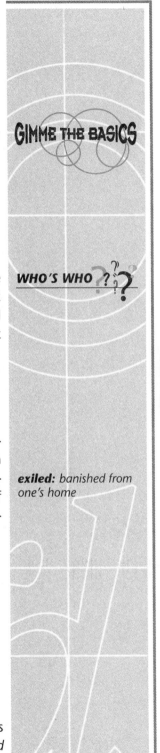

**JOHN:** The apostle John was really close to Jesus during his life on earth. John outlived the other apostles of Jesus and spent most of his life ministering in Asia Minor. These letters, and the Book of Revelation, were written near the end of the first century when John was in his nineties.

**WHO'S WHO ?·?·?**

 **LIGHT, LOVE, AND FAITH**

With the crowning of Emperor Domitian in A.D. 81 the persecution of Christians became state policy. Even though John himself was later **exiled**, the apostle's letters ignore the external threat. John is primarily concerned with the inner life of God's people. He focuses on the need to live in intimate fellowship with God and fellow believers.

***exiled:*** *banished from one's home*

> **Bible Summary: 1, 2, 3 John**
> Each of John's three letters encourages fellowship with the Lord and with other Christians. There are three major themes in John. John wants Christians (1) to live in the light, (2) to live lovingly, and (3) to live by faith.

### What's Up with 1 John?

**1** *Be honest about sin! (1 John 1:8–10).* John tells Christians to be honest with themselves and with God. In saying *"God* is light" with no darkness at all, he reminds us that God sees everything as it really is. The only way to get along with God is to be real, without deceiving ourselves or others.

This is really important when it comes to sin. John says, *"If we claim to be without sin, we deceive ourselves and the truth is not in us"* (1 John 1:8). What are we to do? We need to **confess** our sins—to acknowledge them to God and to ourselves. When we do this, God cleanses us (1 John 1:8–9).

**confess:** to acknowledge or admit

>>>CHECK IT OUT:
1 John 3:18–27;
1 John 4:1–3

228

**OUTSIDE CONNECTION**

**John Wesley:** *He says not, the blood of Christ will cleanse (at the hour of death or in the day of judgment) but it cleanses at the present time.*[6]

2 *Don't love the world (1 John 2:15–17).* Sinful cravings, lust, and bragging about what we have are the results of loving the world more than God. Why is it foolish as well as wrong to adopt the values of human society? John says, *"The world and its desires pass away, but the man who does the will of God lives forever"* (1 John 2:17).

3 *The warning against antichrists (1 John 2:18–23).* John warns his readers against false teachers and others who would lead them astray. How do we avoid these people? By being sensitive to the Holy Spirit within, who provides a built-in spiritual instinct that enables us to distinguish truth from falsehood by a simple objective test. Anyone who denies the divinity of Jesus, who refuses to acknowledge *"that Jesus Christ has come in the flesh"* is a false teacher.

4 *The call to love one another (1 John 4:11–24).* John frequently reminds his readers of the importance of loving one another. God himself is love, so a failure to love fellow Christians is a sign that the believer is out of touch with God.

**OUTSIDE CONNECTION**

**Rachel Scott:** *A friend is someone who can look into your eyes and be able to tell if you're alright or not. . . . A friend is someone who can say something to you without telling them anything and their words hit the spot.*[7]

**OUTSIDE CONNECTION**

**Leon Morris:** *We will never find out what love means if we start from the human end. Only because we have experi-*

enced the love we see in the cross do we love in the distinctively Christian way.[8]

## What about John's Second Letter?

This warm letter (2 John) was written to a woman friend whose family John had come to love (verses 1–3). John is especially pleased that her children are living godly lives (verses 4–6). But John warns against listening to a teacher who denies that in Jesus God became a real human being (verses 7–11). Although John was very old at this time, he was eager to visit this family that had become special to him. There is no substitute for Christian friends in any person's life!

## And How about John's Third Letter?

John expresses best wishes to his friend Gaius (verses 2–4) who has had a ministry in showing hospitality to traveling Christians (verses 5–8). Gaius is one of those humble believers who makes a difference by serving quietly—unlike a local man named Diotrephes who *"loves to be first"*—and whom John will confront when he visits (verses 9–11). Meanwhile, the church is blessed not only to have Gaius, but also a guy named Demetrius who *"does what is good."* John's letter reminds us that being the "big man on campus" doesn't count with God, nor with godly people.

 JUDE

*. . . defend the faith*

| WHO | Jude, a half brother of Jesus, wrote this brief epistle |
|---|---|
| WHAT | about false teachers who were infiltrating the church |
| WHERE | to Christians everywhere |
| WHEN | in the A.D. 80s |
| WHY | to challenge believers to defend the faith. |

>>>CHECK IT OUT:

John 13:34–35

229

GIMME THE BASICS

Why is loving others important for believers?_____

_____

What things make it difficult to love others?_____

_____

What are the benefits to loving others?_____

_____

**GET REAL** Do you have a friend that you have a hard time loving? Are you bullied by a sibling and come close to hating him or her? What's the secret to loving people that are totally unlovable? Here's a hint: Look at them like God does. See them as broken, hurting people. Then, reach out to them. Even if they make fun of you? Yup. Even if their teasing gets worse? You got it. John's words in these passages don't command us to run from people . . . they urge us to love others no matter what.

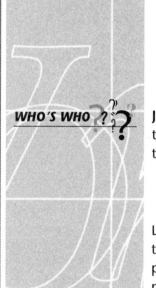

## Bible Summary: Jude

The writer had hoped to write about the glories of salvation, but instead he wound up encouraging his readers to hang in there. Why? Because false teachers were coming into the church, trying to get people to believe lies. So the bulk of Jude's letter is a comparison between false teachers of Jude's day and Old Testament enemies of God, emphasizing the fact that such persons are under the judgment of God.

 **WHO'S WHO** **JUDE:** Early church fathers identify the author of this letter as the half brother of Jesus and brother of James, named in Matthew 13:55 and Mark 6:3.

## ▶▶ SOUNDS JUST LIKE THE CHURCH TODAY

Like Paul, John, and Peter, Jude recognized the danger false teachers posed to the church. Both non-Christian, Jewish, and pagan teachers were active in the first century, busy reinterpreting Christian teachings to fit their own ideas. Jude's letter seems addressed primarily to Jewish Christians. Jude sums up the danger from false teachers and urges believers to stay away from them. Jude closes with advice to believers about how to defeat those who would divide them.

### What's Up with Jude?

Jude's closing advice to his readers is on target for Christians today: *"But you, dear friends, build yourselves up in your most holy faith and pray in the Holy Spirit. Keep yourselves in God's love as you wait for the mercy of our Lord Jesus Christ to bring you to eternal life"* (Jude 1:20–21). We should do that too!

## CHAPTER CHECKUP

1. What are the seven general epistles discussed in this chapter?
2. What is the theme of the Book of James?
3. Why did Peter write about *"all sorts of trials"* that Christians were about to experience?
4. How does the example of Christ's suffering on the cross encourage Christians who suffer unjustly?
5. Why does John warn Christians against deceiving themselves after they sin?
6. Name one test that helps identify false teachers who infiltrate the church.
7. Why does John believe loving our Christian brothers is so important?

### CRASH COURSE

▶ The general epistles in the New Testament include James; 1, 2 Peter; 1, 2, 3 John; Jude; and also Hebrews (covered in the previous chapter).
▶ The epistle of James was the first of the New Testament books to be written. James gives practical advice on how faith in Jesus should be lived.
▶ In Peter's first letter he encourages believers about how to experience persecution, and helps them put suffering in Christian perspective. In Peter's second letter he warns against false teachers, and reminds Christians to live godly lives in view of the coming end of this world.

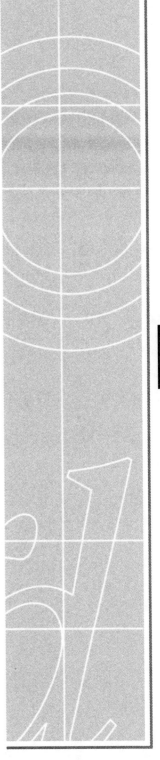

231

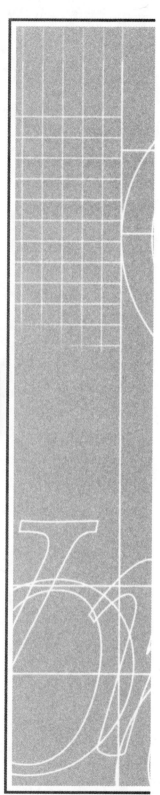

▶ The apostle John wrote three letters that are in the New Testament. In his first letter John emphasizes the importance of loving others and obeying God. In his second letter he encourages a woman whose family he likes. In his third letter he commends his friend Gaius and says he plans to come visit soon.

▶ Jude, a half brother of Jesus, issues an urgent warning against false teachers who reinterpret truths delivered by the apostles.

232

# The End?

## REVELATION

 **LET'S DIVE IN!**

Are you ready for some prophecy?! Alright! You've turned to the right book! The last book of the New Testament, **Revelation**, is a book of prophecy. The events in Revelation's first chapters take place in the past. But most of Revelation is about the future . . . and what will happen at the end of history. The Book of Revelation reminds us that God will one day judge sin, remove evil from his universe, and welcome those who have trusted Jesus as Savior to the new heavens and the new earth that he will create.

*Revelation: disclosure of what was previously unknown*

 **REVELATION**

### . . . stuff that's coming up

| | |
|---|---|
| WHO | The apostle John |
| WHAT | wrote this record of God-given visions |
| WHERE | while exiled on the island of Patmos |
| WHEN | about A.D. 90 |
| WHY | to describe what God will do at the end of history. |

**GIMME THE BASICS**

**predictive prophecy:** *a description of future events*

Much of the Old Testament is known as **predictive prophecy**. In other words, it describes events that will take place in the future. Jesus spoke about the future, and so did writers of the New Testament epistles. But these scattered references did little to fit future events together.

Near the end of the first century, the apostle John was given a vision while he was on the Mediterranean island of Patmos. He saw the resurrected Jesus in his glory, and in a vision he saw history's end. John's description of what he saw helps us to fit earlier prophecies together, and reassures us as well. God truly is in control, and history is moving toward his intended end. When that end comes, God will triumph, and those who have trusted in him will be welcomed to an eternity of blessing and joy.

**>>>CHECK IT OUT:**

Isaiah 65:17–25;
Matthew 24;
2 Peter 3

234

> **Bible Summary: Revelation**
>
> This book can be divided into three main parts: (1) John is given a vision of the risen Christ and is told to write letters to seven churches in Asia Minor; (2) John gets caught up into heaven, and from there he observes terrible punishments that God hurls against the wicked on earth; and (3) the final section of Revelation shows what will happen after Jesus physically returns to earth and describes what eternity holds for both the **lost** and the **saved**.

**lost:** *those who have not trusted Christ*

**saved:** *those who have trusted Christ as Savior and have had their sins forgiven*

 **SEVEN EXAMPLES**

> **Bible Summary: Revelation 1–3**
>
> While on Patmos John was floored by a vision of the risen Christ. Christ dictated letters to seven churches in Asia Minor. Many believe the seven churches are representative either of the spiritual condition of churches from every era, or of the spiritual condition of Christians at different periods in history.

### What's Up with Revelation 1–3?

1 *Jesus shows up (Revelation 1:12–16).* The vision uses symbolic images drawn from the Old Testament to emphasize the divinity of Jesus. John had been close to Jesus while he was on earth. Yet when John saw Jesus in his glory, the apostle *"fell*

*at his feet as though dead"* (Revelation 1:17). The Jesus of history is the eternal God.

**2** God shows John the past, present, and future (Revelation 1:19). Revelation 1:19 says, *"Write, therefore, what you have seen, what is now and what will take place later"* (Revelation 1:19). This verse shows us the different ways John used time in his letter. *"What you have seen"* (past tense) is the vision of Jesus in Revelation 1. *"What is now"* (present tense) refers to the seven churches to whom Jesus will dictate letters (Revelation 2–3). And *"what will take place later"* (future tense) reveals what will happen after the **Church Age** is over (Revelation 4–22).

**3** John writes letters to seven churches (Revelation 2:1–3:22). The seven churches to which the letters are addressed existed in Asia Minor at the time John wrote down what Christ dictated. But the description of the churches, with Christ's warnings and promises, could even apply to churches today.

**Alan F. Johnson:** *Even though the words of Christ refer initially to the first-century churches located in particular places, by the Spirit's continual relevance they transcend that time limitation and speak to all the churches in every generation.*[1]

 **TROUBLE ON THE WAY**

**Bible Summary: Revelation 4–19**
John is taken to heaven, symbolizing the **Rapture** of the church, where he witnesses preparations for really bad judgments about to strike the people left on earth. John does his best to describe what he sees as powerful angels pour out judgment after judgment on a rebellious earth.

During this time of judgment, called the *"Great Tribulation"* or *"the Day of the Lord"* in the Old Testament, Satan gets his troops ready to do battle with God. Satan uses two individuals, the Beast (the Antichrist) and the **False Prophet**, who unite mankind against Israel. Continuous acts of divine judgment destroy the unified religious and political system that the Antichrist establishes. Christ himself returns from heaven with an army of angels and ends the struggle.

>>>**CHECK IT OUT:**

1 Thessalonians 4:13–17

**Church Age:** *from the first century A.D. until Jesus takes Christians to heaven (the Rapture)*

**OUTSIDE CONNECTION**

**Rapture:** *when the church is removed from the earth*

>>>**CHECK IT OUT:**

Revelation 4–19

**False Prophet:** *the second beast of Revelation, it seeks people to follow the Antichrist*

235

# What's Up with Revelation 4–19?

>>>**CHECK IT OUT:**

Revelation 6:12–14

>>>**CHECK IT OUT:**

Revelation 9:20–21

**1** *John uses strange language.* Some people claim Revelation doesn't apply to life here on earth, but it does! John is describing actual events, which will take place here on earth. The difficulty with the language of Revelation is that John was forced to use the vocabulary available to him in the first century.

**2** *The judgments don't work (Revelation 6:15–17).* The nature of the judgments makes it clear that God himself is their source. Even knowing the great day of God's wrath has arrived, the people of earth refuse to repent. They continue in their sins, while trying to call on the mountains to hide them from *"the face of him who sits on the throne and from the wrath of the Lamb!"* (Revelation 6:16).

 **OUTSIDE CONNECTION**

**J. H. Melton:** *The Lord Jesus Christ will either be your Savior or your judge. Your sins will either be judged in Jesus Christ or they will be judged by Jesus Christ. Now he offers his mercy to save you. If you reject his mercy he will judge you in absolute justice and wrath.*[2]

**KEY POINT**

Don't wait to trust Christ until it's too late. Judgment is coming soon.

>>>**CHECK IT OUT:**

Revelation 14:1–5

**3** *The famous 144,000 who convert to Christ (Revelation 7:1–8).* These 144,000 people are Jews, who come from the twelve tribes of Israel. Who are they, and what is their role during this period of terrible tribulation on earth? Well, they're Jews who will convert to Christ during this time. They will witness about him throughout the world.

**OUTSIDE CONNECTION**

**Daymond R. Duck:** *Once God has sealed his 144,000, the whole world will hear his message. Multitudes will believe and be saved. The Antichrist and his False Prophet will be furious and try to stop the revival by forcing new believers to turn away from the faith. They will deny people food and medicine. Executions will be frequent and numerous.*[3]

**4** *There's a party in heaven!* While judgments cause terror for the peoples of earth, John portrays a very different reaction in heaven. There, angels and the saved join in praise of God. Both the judgments and the praise are appropriate, for at last God is acting to establish what is right.

**5** *The end of the Antichrist! (17:1–18:24).* Revelation 17 and 18 are among the most difficult to interpret in Revelation. However, it is clear that the dominant figure—*"Mystery Babylon"*—represents the unification of the Western world under the Antichrist. But the success of this agent of Satan is to be short-lived. All that the Antichrist builds—a one-world religion and a totally materialistic society—soon comes tumbling down.

>>>**CHECK IT OUT:**
Revelation 18:9–24

**6** *Christ wins! (Revelation 19:1–21).* The final scene on earth is that of the Antichrist and his forces gathered to fight Christ, who returns to earth at the head of the armies of heaven. The Antichrist and False Prophet are immediately thrown alive into the **Lake of Fire** (ouch!), and their armies are destroyed.

**Lake of Fire:** *the final destination of Satan and his followers*

**Alan F. Johnson:** *John is showing us the ultimate and swift downfall of these evil powers by the King of kings and Lord of lords. They have met their master in this final and utterly real confrontation.*[4]

OUTSIDE CONNECTION

 **PEACE AT LAST**

Bible Summary: Revelation 20–22
Finally Jesus rules on earth, fulfilling the predictions of the Old Testament prophets. The reign will last for a thousand years (a millennium), during which Satan will be tied up. At the end of the millennium Satan is released and deceives human beings (again) into rebelling against God. This time God responds by putting an end to the universe. Lost human beings are called before God's throne for final judgment, and all those who have not trusted Christ as Savior are sent to the lake of fire. God then creates a new and perfect universe, to be populated by the saved for ever and ever.

>>>**CHECK IT OUT:**
Revelation 20–22

**Duffy Robbins:** *Someday in eternity, we'll all enjoy a big party in the presence of God. We won't need Bibles and we won't need prayers, because we'll be with him. Won't that be something! A party in the throne room of almighty God! I'll guarantee you that nobody is going to sleep through that one!*[5]

OUTSIDE CONNECTION

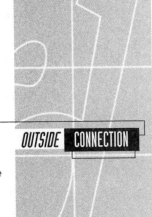

## What's Up with Revelation 20–22?

**Millennium:**
*thousand-year reign of Christ on earth*

**1** The **Millennium** *(Revelation 20:1–6)*. This is the only passage in the Bible that speaks specifically of a thousand-year period. Some have dismissed the idea of a millennial reign of Christ for this reason. However, the Old Testament prophets pictured just such a rule of the Messiah, and Christ's reign on this earth is mentioned dozens of times.

**2** *Satan's doom (Revelation 20:7–10)*. Satan began his existence as a bright and powerful angel, who then rebelled against God and tricked Adam and Eve into joining his side. But from the very beginning Satan's destruction has been something he couldn't avoid.

**3** *God's final judgment of the lost (Revelation 20:11–14)*. John speaks of two books that will be referred to at the final judgment. One book, the book of life, is a record of the deeds of every human being. The other book is called the *"Lamb's book of life,"* or Christ's book of life, where the names of those

238

Why do you think people get excited about heaven?_____ **Your Move**

_____

What do you think heaven will be like?_____

_____

Why did God make heaven?_____

_____

**GET REAL**

Heaven. Think about that word for a moment. Everything we believe as Christians leads us to hope for that day when we'll finally enter God's perfect kingdom. He's got the perfect place waiting for us. So, why does he let us know about it now? Simple. It helps us keep going. Look, being a Christian can be really tough. God wants us to know what's waiting for us so we'll be able to endure all the junk we face here. Are you really discouraged? Are you feeling good? Whatever you face, remember this: You've got another home. There's a better place waiting for you.

who have trusted Christ and whose sins have been paid for are written. Anyone judged on the basis of what he or she has done is condemned to the lake of fire. At that time all will know that hell is not fiction; it's totally real.

**David Hocking:** *Those who are cast into hell are not annihilated as some religious groups teach. They experience torment forever and ever; it is an everlasting fire into which they are cast. Satan deserves it, and the justice of God demands it.*[6]

**OUTSIDE CONNECTION**

**4** *God's new heaven and new earth (Revelation 21:1–22:6).* We can't fully know how wonderful eternity will be until we get there. But these last chapters of the Bible tell us that it will be beyond our imagination.

### What Will Heaven Be Like?

- God himself will be with us.
- God will wipe away every tear.
- There will be no more death, mourning, crying, or pain.
- The glory of the Lord will provide its light.
- Nothing impure will ever enter it.
- No longer will there be any curse.
- The throne of God will be in the city, and we will serve him.
- We will reign forever and ever.

**5** *Jesus is coming soon (Revelation 22:12–21).* Revelation closes with a wonderful promise. Jesus says he is coming. He is coming *soon.* So, if you know Christ, you've got something to look forward to!

## CHAPTER CHECKUP

1. What is the subject of Revelation?
2. What is special about Jesus when John sees him?
3. Will the terrible judgments predicted for history's end cause sinners to repent?
4. Who is the Antichrist and what does he do?

239

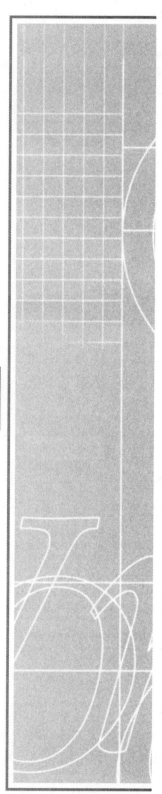

5. What is the Millennium?
6. What is the fate of those who fail to trust Christ in the final judgment?
7. What is the destiny of those who have trusted Christ and whose names have been written in the Lamb's book of life?

**CRASH COURSE**

▶ Much of Revelation is called "predictive prophecy." The prophecy in Revelation reveals what will happen at history's end.

▶ God will bring devastating judgments on those who continue to rebel against him. Satan will give supernatural powers to the Antichrist who will build a one-world political and economic empire.

▶ God will destroy the Antichrist and his forces when Jesus returns personally to set up a thousand-year reign on earth. Satan will lead a final rebellion at the end of Christ's reign and will be sent to the lake of fire. This universe will be dissolved, and the dead will be revived to face God's judgment.

▶ Those who have failed to trust in God during their lives will be judged by their actions, and sent to the lake of fire forever. Those who have trusted in God will be welcomed into a new heaven and earth which God will create, and they will be with him eternally in glory.

# ANSWERS

## CHAPTER 1: HOW IT ALL BEGAN

1. If God did not create and the universe "just happened," life has no meaning or purpose, and death is the end. If an all-knowing, all-loving, all-powerful God did create the universe, then life does have meaning, and we can look forward to living in heaven some day.
2. Human beings are special because we were created in the image of God. (Genesis 1:26–27)
3. The evils in society and our own tendency to sin are a consequence of the fall. (Genesis 4)
4. The fall was the choice of Adam and Eve to disobey God. The fall corrupted human nature and gave all human beings a sinful nature. (Ephesians 2:1–4)
5. The flood tells us that God is a moral judge who will punish sin. (Genesis 6:5–7)

## CHAPTER 2: SETTING THE COURSE

1. God chose Abraham to receive special promises, and Abraham responded to God with faith. (Genesis 15:6)
2. A covenant is a commitment, contract, oath, or treaty. The biblical covenants are commitments made by God. (Hebrews 6:13–20)
3. The Abrahamic Covenant is important because it spells out what God has committed himself to do through Abraham and his descendants. (Genesis 1–3)
4. The Abrahamic Covenant passed to Isaac, Jacob, and to the Jewish people who descended from them. (Genesis 21–50)
5. Faith is important because God will declare those who have true faith to be righteous. (Romans 4: 18–25)

## CHAPTER 3: THE LONG TRIP HOME

1. Moses is important because God used him to deliver the Israelites from slavery, to give Israel his law, and to write the first five books of the Old Testament. (Exodus 3–5)
2. A miracle is an event caused directly by God to accomplish a purpose of his own. There are many miracles in the Old Testament, including the swarm of locusts (Exodus 1:13–14) and the parting of the Red Sea (Exodus 14:21–31).
3. God struck Egypt with a series of plagues that forced Pharaoh to release his Hebrew slaves. (Exodus 7:3)
4. The first four commandments tell us how to have a good relationship with God; the rest are about how to have good relationships with other people. (Exodus 20:1–17)

## CHAPTER 4: EXTREME ADVENTURE!

1. The theme of Leviticus is holiness.
2. Important terms linked with the teaching of Leviticus on sacrifice include guilt, blood, atonement, and forgiven. These are important because they lay the foundation for understanding the meaning of Jesus' death on the cross. (Leviticus 1–5, 16)
3. Ritual laws defined actions that made an Israelite ritually unclean. Moral laws defined acts that were sin (compare Leviticus 11 with Leviticus 18).
4. The Israelites refused to obey God when he commanded them to enter Canaan. (Numbers 14)
5. Love motivated the giving of the law, as God revealed to Israel the way to experience his blessings. Also, love for God is the only motive that will produce true obedience to the law God gave. (Deuteronomy 11)

## CHAPTER 5: CONQUEST AND COLLAPSE

1. The main message of Joshua is that obedience brings victory, and disobedience brings defeat. (Joshua 6–8)
2. The main message of Judges is that commitment to worshiping and obeying God is essential to maintain a just society. (Judges 3:6–15)
3. The judges of Israel were military, political, and religious leaders. They offered the Israelites someone to turn to for moral and spiritual leadership. (Judges 6:1–8)
4. The main message of the Book of Ruth is that godly people can live meaningful lives even in a corrupt society. (Ruth 3)

## CHAPTER 6: A NEW BEGINNING

1. The three key figures in the transition to monarchy are Samuel, Saul, and David.
2. When Samuel was born, Israel was a loose confederation of poverty-stricken tribes oppressed by foreign enemies. (1 Samuel 2:12–4:27)
3. When David died, Israel was a wealthy, powerful nation whose territory had been expanded tenfold. (1 Chronicles 18)
4. The Davidic Covenant established the fact that it would be a descendant of David who would fulfill the promises God had made to Abraham. (2 Samuel 7)
5. A study of David's life teaches the importance of loving God, the vulnerability of the greatest saints to sin, and the willingness of God to forgive those who confess their sins to him. (Psalm 51)

## CHAPTER 7: ISRAEL AT ITS BEST

1. The two kings who ruled Israel during the golden age were David and Solomon. (1 Chronicles–2 Chronicles 10)
2. The golden age was marked by prosperity, military strength, and literary accomplishment. (1 Kings 4:20–34)
3. Books of Bible poetry associated with the golden age are Proverbs, Psalms, Ecclesiastes, and the Song of Songs.
4. The themes of these books are:
   Job: faith's response to suffering (Job 1–2)
   Psalms: personal relationship with God; worship (Psalm 9)
   Proverbs: guidance in making wise and right choices (Proverbs 1:1–6)
   Ecclesiastes: there's no meaning in life apart from a relationship with God (Ecclesiastes 1:1–11)
   Song of Songs: married love (Song of Songs 4)

## CHAPTER 8: THE KINGDOM UP YONDER: ISRAEL

1. All the kings of Israel were evil and maintained the false religious system set up by Jeroboam I. (2 Kings)
2. Jonah and Amos.
3. Jonah's mission to Nineveh was to show God's willingness to withhold punishment of those who would repent. Amos's preaching condemned Israel's false religion and social injustice. (Jonah 4; Amos 4)
4. The "day of the LORD" is any period in which God acts directly to accomplish his plans. (Amos 5:18–27)
5. The sins of Israel which demanded God's judgment included false religion, immorality, and injustice. (Amos 2)

## CHAPTER 9: THE KINGDOM ON THE SOUTH SIDE: JUDAH

1. 2 Kings and 2 Chronicles record the history of Judah after the division of Solomon's kingdom.
2. Godly kings stimulated religious revivals, which permitted God to act for his people. (2 Chronicles 19:20)
3. Pagans turn to occult practices to seek supernatural guidance. God provided his people with prophets through whom he could speak. (Deuteronomy 18:9–22)
4. The true prophet was to be an Israelite who spoke in the name of the Lord, whose message was in harmony with Scripture, and whose predictions came true. (Deuteronomy 18:19–22)
5. Joel, plague of locusts (Joel 1); Obadiah, judgment on Edom (Obadiah 1); Micah, the Savior to be born in Bethlehem (Micah 5:2); Isaiah, God's sovereign rule (Isaiah 44).

## CHAPTER 10: THE KINGDOM LIVES!

1. Revival under Hezekiah saved Judah from destruction by Assyria. (2 Chronicles 29–32)
2. The prophets of Judah pointed to idolatry and the worship of pagan deities. (Isaiah 1)
3. Nahum, Zephaniah, Habakkuk, and Jeremiah all preached in the surviving kingdom of Judah.
4. Ezekiel preached to the exiles in Babylon before the fall of Jerusalem. (Ezekiel 1:1)

## CHAPTER 11: EXILE AND RETURN

1. Lamentations expresses the despair of the Jews taken captive to Babylon.
2. The Book of Daniel contains a specific prediction about the date of the entrance of the Messiah into Jerusalem. (Daniel 9:20–27)
3. The books of Ezra and Nehemiah tell of the return to Judah.
4. The book of Esther teaches that God is in control of every aspect of our lives.
5. Zechariah and Haggai encouraged the people to finish building God's temple.

## CHAPTER 12: JESUS: THE REAL DEAL

1. Jesus Christ is the main person in the New Testament.
2. Psalm 2:7; 45:5, 6; Isaiah 7:14; 9:6, 7; Micah 5:2; and Malachi 3:1 all indicate that the Messiah will be God himself.
3. John 5:17, 18; 8:58, 59; Matthew 16:16, 17; and Matthew 26:63, 64 all report Jesus' claim to be God.
4. Philippians 2 says that "being in very nature God" Jesus was made "in human likeness."
5. The resurrection proved that Jesus was truly God. (Romans 1:1–4)

## CHAPTER 13: THE LIFE OF CHRIST: PART 1

1. The Gospel of John is not in chronological order.
2. The two genealogies of Jesus are different because one genealogy is Mary's and the other is from Jesus' stepfather, Joseph. (Matthew 1:1–17; Luke 4:21–38)
3. The appearances of angels marked Jesus' birth as unusual. (Matthew 1:15, 24; Luke 1:11, 26–38)
4. The message of John the Baptist was, "Repent, because the Messiah is about to appear." (Matthew 3:2)
5. God spoke from heaven, and the Holy Spirit descended as a dove. (Matthew 3:16–17)
6. To deliver us from our sins Jesus needed to be without sin. (Hebrews 4:14–16)

## CHAPTER 14: THE LIFE OF CHRIST: PART 2

1. The disciples were twelve men, specially chosen by Jesus. They followed Christ from the beginning of his ministry. (Mark 3:13–19)
2. The Pharisees and Sadducees were religious parties in Jesus' time.
3. Jesus performed miracles of healing, control of nature, control of demons, and power over death. (Mark 4; 5)
4. The Beatitudes define what God values in human beings. (Matthew 5:1–10)
5. Jesus explained the law and exposed its true meaning. (Matthew 5:17–47)
6. God's character as Father helps define the relationship he wants with human beings. (Matthew 6)
7. The Pharisees started the rumor that Jesus' miracles were performed by Satan's instead of God's power. (Matthew 12:22–32)

## CHAPTER 15: THE LIFE OF CHRIST: PART 3

1. The Pharisees brought the false charges against Jesus. (John 8)
2. The fact that Jesus had not "studied" allowed the Pharisees to say Jesus was not qualified to teach. (Matthew 13:53–58)
3. Jesus began to use parables after the crowds had refused to acknowledge him as the Messiah. (Matthew 13)
4. The subject of Jesus' parables was the kingdom of God. (Matthew 13)
5. The mark of a true disciple is the belief that Jesus is God the Son. (Matthew 16:13–20)
6. The key to greatness for a disciple of Jesus is willingness to serve others. (Matthew 20:20–28)
7. Jesus' "new commandment" was to love one another as he had loved them. (John 13:33–34)

## CHAPTER 16: THE LIFE OF CHRIST: PART 4

1. His triumphal entry into Jerusalem began Jesus' last week on earth. (Matthew 21)
2. Jesus called the Pharisees hypocrites. (Matthew 23)
3. In the Jewish courts he was charged with blasphemy. Pilate charged him with being a king and rival of Caesar. (John 19)
4. The body was taken down from the cross and sealed in a tomb. (John 27:32–66)
5. The Bible views Jesus' death as a sacrifice for sins, made on our behalf. (Hebrews 10)
6. Jesus is alive to save and to guard us. (Hebrews 7:11–28)

## CHAPTER 17: CHURCH ON FIRE!

1. Acts is a historical narrative. (Acts 1:1–2)
2. The coming of the Holy Spirit provides the disciples with power to witness to Christ. (Acts 1:8; Acts 2:1–12)
3. Jesus is a historical person who was crucified, rose, and saves those who trust in him. (Acts 2:14–41)
4. Cornelius was the first Gentile convert. (Acts 10)
5. Three of Paul's missionary journeys are reported in Acts. (Acts 13–19)
6. It determined that a person did not have to adopt Jewish practices to be a Christian. (Acts 15)
7. At the end of the Book of Acts, Paul is imprisoned in Rome. (Acts 28)

## CHAPTER 18: EXPLAINING THE GOSPEL

1. The epistles are letters of correspondence.
2. The theme of Paul's letter to the Romans is righteousness. (Romans 1:16–17)
3. Romans teaches us that no human being is righteous, God requires us to be righteous, and God will declare those who trust in Jesus to be righteous. (Romans 3)
4. Our sinful nature. Ever since the fall humans have been inheritors of original sin. This means that humans are flawed and in need of redemption. (Romans 5:12–20)
5. People have their own sense of right and wrong, and all have acted against their own standards. (Romans 2:12–16)
6. God's law is meant to convince us that we are sinners and cannot help ourselves. (Romans 3:19–20)
7. The theme of Paul's letter to the Galatians is the inadequacy of the law vs. the power of the Holy Spirit and grace.
8. Relating to God through the law involves dependence on our own self-effort. Relating to God through the Spirit involves relying on God to do in us what we cannot do alone. (Romans 8)

## CHAPTER 19: LETTERS ON THE CHRISTIAN LIFE

1. 1, 2 Corinthians; 1, 2 Thessalonians
2. Paul's solution was to expel Christians who refuse to stop sinning. (1 Corinthians 5)
3. They thought it indicated a special closeness to God. (1 Corinthians 12:1–11)
4. God loves cheerful givers, we can meet the needs of others by giving, and God can provide for all our needs. (2 Corinthians 8–9)
5. God did not answer Paul's prayer for healing in order to keep him from becoming proud and to teach him to rely on God. (2 Corinthians 12)

## CHAPTER 20: LETTERS FROM PRISON

1. The theme of Ephesians is the church of Jesus Christ as a living entity. (Ephesians 4)
2. Faith produces works. (Ephesians 2:8–10)
3. A husband's responsibility is to love his wife as Christ loved the church. (Ephesians 5:25)
4. To gain freedom from anxiety, Christians can present requests to God with thanksgiving. (Philippians 4:8–9)
5. In the Book of Colossians Paul battles a heresy that says that everything material is evil and only the nonmaterial can be spiritual or good.
6. Colossians 1:15–17 shows that Jesus is God.
7. Fake Christians live by lists of do's and don'ts; real Christians show love, compassion, and forgiveness toward others. (Colossians 2:6–23)

## CHAPTER 21: LETTERS TO FRIENDS

1. The three pastoral letters are 1, 2 Timothy and Titus.
2. The widows' ministry was teaching younger women. (2 Titus 2:3–5)
3. Love of money is the root of all kinds of evil. (1 Timothy 6:3–10)
4. Also involved in Christian teaching is teaching to live in harmony with the truth. (2 Timothy 2)
5. One justified by faith expresses that reality through good works. (James 2)
6. Philemon and Onesimus had become brothers in Christ. (Philemon 12–16)

## CHAPTER 22: DEFINING JESUS

1. Hebrews is addressed to Jewish Christians.
2. Hebrews was intended to show that Christianity and Christ are better than Judaism. It was also intended to convince Jewish Christians not to go back to Judaism.
3. Jesus brought a better revelation and offered an atoning sacrifice. (Hebrews 1)
4. It saves us from sin once and for all, and it works an inner transformation by writing God's law within our hearts. (Hebrews 8)
5. This shows that the sacrifice was complete and that we truly are forgiven. (Hebrews 10:1–18)
6. Hebrews 11 explores the significance of faith.
7. All loving fathers discipline or train their children, and hardships are evidence of God's discipline in our lives. (Hebrews 12)

## CHAPTER 23: PRACTICAL STUFF

1. The seven epistles discussed in this chapter are James; 1, 2 Peter; 1, 2, 3 John; and Jude.
2. The theme of the book of James is faith at work.
3. Christians need to understand how to relate to suffering. (1 Peter)
4. God turned the injustice into good, and can do the same for us. (1 Peter 3:13–18)
5. We need to confess our sins to remain in fellowship with God. (1 John 1:9)
6. Ask this question: Are they willing to confess that Jesus is God come in the flesh? (1 John 4:1–6)
7. Love is God's nature and he commands us to love our brothers. (1 John 4:16–21)

## CHAPTER 24: THE END?

1. The subject of Revelation is the events to take place at history's end. (Revelation 2:19)
2. Jesus is seen in his essential nature; he is so glorious John is stunned. (Revelation 1:9–20)
3. Even in the face of the terrible judgments, the sinners will not repent. (Revelation 9)
4. The Antichrist will be a human being in league with Satan, who will claim the benefits of Christ and demand to be worshiped. (Revelation 13)
5. The Millennium will be the thousand-year period during which Jesus will rule on earth, fulfilling Old Testament prophecy. (Revelation 20:1–6)
6. Those who don't trust Christ are thrown into the lake of fire. (Revelation 20:11–15)
7. Those who have trusted Christ will spend eternity with God in the new heaven and earth God will create. (Revelation 21–22)

# EXPERTS

**Thomas à Kempis** was a priest around the early 1400s. He is well known for his compilation of simple truths about living like Jesus.

**Michelle Akers** is a pro soccer player, Olympic Gold Medalist, and the U.S. team's leading goal scorer.

**Kay Arthur** is a well-known Bible teacher, best-selling author, and the founder of Precept Ministries.

**St. Augustine** (354–430) was an early church father. He wrote *The Confessions*, a book describing his spiritual journey.

**Tim Baker** is the associate pastor of Hope Fellowship in Longview, Texas. A writer, Tim has contributed over one hundred youth devotionals and youth ministry curriculums.

**William Barclay** (1907–1978) was a theologian, broadcaster, commentator on the New Testament, and professor of divinity and biblical criticism at Glasgow University.

**F. F. Bruce** (1910–1990) was Rylands Professor of Biblical Criticism and Exegesis at the University of Manchester in England and author of many Bible commentaries.

**Tony Campolo** is professor of sociology at Eastern College and author of several best-selling books.

**Cris Carter** is wide receiver for the Minnesota Vikings.

**Edmund P. Clowney**—Emeritus professor of practical theology, former president of Westminster Theological Seminary, and author of several commentaries on the Bible.

**Trent Dilfer** is quarterback for the Baltimore Ravens.

**Daymond R. Duck** is a Bible teacher and author of *Revelation: God's Word for the Biblically-Inept.*

**Norman L. Geisler** is the author or coauthor of fifty books and had been a graduate teacher for over forty years.

**Billy Graham** is a world-famous evangelist and best-selling author of several books.

**Everett F. Harrison** is a Bible expositor and author of several books.

**David Hocking** is a pastor, radio host, and director of Hope for Today Ministries.

**Alan F. Johnson** is professor of New Testament and Christian ethics at Wheaton College and Graduate School.

**Kevin Johnson** is a full-time writer and speaker to teenagers.

**Craig S. Keener** is Professor of New Testament at Eastern Seminary in Wynnewood, Pennsylvania, an ordained minister in the National Baptist Convention, and author of several books.

**Helen Keller** (1880–1968) was a leading advocate for people with disabilities. When she was nineteen months old, a fever struck and took away her eyesight and hearing. With the help of a devoted teacher, Anne Sullivan, she eventually graduated from Radcliffe College with top honors. Her books include *The Story of My Life, Midstream: My Later Life,* and *Helen Keller in Scotland.*

**William Law** (1686–1761) studied in England in the early 1700s and was a university preacher and teacher. Law served as a private tutor and used his books to preach to the masses.

**C. S. Lewis** (1898–1963) taught at Oxford, was professor of Medieval and Renaissance English at Cambridge, a Christian apologist, and best-selling author.

**Paul Little** is associate professor of evangelism at Trinity Evangelical Divinity School and 25-year staff member with InterVarsity.

**Max Lucado** is a pastor and one of today's most well-known Christian writers.

**Ron Luce** is a youth leader and director of Acquire the Fire youth conferences.

**Martin Luther** (1483–1546) was a Protestant reformer, theologian, and leader in church reform in the early 1500s.

**Peter Marshall** is a Presbyterian minister, an evangelist, and a writer.

**Josh McDowell** is an internationally known speaker and author or coauthor of over fifty books.

**J. Vernon McGee** is a former pastor and host of the *Thru the Bible* radio show.

**J. H. Melton** is a graduate of Southwestern Baptist Theological Seminary and former chairman of the Department of Bible at Baptist Bible College in Springfield, Missouri.

**Dwight L. Moody** (1837–1899) was an evangelist and missionary during the mid-1800s.

**Leon Morris** is a leading New Testament scholar and principal of Ridley College in Melbourne, Australia.

245

EXPERTS • LEARN THE WORD

**John Paul III** was pope during the mid-1500s and active in the Council of Trent. He encouraged Michelangelo to continue his work on the Sistine Chapel.

**J. Dwight Pentecost** is the author of many books and professor at Dallas Theological Seminary.

**Larry Richards** is best-selling author of over 175 books on the Bible. He is general editor of the *God's Word for the Biblically-Inept* series.

**Duffy Robbins** is chair of the Youth Ministry Department at Eastern College in St. Davids, Pennsylvania, and author of many books on youth ministry.

**Charles C. Ryrie** is author of many books and seminary professor of Systematic Theology.

**Rachel Scott** was martyred during the massacre at Columbine High School in Colorado.

**Lewis Smedes** is the author of ten books and senior professor at the Graduate School of Psychology at Fuller Theological Seminary in Pasadena, California.

**R. C. Sproul** is a theologian, minister, and chairman of the board for Ligonier Ministries.

**Ray C. Steadman** is a prolific writer and longtime pastor of Peninsula Bible Fellowship in Palo Alto, California.

**Charles Swindoll** is the author of numerous books on Christian living and president of Dallas Theological Seminary.

**Joni Eareckson Tada** is the author of several best-selling and award-winning books, and president of Joni and Friends, an organization enhancing the advancement of Christian ministry within the disability community.

**Michael Tait** is a singer with the Christian music group DC Talk.

**Mother Teresa** (1910–1997) was a nun in Calcutta, India. She is widely known for her efforts in reaching the poor in India.

**John Wesley** (1703–1791) was an evangelist and the founder of Methodism.

**Warren Wiersbe** is a pastor and author of many popular Bible commentaries.

**Michael Yaconelli** is the author of many books and the owner of Youth Specialties, a ministry serving youth workers.

**Ronald F. Youngblood** is a preacher, author, editor, and professor of Old Testament at Bethel Seminary in San Diego, California.

> Note: To the best of our knowledge, all of the above information is accurate and up to date. In some cases we were unable to obtain biographical information.
> —THE STARBURST EDITORS

# ENDNOTES

## INTRODUCTION

1. Helen Keller, *The Story of My Life 1880–1968* (Garden City, NY: Doubleday, 1954), <http://www.bible-history.com/quotes/helen_keller_1.html> (17 July 2001).
2. Duffy Robbins, *Going the Distance* (Grand Rapids, MI: Zondervan, 1991), 3.

## CHAPTER 1: HOW IT ALL BEGAN

1. Billy Graham, *Billy Graham Answers Your Questions* (Grand Rapids, MI: Zondervan), 165.
2. R. C. Sproul, *Reason to Believe* (Grand Rapids, MI: Zondervan, 1978), 113.
3. Ray C. Steadman, "How to Worship," sermon, <http://www.pbc.org/dp/steadman/psalms/0389.html> (18 July 2001).
4. Ronald F. Youngblood, *The Book of Genesis* (Grand Rapids, MI: Baker Book House, 1991), 23.
5. Kevin Johnson, *Look Who's Toast Now* (Minneapolis, MN: Bethany House, 1997), 81.
6. Josh McDowell, *The New Evidence That Demands a Verdict* (Nashville, TN: Thomas Nelson, 1999), 377.

## CHAPTER 2: GETTING THE COURSE RIGHT

1. Max Lucado, *The Applause of Heaven* (Nashville, TN: Word, 1999), 32.
2. Kay Arthur, *Lord, Where Are You?* (Colorado Springs, CO: Waterbrook, 2000), 118.
3. Duffy Robbins, *Going the Distance* (Grand Rapids, MI: Zondervan, 1991), 22.
4. Mother Teresa, *A Gift from God* (New York: Harper & Row, 1975), 37.

## CHAPTER 3: THE LONG TRIP HOME

1. Kay Arthur, *Lord, I Want to Know You* (Colorado Springs, CO: Waterbrook, 2000), 63.
2. Norman L. Geisler, quoted in Larry Richards, *The Bible: God's Word for the Biblically-Inept* (Lancaster, PA: Starburst, 1998), 28.

3. Bob Briner, *Roaring Lambs: A Gentle Plan to Radically Change Your World* (Grand Rapids, MI: Zondervan, 1993), 23.

## CHAPTER 4: EXTREME ADVENTURE

1. Joni Eareckson Tada, *The Women's Devotional Bible* (Grand Rapids, MI: Zondervan, 1995), 123.
2. Josh McDowell, quoted in Josh McDowell and Kevin Johnson, *God's Will, God's Best* (Minneapolis, MN: Bethany House, 2000), 133.

## CHAPTER 5: CONQUEST AND COLLAPSE

1. McDowell, quoted in McDowell and Johnson, *God's Will, God's Best*, 38–39.
2. Martin Luther, quoted in *The 365-Day Devotional Commentary* (Colorado Springs, CO: Chariot/Victor, 1989), 343.

## CHAPTER 6: A NEW BEGINNING

1. Duffy Robbins, *Going the Distance* (Grand Rapids, MI: Zondervan, 1991), 110.
2. Michelle Akers, *Christian Sports Flash*, "Michelle Akers—Hot Seat," <http://www.gospelcom.net/gf/sf/sports/hotseat/michelleakersprofile.html> (2 February 2001).
3. St. Augustine, quoted in The *365-Day Devotional Commentary* (Colorado Springs, CO: Chariot/Victor, 1989), 207.

## CHAPTER 7: ISRAEL AT ITS BEST

1. Charles Swindoll, *God's Masterwork*, vol. 1 (Nashville, TN: Word, 1997), 98.
2. Max Lucado, *The Applause of Heaven* (Nashville, TN: Word, 1999), 5.
3. Paul Little, *How to Give Away Your Faith* (Downers Grove, IL: InterVarsity, 1988), 181.
4. Swindoll, *God's Masterwork*, 52.
5. Larry Richards, *The Nelson Illustrated Bible Handbook* (Nashville, TN: Thomas Nelson, 1997), 270.
6. Graham, *Billy Graham Answers Your Questions*, 17.

7. McDowell, quoted in McDowell and Johnson, *God's Will, God's Best*, 146.

### CHAPTER 8: THE KINGDOM UP YONDER: ISRAEL
1. Swindoll, *God's Masterwork*, 83.
2. Warren Wiersbe, *Wiersbe's Expository Outlines* (Colorado Springs, CO: Chariot/Victor, 1992), 601.
3. Billy Graham, *Peace with God* (Nashville, TN: Word, 2000), 38.

### CHAPTER 9: THE KINGDOM ON THE SOUTH SIDE: JUDAH
1. King Solomon, Proverbs 14:34.
2. Ron Luce, *Inspire the Fire* (Orlando, FL: Creation House, 1994), 154.
3. John Alexander, quoted in *Christianity Today*, 9 February 1998, 78.
4. Swindoll, *God's Masterwork*, 96.

### CHAPTER 10: THE KINGDOM LIVES!
1. Warren Wiersbe, *Wiersbe's Expository Outlines* (Colorado Springs, CO: Chariot/Victor, 1992), 358.
2. R. C. Sproul, *Choosing My Religion* (Grand Rapids, MI: Baker, 1995), 3.20.
3. McDowell, quoted in McDowell and Johnson, *God's Will, God's Best*, 61.
4. Norman L. Geisler, *Miracles and Modern Thought* (Grand Rapids, MI: Zondervan, 1982), 260.
5. Wiersbe, *Wiersbe's Expository Outlines*, 522.

### CHAPTER 11: EXILE AND RETURN
1. Luther, quoted in *The 365-Day Devotional Commentary*, 1075.

### CHAPTER 12: JESUS: THE REAL DEAL
1. John F. MacArthur Jr., *God With Us* (Grand Rapids, MI: Zondervan, 1997), 46.
2. C. S. Lewis, *Christian Reflections* (Grand Rapids, MI: Eerdmans, 1994), 137.
3. Max Lucado, *Six Hours One Friday* (Sisters, OR: Multnomah, 1989), 73–74.
4. Toby McKeehan, *Squares Music Online*, "Artist Interview," <http://www.spank.com/squares/talk_dctalk2.html> (18 July 2001).

### CHAPTER 13: THE LIFE OF CHRIST: PART 1
1. Sproul, *Choosing My Religion*, 5.14.
2. J. Dwight Pentecost, quoted in J. W. Shepherd, *The Christ of the Gospels* (Grand Rapids, MI: Eerdmans, 1988), 91.
3. Tony Campolo, *Following Jesus without Embarrassing God* (Nashville, TN: Word, 1997), 230.
4. Duffy Robbins, *Going the Distance* (Grand Rapids, MI: Zondervan, 1991), 85.

### CHAPTER 14: THE LIFE OF CHRIST: PART 2
1. Charles C. Ryrie, *The Miracles of Our Lord* (Neptune, NJ: Loizeaux Bros., 1988), 11.
2. Max Lucado, *A Gentle Thunder* (Nashville, TN: Word, 1995), 19.
3. J. Dwight Pentecost, *The Words and Works of Jesus Christ* (Grand Rapids, MI: Zondervan, 1981), 159.
4. Warren Wiersbe, *Wiersbe's Expository Commentary* (Colorado Springs, CO: Chariot/Victor, 1997), 22.
5. Cris Carter, *Christian Sports Flash*, "Cris Carter Interview," <http://www.gospelcom.net/gf/sf/sports/profiles/criscarter.html> (2 February 2001).
6. Wiersbe, *Wiersbe's Expository Commentary*, 25.
7. Michael Tait, *Squares Music Online*, "Artist Interview," <http://www.spank.com/squares/talk_dctalk2.html> (18 July 2001).

### CHAPTER 15: THE LIFE OF CHRIST: PART 3
1. Max Lucado, *Six Hours One Friday* (Sisters, OR: Multnomah, 1989), 73.
2. Pentecost, *Words and Works*, 213.
3. Kevin Johnson, *Look Who's Toast Now* (Minneapolis, MN: Bethany House, 1997), 7.
4. Warren Wiersbe, *Wiersbe's Expository Commentary*, 58.
5. Trent Dilfer, *Christian Sports Flash*, "Trent Dilfer Interview," <http://www.gospelcom.net/gf/sf/sports/profiles/trentdilfer.html> (2 February 2001).
6. Pentecost, *Words and Works*, 311.
7. John Wesley, quoted in *The 365-Day Devotional Commentary* (Colorado Springs, CO: Chariot/Victor, 1989), 671.
8. Max Lucado, *A Gentle Thunder* (Nashville, TN: Word, 1995), 160.
9. Thomas à Kempis, *The Imitation of Christ* (Nashville, TN: Thomas Nelson, 1999), 6.1.

### CHAPTER 16: THE LIFE OF CHRIST: PART 4
1. Pentecost, *Words and Works*, 455.
2. McDowell, quoted in McDowell and Johnson, *God's Will, God's Best*, 77.
3. Max Lucado, *No Wonder They Call Him the Savior* (Sisters, OR: Multnomah, 1998), 140.
4. F. F. Bruce, *The Gospel of John* (Grand Rapids, MI: Eerdmans, 1983), 90.
5. McDowell, *The New Evidence That Demands a Verdict*, 205.
6. Peter Marshall, *The First Easter* (Grand Rapids, MI: Chosen Books, 1995), 13.

## CHAPTER 17: CHURCH ON FIRE!

1. F. F. Bruce, *New Testament History* (New York: Doubleday, 1980), 215.
2. Little, *How to Give Away Your Faith*, 44.
3. Tim Baker, *Extreme Faith* (Nashville, TN: Thomas Nelson, 2000), 139.
4. Wiersbe, *Wiersbe's Expository Commentary*, 441.
5. Craig S. Keener, *The IVP Bible Background Commentary* (Downers Grove, IL: InterVarsity, 2000), 354.
6. Ron Luce, *Inspire the Fire* (Orlando, FL: Creation House, 1994), 71.
7. Wiersbe, *Wiersbe's Expository Commentary*, 492.

## CHAPTER 18: EXPLAINING THE GOSPEL

1. Max Lucado, *In the Grip of Grace* (Nashville, TN: Word, 1996), 33.
2. Wiersbe, *Wiersbe's Expository Commentary*, 519.
3. Everett F. Harrison, *The Expositor's Bible Commentary* (Winona Lake, IN: BMH Books, 1976), 23.
4. Wiersbe, *Wiersbe's Expository Commentary*, 519.
5. Lucado, *In the Grip of Grace*, 92.
6. Wiersbe, *Wiersbe's Expository Commentary*, 519.
7. Lucado, *In the Grip of Grace*, 141
8. Harrison, *The Expositor's Bible Commentary*, 31.
9. Wiersbe, *Wiersbe's Expository Commentary*, 521.
10. Lucado, *In the Grip of Grace*, 92.
11. Wiersbe, *Wiersbe's Expository Commentary*, 719.

## CHAPTER 19: LETTERS ON THE CHRISTIAN LIFE

1. Graham, *Billy Graham Answers Your Questions*, 86.
2. Wiersbe, *Wiersbe's Expository Commentary*, 678.
3. Dwight L. Moody, quoted in *The 365-Day Devotional Commentary* (Colorado Springs, CO: Chariot/Victor, 1989), 954.
4. Martin Luther, *The Best of All His Works* (Nashville, TN: Thomas Nelson, 1989), 276.
5. Kevin Johnson, *Look Who's Toast Now* (Minneapolis, MN: Bethany House, 1997), 98.
6. C. S. Lewis, quoted in *The 365-Day Devotional Commentary* (Colorado Springs, CO: Chariot/Victor, 1989), 1025.

## CHAPTER 20: LETTERS FROM PRISON

1. Lewis Smedes, quoted in *Christianity Today*, 13 November 1995, 69.
2. Pope John Paul III, quoted in *Christianity Today*, 13 November 1995, 69.
3. Duffy Robbins, *Going the Distance*, (Grand Rapids, MI: Zondervan, 1991), 113.
4. Edmund P. Clowney, quoted in *Christianity Today*, 27 April 1998, 78.
5. Warren Wiersbe, *Be Confident* (Colorado Springs, CO: Chariot/Victor, 1997), 18.
6. Ibid., 89.

## CHAPTER 21: LETTERS TO FRIENDS

1. Duffy Robbins, *Going the Distance* (Grand Rapids, MI: Zondervan, 1991), 71.
2. William Barclay, *Letters to Timothy, Titus, and Philemon* (Louisville, KY: John Knox Press, 1975), 36.
3. McDowell, quoted in McDowell and Johnson, *God's Will, God's Best* (Minneapolis, MN: Bethany House, 2000), 146.
4. J. Vernon McGee, *The Epistles of 1, 2 Timothy, Titus, & Philemon* (Nashville, TN: Thomas Nelson, 1997), 66.
5. Warren Wiersbe, *Be Rich* (Colorado Springs, CO: Chariot/Victor, 1982), 26.
6. William Barclay, *Letters to Timothy, Titus, and Philemon* (Louisville, KY: John Knox Press, 1975), 256.
7. Little, *How to Give Away Your Faith*, 37.

## CHAPTER 22: DEFINING JESUS

1. Billy Graham, quoted in Rick Lawrence, *Trendwatch* (Loveland, CO: Group Publishing, 2000), 121.
2. Leon Morris, quoted in Leon Morris and Donald W. Burdick, *The Expositors Bible Commentary*, "Hebrews and James" volume (Grand Rapids, MI: Zondervan, 1996), 32.
3. F. F. Bruce, *Epistle to the Hebrews* (Grand Rapids, MI: Eerdmans, 1997), 102.
4. McDowell, quoted in McDowell and Johnson, *God's Will, God's Best*, 139.
5. F. F. Bruce, *Epistle to the Hebrews*, 173.
6. Kay Arthur, *Lord, I Want to Know You* (Colorado Springs, CO: Waterbrook, 2000), 157.
7. Michael Yaconelli, *Dangerous Wonder* (Colorado Springs, CO: NavPress, 1998), 40.

## CHAPTER 23: PRACTICAL STUFF

1. Leon Morris, *New Testament Theology* (Grand Rapids, MI: Zondervan, 1998), 313.
2. C. S. Lewis, *Miracles* (New York: Collier Books, 1947), 181.
3. Ron Luce, *Inspire the Fire* (Orlando, FL: Creation House, 1994), 171.
4. William Law, quoted in *Christianity Today*, 19 June 1995, 33.
5. Kevin Johnson, *Look Who's Toast Now* (Minneapolis, MN: Bethany House, 1997), 125.
6. John Wesley, *The Works of John Wesley* (Nashville, TN: Abingdon, 1998), 6:15.
7. Rachel Scott, quoted in Beth Nimmo and Darrell Scott, *Rachel's Tears* (Nashville, TN: Thomas Nelson, 2000), 86.
8. Leon Morris, *New Testament Theology* (Grand Rapids, MI: Zondervan, 1998), 290.

## CHAPTER 24: THE END?

1. Alan F. Johnson, *The Expositor's Bible Commentary*, Volume 10 (Winona Lake, IN: BMH Books, 1976), 432.
2. J. H. Melton, *52 Lessons in Revelation*, 93.
3. Daymond R. Duck, *Revelation for the Biblically-Inept* (Lancaster, PA: Starburst Publishers, 1998), 109.
4. Johnson, *The Expositor's Bible Commentary*, 576.
5. Duffy Robbins, *Going the Distance* (Grand Rapids, MI: Zondervan, 1991), 47.
6. David Hocking, *The Coming World Leader* (Sisters, OR: Multnomah, 1988), 288.

# INDEX

Boldface numbers refer to defined (What?) terms in the sidebar.

## A
Aaron, 21, 29
Abba, **152**
Abel, 8
Abraham (Abram), 10, 13–16, 19
  descendants as God's chosen, 13, 15, 19, 111
  faith of, 222–223
  Jesus as descended from, 15
  Jesus referring to, 117
  Jews, as father of, 13, 15, 19, 111
  and Melchizedek, 215
Abrahamic Covenant, **14**, 16, 24
Absalom, 53
Acquitted, **168**
Acrostic poems, **100**
Acts, Book of, 114, 157–168, 169
  Christianity, converts to, 160
  Church, the first, 160
  Gentiles, salvation of, 162–163
  Holy Spirit, appearance and promise of, 159
  James, martyrdom of, 163
  Luke as author, 157
  Paul, arrest and martyrdom of, 166–168
  Paul (Saul), conversion of, 161
  Paul's missionary journeys, 163–166
  Peter, sermons of, 159–160
  Samaritans, conversion of, 161
  Stephen, martyrdom of, 159, 160
A.D., **xii**
Adam:
  creation of, 5
  the fall, 7–8
  temptation of, 6–7
Adultery, 111
  Jesus regarding, 141
  the Ten Commandments, 24
Africa, Christianity in, 168
Agrippa, King (Herod Agrippa II), 166–167
Ahab, King, 67–68
Ahaz, King, 68, 81
Ai, city of, 38, 43
Akers, Michelle, on closeness to God, 51
Alexander, John, on repentance, 80
Alienation, **171**
Allegory, **63**
Alms, **136**
Altar:
  fire from heaven burning, 68
  (See also Sacrifice)
Amalekites, 48
Amaziah, 71
Amon, King, 89

Amos, Book of, 2, 70–72
Amos, writing prophet, 67
Andrew, 131
Angel(s), 125
  archangel, 186
  at end time, 236
  Jesus greater than, 213
  at Second Coming, 186
  twelve legions of, 152
  visitations at Jesus' birth, 124
Animals:
  clean and unclean, 162
  Noah's ark, 8–10
  in Peter's vision, 162
  (See also specific animals)
Animal sacrifice, 111, 218
  the first, 8
  lamb at Passover, 22
  meat from, selling, 181–182
  temple, 150
Anna, 124
Anointed, **45**
"Anointed One," 116
Antichrist, 187
  end of, 237
Antichrists, 228
Aphrodite, **180**
Apocalyptic, **236**
Apostles, **159**
  false, 184
  Letters by, 114
  (See also Disciples; individual names)
Arabs, 15
Archaeologists, xiv, 101
Archangel, 186
Ark, Noah's, 8–10
  illustration of, 9
Ark of the covenant, **47**, 54
Arrogance, 173
Arthur, Kay:
  on being right with God, 217
  on faith, 15
  on the name Jehovah, 21
Asia Minor, 190
Assyrian Empire:
  Israel, conquest of, 71–72, 75, 81, 82–83, 85–86
  Nineveh as capital, 68–70, 87–88
Assyrians, 65
Athletes, 204
Atonement, **214**
Augustine, Saint, on confessing sin, 53

## B
Baal, **67–68**
Babylonian Empire, 14, 50, 66
  Daniel as official, 101
  Jerusalem, conquest of, 86
  Judah, invasion and conquest of, 75, 90–91, 92, 94–95, 99
  timeline for captivity and return of Jews, 104
  (See also Nebuchadnezzar, King)

Baker, Tim, on passion for God, 161
Balaam, 33
Balak, 33
Baptism:
  of Jesus, 126
  John the Baptist, 125–126
Barclay, William:
  on Christians and sin, 201
  on moral change, 207
Barnabas, 161
Bartholomew, 131
Bathsheba, 53
B.C., **1**
Beast (See Antichrist)
Beatitudes, **135**
Beauty, 173
Beelzebub, 137
  (See also Satan)
Belief and Unbelief, 123
  (See also Unbelievers)
Believers (see Christians)
Bethel, 14, 67, 71
Bethlehem, 116
  in Old Testament prophecy, 140
Bible, 16
  composition of, xii–xiii
  as message from God, xii–xiii
  New International Version (NIV), xiv
  sex roles in, 17
  study, importance of, 205
  study of, xiii–xiv
  timelines in, xiv
  (See also New Testament; Old Testament)
Birthright, **17**
Blasphemy, **153**
Blessing(s), **17**
  Christians as given, 190
  endless, 83
  for obedience, 31, 108
Blind and mute man, 137–138
Blood atonement (see Sacrifice)
Boastfulness, 173
Boaz, 42–43
Body of Christ, **182**
Bones, in Ezekiel's visions, 95–96
Born again (see Salvation; Saved)
Bread, temptation of Jesus, 127
Briner, Bob, on committing to God, 23
Bruce, F. F.:
  on disciples' public witness, 160
  on God's love, 155
  on Jesus as priest, 216
  on unbelief, 214–215

## C
Caesar, Paul as appealing to, 166–167
Caesarea, 123
  Paul in, 166–167

Caesarea Philippi, 144
Cain, 8
Calves:
  the golden calf, 26
  idols, 66
Campolo, Tony, on temptation of Jesus, 127
Cana, wedding at, 133
Canaan, 14, 20, 214
  Abraham entering, 13
  Joshua conquering, 37–39
  Philistines warring with, 42
  as promised land, 27, 28, 31–32, 33
  (See also Israel; Promised land)
Canaanites, 35, 40–41
Carmel, Mount, 68
Carter, Chris, on glorifying God, 136
Caught up, **186**
Centurion, Cornelius as (see Cornelius)
Ceremonial law, 29
Chambers, Oswald, 187
Chief priests, 150
  (See also Religious leaders)
Childbirth, after the fall, 7
Christ, 116
  (See also Jesus Christ)
Christian freedom, 181–182
Christianity:
  Abraham as founder of, 15
  beginnings of, 157
  conversion of priests and Pharisees, 160
  Jewish roots of, 157
  Roman Empire, spread in (see Roman Empire)
  (See also Church)
Christian martyrs (see Martyrs)
Christians:
  attitude for, 226–227
  beliefs of, 115, 147–148
  blessings given, 190
  character of, 201, 226
  faith, living, 222–224 (See also Faith)
  fake and real, 197, 205
  fellowship, 160
  and God's will, 145
  Holy Spirit and, 158, 207
  imitation of Christ, 191, 193
  living your faith, 206, 207, 215–216
  loving each other, 146, 228–229
  Paul's advice for, 201
  persecution of, 160, 203, 224–225
  resting, importance of, 214
  seeking God, 125
  sin and, 201
  suffering inevitable for, 192, 225
  teenagers, 162
  witness, effectiveness of, 141
  (See also Witness)
  (See also Church)

# IT'S THE BIBLE MADE EASY!

The *God's Word for the Biblically-Inept™* series is already a best-seller with over 300,000 books sold! Designed to make reading the Bible easy, educational, and fun, this series of verse-by-verse Bible studies, topical studies, and overviews mixes scholarly information from experts with helpful icons, illustrations, sidebars, and time lines. It's the Bible made easy!

## God's Word for the Biblically-Inept™ Series

| TITLE | ISBN | TITLE CODE | PRICE |
|---|---|---|---|
| **Acts** by Robert C. Girard | 189201646X | **GWAC** | $17.99 |
| **The Bible** by Larry Richards | 0914984551 | **GWBI** | $16.95 |
| **Daniel** by Daymond R. Duck | 0914984489 | **GWDN** | $16.95 |
| **Genesis** by Joyce Gibson | 1892016125 | **GWGN** | $16.95 |
| **Health & Nutrition** by Kathleen O'Bannon Baldinger | 0914984055 | **GWHN** | $16.95 |
| **John** by Lin Johnson | 1892016435 | **GWJN** | $16.95 |
| **Life of Christ, Volume 1,** by Robert C. Girard | 1892016230 | **GWLC** | $16.95 |
| **Life of Christ, Volume 2,** by Robert C. Girard | 1892016397 | **GWLC2** | $16.95 |
| **Mark** by Scott Pinzon | 1892016362 | **GWMK** | $17.99 |
| **Men of the Bible** by D. Larry Miller | 1892016079 | **GWMB** | $16.95 |
| **Prophecies of the Bible** by Daymond R. Duck | 1892016222 | **GWPB** | $16.95 |
| **Revelation** by Daymond R. Duck | 0914984985 | **GWRV** | $16.95 |
| **Romans** by Gib Martin | 1892016273 | **GWRM** | $16.95 |
| **Women of the Bible** by Kathy Collard Miller | 0914984063 | **GWWB** | $16.95 |

For purchasing information see page 258 • Learn more at **www.biblicallyinept.com**

# Purchasing Information

### www.starburstpublishers.com

Books are available from your favorite bookstore, either from current stock or special order. To assist bookstores in locating your selection, be sure to give title, author, and ISBN. If unable to purchase from a bookstore, you may order direct from STARBURST PUBLISHERS. When ordering please enclose full payment plus shipping and handling as follows:

| **Post Office (4th class)** | **United Parcel Service (UPS)** | **Canada** | **Overseas** |
|---|---|---|---|
| $3.00 with a purchase of up to $20.00 | $5.00 (up to $20.00) | $5.00 (up to $35.00) | $5.00 (up to $25.00) |
| $4.00 ($20.01–$50.00) | $7.00 ($20.01–$50.00) | 15% ($35.01 and up) | 20% ($25.01 and up) |
| 8% of purchase price for purchases of $50.01 and up | 12% ($50.01 and up) | | |

Payment in U.S. funds only. Please allow two to four weeks minimum for delivery by USPS (longer for overseas and Canada). Allow two to seven working days for delivery by UPS. Make checks payable to and mail to:

**Starburst Publishers®**
P.O. Box 4123
Lancaster, PA 17604

Credit card orders may be placed by calling 1-800-441-1456, Mon–Fri, 8:30 A.M. to 5:30 P.M. Eastern Standard Time. Prices are subject to change without notice. Catalogs are available for a 9 x 12 self-addressed envelope with four first-class stamps.